Who Knows the Shape of God?

Homilies and Reflections for Year B

Breaking Open the Word

Who Knows the Shape of God?

Homilies and Reflections for Year B

Corbin Eddy

NOVALIS

© 2002 Novalis, Saint Paul University, Ottawa, Canada

Cover design: Blair Turner
Cover art: sculpture entitled "Delivery" by Julie Campagna, photographed by Wally Moss
Layout: Suzanne Latourelle, Francine Petitclerc
Editor: Bernadette Gasslein

Business Office:
Novalis
49 Front Street East, 2nd Floor
Toronto, Ontario, Canada
M5E 1B3
Phone: 1-800-387-7164 or (416) 363-3303
Fax: 1-800-204-4140 or (416) 363-9409
E-mail: cservice@novalis.ca
www.novalis.ca

National Library of Canada Cataloguing in Publication

Eddy, Corbin, 1942–
    Who knows the shape of God? : homilies and reflections
for year B / Corbin Eddy.

(Breaking open the Word)
Includes bibliographical references.
ISBN 2-89507-044-X

    1. Church year sermons. 2. Sermons, Canadian (English).
3. Catholic Church—Sermons. I. Title. II. Series.

BX1756.E36W43 2002   252'.6   C2002-904752-8

Printed in Canada.

We acknowledge the financial support of the Government of Canada through the Book Publishing Industry Development Program (BPIDP) for our publishing activities.

10 9 8 7 6 5 4 3 2 1   10 09 08 07 06 05 04 03 02

*to the people of
St. Basil's Parish,
Ottawa*

Table of Contents

Introduction

A friend of mine used to love quoting his father, from whom he had inherited many important values and approaches to life, along with a few he thought he should probably get over as the years passed. His father was clearly a character about whom there were many colourful stories to be told, some of which related to his driving. For example, he had the habit of speeding up at the sight of an amber or yellow light. Sometimes he didn't quite make it through the intersection before the light had turned red. "That's okay," he'd say, "it was only pink." At other times, when frustrated with trying to find a parking place, he would simply pull in wherever and go about his business. It didn't matter that he was blocking a driveway or a fire hydrant. He'd just be a minute. "When in doubt," he'd say, "just stop and get out. That's being parked."

Yet, as well as my friend remembers his father and his rather casual approach to driving, he would be hard pressed to describe the specifics of that approach. He just knew what his father used to say, or how he used to think or what he used to do. That it was the intersection of Elm and First Avenue where he darted through a "pink light," or that it was on the sidewalk in front of the public library where he simply stopped the car and got out, didn't really matter. What he was accurately communicating was his father's carefree, even cavalier, approach to driving. My friend, in his delight about remembering his father, could happily spin out all kinds of good stories. Were they true? Of course. Were they accurate in every detail? Were they in chronological order? Probably not. One thing reminded him of another which reminded him of something else. Before we knew it he was weaving a big story that reflected the truth of his father's character and personality in all kinds of interesting events and amusing antics. That everything wasn't exactly right didn't detract at all from the overall truth of his life, his character and the legacy he had left to his son.

The gospel accounts of Jesus' life and ministry reflect something of this same dynamic and creative process of remembering, interpreting, and passing on a revered person's life and spiritual legacy.

This is especially clear when we compare the four gospels. They clearly show a lack of precision and consistency about the exact sequence of events, and even the precise formulation of Jesus' teaching. At the heart of the story's telling there is, however, a remarkably consistent power and energy. In their foundational theology of who Jesus is and what he means for the world, the four gospels demonstrate remarkable agreement.

Specific sayings of Jesus and anecdotes about him seem to have circulated widely in the Mediterranean world. A large body of material about what Jesus said and did, as well as traditions about what happened to him, was accumulated in much the same way as stories were collected about other important figures. Sayings of rabbis and philosophers and deeds of important men and women favoured by the gods were common, and bore witness to traditional faith and values in all the ancient cultures and spiritual systems of thought and practice. They were organized to promote and defend the framework of cultural and religious convictions to which they witnessed.

When it comes to Jesus, however, there is an important, even defining, difference. Like my friend's father, Jesus was a "character" about whom there were stories to be told and from whom there were lessons to be learned. But, unlike my friend's father, *Jesus is risen*. He lives in a way that my friend's father does not. He lives in a way that utterly transcends the ways in which long-dead teachers and heroes live on. At the heart of the Christian faith is the conviction that death was unable to hold Jesus in its grasp, that God had raised and exalted him to his own right hand, and that Jesus would come again to usher in the final and complete reign of God, which his earthly life foreshadowed. Jesus is not a dead hero, however powerful and inspiring. He is not a dead teacher, however insightful and inspiring. The Christian missionary proclamation does not revolve around the memory of a good and holy man, now gone, of whom we have reminiscences that could have some contemporary moral or spiritual application. Jesus is alive and at the right hand of the Father in heaven, a position from which "he will come again in glory to judge the living and the dead."

The earliest generation of believers expected that this great return would take place in the immediate future. With Christ's reappearance, God would establish his rule, his reign, his kingdom, in place of the cultural, political and religious structures that had dominated the earth and its history until that time. Since that transformation would occur within their lifetime, they had little need to be occupied with specific details about what happened in the past. The signs, miracles, sayings and experiences of the earthly Jesus were but dim foreshadowings of what his final coming would bring. With the kingdom of God fully and finally in place, would anyone really care about the foreshadowing and promise offered in the life and teaching of the earthly Jesus? A promise fulfilled clearly overshadows the promise itself. Had the promise been fulfilled as originally anticipated, there would have been no need for the gospels.

As the fulfillment of the promise was taking more time than anticipated, however, the promise needed to be clearly formulated so that it could be proclaimed to successive generations of believers. Hope needed to be kept alive. People needed to find a way to live that was consistent with their hope: hence the gospels. *The gospels' primary focus is not to preserve the past but to articulate the promise.* The events of Jesus' life in which God revealed his divine sonship, stories that demonstrated his healing and liberating power, examples of his spiritual and ethical teaching—all these would be useful, especially for new generations of believers living "in the meantime." As that "meantime" stretched out, they felt the need to articulate the promise more and more clearly.

Almost all scholars believe that Mark's gospel is the first to be written. Because it forms the heart of the lectionary for Cycle B, it is important for homilists and catechists to look at its original spirit and purpose so they can preach and teach from it with integrity.

Early sources indicate that Mark's gospel was written during the decade AD 60–70. Most likely it was originally directed to the church in Rome. Peter and Paul are believed to have been martyred in the persecution following the great fire in AD 64, which would clearly have been a dramatic and traumatic moment in the life of the early church. Mark's gospel is directed to a church in crisis.

In his commentary entitled *The Gospel of Mark*, John Donahue S.J. sets the stage as follows:

> The shadow of the cross, opposition from powerful leaders, divisions among Jesus' followers, persecutions, and betrayals— all these themes in Mark's gospel would have been especially

meaningful to an early Christian community that had suffered for the name of Jesus and was expecting even more suffering. These themes fit well with the experience of Christians at Rome in the late 60s of the first century C.E. There is solid historical evidence that the Christian community at Rome faced persecutions, brutal executions, and intrafamilial betrayals some time after the great fire of 64 C.E. under Nero. According to the Roman historian Cornelius Tacitus who wrote around 115 C.E., the emperor Nero fixed the guilt on the Roman Christians (Ann.15.44). Tacitus described the procedure used in arresting the Christians as follows: 'First, then, the confessed members of the sect were arrested; next on evidence furnished by them a large multitude was convicted not so much on the count of arson as hatred of the human race.' Tacitus goes on to recount the horrible punishments inflicted on them: 'they were covered with wild beasts' skins and torn to death by dogs; or they were fastened on crosses, and when daylight failed were burned to serve as lamps by night.' ... It is in this atmosphere that Mark's gospel very likely took shape. This setting fits remarkably with Jesus' 'prophecies' to his disciples in Mark 13:9-13. In the context of proclaiming the gospel in a predominantly Gentile milieu the Roman Christians were forced to bear witness before Roman officials (see 13:9-11). There were intrafamilial betrayals (see 13:12) and they were 'hated by all for my sake.'

Donahue goes on to describe other suggestions that the gospel may have originally been directed to a community in Palestine that would have experienced the horrors of the First Jewish War and the destruction of the temple. This would explain some of the local references to Galilee and to the Jerusalem temple, as well as the apocalyptic features that are so prominent in Mark, which would resonate more clearly with Jewish expectations.[1]

The traditions surrounding the earthly life of Jesus leading up to his death and resurrection were organized and arranged to provide direction, meaning and encouragement to a community whose faith and hope were being profoundly tested. Mark presents the image of the cross as central to the earthly experience of Jesus. Discipleship and the cross are virtually synonymous. The earthly Jesus proclaimed and lived his vision of the reign of God in anticipation of its final fulfillment, even though it cost him his life. He himself was persecuted, betrayed and executed, and warned his disciples, as slow as they were to get the message, that the same level of commitment and dedication would be required of them. Believers would be called upon to live the cross in their own way, in their own time and place. They would be invited to live in anticipation of God's kingdom, whatever the cost. His disciples would continue to bear the cross of Christ. He would be going before them. They would be following him. They would want to keep their eyes on him. They would want to be up to the challenge; they would want to keep "in shape."

It is this sense of being "in shape" that inspired the title of this collection of homilies and reflections rooted in Mark's theology. "Who knows the shape of God?" Mark claims to know it. The shape of God is Jesus; the shape of Jesus is cruciform. Sometimes subtly and sometimes blatantly, Mark notes that the first disciples had a hard time understanding this "cruciform messiah, this cruciform Son of God." In doing so, he draws readers of all generations into the story with the same question, the same challenge:

Are you in shape to be a follower of Jesus?

To take up your cross and to follow Jesus means becoming cruciform yourself, letting your own story be shaped by his, expressing in your own body language the "divinity" of openness, inclusivity and vulnerability. It has never been an easy lesson to learn, but according to Jesus, that's what it means to be "in shape." Victory, glory and grace flow from a cross-shaped God.

In the First Eucharistic Prayer for Masses of Reconciliation, we address the Father in these words:

> Nailed to a cross, Jesus your Son stretched out his arms between heaven and earth in the everlasting sign of your covenant ...
> We celebrate his death and resurrection and look for the coming of that day when he will return to give us fullness of joy ...
> Father, look with love on those you have called to share in the one sacrifice of Christ ...

Mark's own faith in a "cross-shaped" messiah who is living and going before disciples of every age coloured his presentation of materials recalling Jesus' earthly career. This faith gave him the necessary freedom to use and to shape these traditions to the specific situation and community he was trying and hoping to get "in shape."

It was likewise the limitations, slowness to believe, and fear of the men and women who were Jesus' first disciples—but who subsequently were ready to die for their faith—that would be a source of hope to the doubting and struggling church to whom he originally addressed his work, a community trying in their own time to keep "in shape."

In Mark's resurrection account, a mysterious man in a white robe sitting at the right of the tomb proclaims the news of Jesus' resurrection to the women who came out to the tomb.

> "Do not be alarmed," he declared. "You are looking for Jesus of Nazareth, who was crucified. He has been raised; he is not here. Look, there is the place they laid him. But go, tell his disciples and Peter that he is going ahead of you to Galilee; there you will see him, just as he told you."

Note their response to the good news:

> They went out and fled from the tomb, for terror and amazement had seized them; and they said nothing to anyone, for they were afraid.

At least at this point, they were clearly not in shape for their mission. They were not prepared to risk believing in the form his life and death had taken and to allow themselves to be conformed to his spirit. They had to grow into their mission. Only gradually did they get in shape for it. They must have, because the word got out.

We will probably never be sure about the original context out of which Mark's writing arose. Whatever the situation might have been, or the location of the original audience, the result was something new within the Christian community: a collection of the words and deeds of Jesus, along with some traditions about things that happened to him (e.g., baptism, transfiguration, crucifixion), arranged as a story imprinting on the faith a self-understanding that would have profound and lasting consequences. What we experience in the Gospel of Mark is a new literary attempt within the Christian community to communicate the truth of Jesus of Nazareth—not truths about him, but an ongoing, dynamic, living truth.

It would be difficult to overestimate the importance of this small book. The entire history of Christianity has been enormously influenced by the gospel tradition of which Mark's is almost universally understood to be the first example. Modern commentators have also suggested that it would be difficult to overestimate the artistic and theological capacity of this remarkably committed and insightful Christian who first conceived the idea of putting unconnected traditions about Jesus into a larger framework to serve a struggling and needy community. What commentators in the past may have thought to be uneven and awkward transitions and unresolved tensions in the text are actually at the heart of its paradoxical interest, dramatic power and crisis orientation.[2]

Although originally directed to a particular time and place, Mark's message is for disciples of all time. There are as many Galilees as there are futures into which disciples step, however fearfully or awkwardly. The risen Christ goes before his disciples in every age. He continues to teach and guide in the same spirit as he did before his crucifixion. Consistent with the activities of his earthly ministry, he continues to teach and guide his disciples, but now he does it as living Lord. This conviction inspired and compelled early Christian teachers to reshape the traditions they had received to reflect and communicate their perennial value. The gospels are a living proclamation of a living Lord. In their ongoing proclamation they come alive anew.

Here are two clear invitations to enter into gospel action that we'll hear again during the course of the year.

> "If any want to become my followers, let them deny themselves and take up their cross and follow me. For those who want to save their life will lose it, and those who lose their life for my sake, and for the sake of the gospel, will save it. For what will it profit them to gain the whole world and forfeit their life? Indeed, what can they give in return for their life? Those who are ashamed of me and of my words in this adulterous and

sinful generation, of them the Son of Man will also be ashamed when he comes in the glory of his Father with the holy angels." (Mark 8.34-38)

"Truly I tell you, there is no one who has left house or brothers or sisters or mother or father or children or fields, for my sake and for the sake of the good news [gospel], who will not receive a hundredfold now in this age—houses, brothers and sisters, mothers and children, and fields with persecutions—and in the age to come eternal life. But many who are first will be last, and the last will be first." (Mark 10.29-31)

Powerful challenges! The gospel or good news is clearly not just a story from the past, but a story that has begun with the life, death and resurrection of Jesus and continues to invite the ongoing participation of its hearers. It reaches forward, including and incorporating the lives of those in the process of being transformed by embracing the cross in their own lives.

I love the inclusion within the gospel text of an anonymous woman who anointed Jesus at Bethany in the house of Simon the leper. She "came with an alabaster jar of very costly ointment of nard, and she broke open the jar and poured the ointment on his head." "She has done what she could," Jesus proclaimed in defence of her extravagant outpouring of love and respect. "She has anointed my body before-hand for its burial. Truly I tell you, wherever the good news [gospel] is proclaimed in the whole world, what she has done will be told in remembrance of her." (Mark 14.3-9) Her loving and wholehearted identification with the glory that is to arise out of the experience of the cross, which she herself is sharing, is truly remarkable. She is clearly part and parcel of the gospel.

In situating what may have been the original context of Mark's work in the persecution of Nero, Father Donahue points to another wonderful and very different subsequent example of the inclusion of others into the gospel—good news. He refers to Peter's martyrdom, which may have played a part in motivating the author to produce this first of the four canonical gospels. More than rehabilitated after his denial of Jesus, and from the fears, doubts and weaknesses evident throughout the gospel, Peter must have been thoroughly transformed to live out the mystery of the cross in his own body. In writing to the Corinthian Christians in the late first century AD, Clement, the bishop of Rome, reported that "by reason of jealousy and envy the greatest and most righteous pillars of the church were persecuted and contended even to death." (1 Clement 5:2) His praise of Peter's heroism in the face of suffering is particularly moving. "Having borne his testimony, he went to his appointed place of glory." Peter's story continues to proclaim good news possibilities. He "contended even to death and took his appointed place of glory." Mark's gospel that features Peter in such an unflattering light can be seen as a prelude to his ultimate heroic triumph.

I believe that it is in understanding Mark's text as a prelude to the ongoing life and commitment of the church that we best connect with his creative intentions. We can take our cue from the grammatical fragment with which it begins. Although not separated from the text, it serves as the book's title.

"The beginning of the good news [gospel] of Jesus Christ, the Son of God."

The title of Mark's work is not "The Gospel of Jesus Christ," but "The Beginning of the Gospel, The Beginning of the Good News."

Eugene LaVerdiere expresses this understanding of Mark's point of view very succinctly when he describes how the beginning ends.

"The *beginning* of the gospel of Jesus Christ" *ends* after Jesus' burial with the visit of women to his tomb, with a young man's proclamation of his resurrection and with the flight of the women from the tomb, "saying nothing to anyone because they were afraid." (Mark 16.1-8) "The *beginning* of the gospel of Jesus Christ the Son of God" *ends* with the silence of the women. This does appear to be a strange ending for a story that was announced as gospel or good news. But we have to remember that *this ending is not the end of the gospel, but only the end of the "beginning of the gospel."* The good news goes on in the lives of all who live and serve in the spirit of the cross, in the hope of resurrection.[3]

Mark's work is not the gospel, but the "beginning of the gospel." The gospel continues in the lives of all who discover and live out paradoxical good news in the prospect of "denying themselves" and "taking up their cross" in favour of real life—risen life. The good news continues to be told in the lives of believers who, having overcome "terror and amazement," are in touch with Jesus who "goes before them," and in faith and hope come to recognize the futility of "gaining the whole world and losing their own lives" in the process.

I recently attended an ordination in Iowa. The gathering song for the Eucharist at which one of the newly ordained priests presided the next day was "Bless This Feast" by James Hansen (OCP, 1998). It begins: "Welcome this moment, this day of sweet grace."

Verse three continues:

Freedom to captives, good news to the poor,
lighting the darkling, unsighted, unsure.
Telling the story: love without end,
Breath of creation, all life to defend.
Telling the covenant story again;
Exodus journey for women and men.
Telling once more and hearing the Word—
Whose shining conclusion has yet to be heard.

It struck me as we were singing that this is decidedly Markan. The shining conclusion of the oft-proclaimed word has yet to be heard. The gospel continues to be written with our own rising above fear and doubt and cynicism to connect with the risen Jesus himself and to become a part of the ongoing telling of "good news," to become "gospel people."

I hope that these reflections, which derive from my own ministry of gospel proclamation Sunday after Sunday, are true to the kind of momentum that Mark sets up for us. I hope that they will encourage ongoing "gospel" living in their readers.

Many of these reflections derive from homilies preached at Saint Basil's Parish in Ottawa, where I served as pastor. Ron Warren took the trouble week after week to record them for ill and housebound parishioners and for anyone else who wished to hear them. Michelle

Rocheleau subsequently transcribed them. Some of these were now dated or so parish-specific that I could not build on them for publication in this form, but had to begin again. Readers will likely be able to distinguish between the two types of reflections. None of them was actually preached "as is" and are now presented more to be read than heard. Most of them carry too many ideas for a single homily, but I hope that they still retain a certain conversational quality that they had in the beginning. I am very grateful to Ron and Michelle for making it possible for me to retrieve what I tried my best to proclaim to a wonderfully living and active community of faith as a foundation for what is offered here. I am also very grateful to Bernadette Gasslein for her careful editing both of my revisions of initially oral material and of those which came "from scratch." Her insights and suggestions have always been challenging and constructive.

A final word about Mark: The French have a wonderful way of expressing what I understand to be his underlying open-endedness:

> "C'est à suivre."
> It's to follow.
> To be continued…
> The best is yet to come.

> "Welcome this moment of sweet grace…
> whose shining conclusion has yet to be heard."
> So be it! Amen.

Corbin Eddy
Saint Mary's Seminary and University
Baltimore, Maryland

June 29, 2002
Solemnity of Sts. Peter and Paul, Apostles

Centring Vision

First Sunday of Advent

Isaiah 63.16b-17; 64.1, 3-8
Psalm 80
1 Corinthians 1.3-9
Mark 13.31-37

As intense as today's scriptures are, there's nothing really scary about them. As clear and unequivocal as they are, there's nothing bombastic or threatening. They do, however, communicate a strong and vigorous message, a judgment call, however gently expressed.

I read last week about an 80-year-old woman named Dorothy who was experiencing a moment of real crisis. She had lived in the same tenement-style apartment building for almost 50 years. She had raised both of her children there; her husband had died there. Today was the day to move on. She had to go. She could no longer live on her own. She was heading to what we call "a home." She was standing at a window looking out. "Come on, Dorothy," her daughter-in-law said. "It's time to go."

"Not until I've frozen my memories," Dorothy replied.

She was standing at the window "freezing her memories." What a moment! It's no wonder that her daughter-in-law's eyes filled with tears. Everything of real value was past for this elderly woman and she wanted to make sure she didn't lose it. She was stepping out into her future with, at best, a sense of resignation, but with little more. I'll bet there's not one person in this congregation who doesn't know some-one who has had a day like Dorothy's—little or no joy or hope for the future, at best resignation, at worst bitter despair.

The priests of the diocese were on retreat a few weeks ago. In his very first conference with us, the retreat director asked us to write down our feelings at that very moment about ourselves, our ministry, our priesthood. "Don't think real hard. Just write. Jot your feelings down. Be quick. Be spontaneous. No forethought that might tame or soften them." He didn't ask us to share our jottings, but went on to describe his experience working with priests. He started talking about the situation as, from his experience, he guessed it might be among us. Probably a lot of work, with fewer people to do it, people who were, on the average, older. He anticipated, too, that there would be a lot of wondering about where it's all going, a strong sense of duty, some tiredness, some disappointment due to a lack of positive encouragement from those in authority. He even suggested that we might be bored! We do the same things—even very holy things—so often that there ceases to be much new life in them. We may be in a kind of rut. Although that doesn't sound very spiritual, some of us were shaking our heads in agreement. Most of us didn't, in fact, have those words in our jottings, but we could identify with what he was saying and recognize the dangers he was pointing out. His response? He called us back to personal prayer, and reminded us of the foundational value of daily meditation.

Further reflection on my own experience helped me realize that he wasn't just talking about priests. He was talking about all kinds of people. There are surely married people who are in a rut and who live their relationship in ways that are not particularly creative or enthusiastic. There could well be married people who are bored.

What about the other professions? Don't all kinds of people experience the same kind of thing? Boredom. Ennui. Fatigue. No real sense of creative positive energy—no hope—no centring vision.

People live this experience concretely in different ways. Some slow down and get passive—a low-grade depression. Others speed up and get going so fast that they're afraid to stop, because if they stopped they might discover that they were going in the wrong direction. Both cases lack hope—a centring vision.

Various forms of consumption might be another "out." There is always more to experience, more things to try, more things to buy, more places to go—all to distract from any real depth. Today's Advent scriptures stand in direct opposition to that kind of living.

You, O Lord, are our father;
"Our Redeemer from of old" is your name …
O Lord, you are our Father;

we are the clay, and you are our potter;
we are all the work of your hand. (Isaiah 63.16b; 64.8)

Lord, make us turn to you; let us see your face and we shall
be saved. (Psalm 80)

He will also strengthen you to the end, so that you may be
blameless on the day of our Lord Jesus Christ. God is
faithful; by him you were called. (1 Corinthians 1.8-9)

"Heaven and earth will pass away, but my words will not
pass away … Keep alert … What I say to you I say to all:
Keep awake." (Mark 13.31, 37)

Keep awake. You never know when the Lord is coming. Shake
yourself a bit. Isn't this what prayer and meditation are finally all about?
Don't just freeze your memories.
Don't let yourself feel victimized or sorry for yourself.
Don't give in to low-grade depression.
Don't just drive yourself.
Don't just look for new ways to stimulate yourself.
Be creative. Be really creative. PRAY. You've got a big future ahead.
Don't give the past full reign in determining your future, however
wonderful your memories might be, or however complex, confusing
or even sinful those memories might be. Live in hope. Believe that
your future can be shaped by the creative spirit of the Lord. Be awake
and alert to its possibilities. Eternal life, after all, is going to last a long
time!

In focusing on the value of meditation and prayer, the retreat master may have been right on target.

I found a story in one of the little monthly devotional books that
come in the mail from time to time. A time management expert who
asked a seminar group to brainstorm all the things they could do in an
hour received a great variety of responses from the group—walk the
dog, nap, pay bills, clean the fish tank … you can add your own items to
the list. When the leader asked what activity would have the longest-
term impact on their lives, the response, after some discussion, was *pray*.

There was certainly no consistency in the room about what it meant to pray, but the value of prayer clearly had power and energy for them. Meditation, a sense of depth, a kind of centring, a conscious movement of hopeful connectedness to God.

> Lord, make us turn to you; let us see your face and we shall be saved. (Psalm 80)

Wouldn't that be a wonderful prayer for Dorothy to say? Dorothy, who, clinging to frozen memories, finds the future so empty? Wouldn't it be a wonderful prayer for priests on retreat, as they grapple with their busyness and the stresses and tensions of their ministry? Wouldn't it be a wonderful prayer for all of us as we look for energy and joy in our future?

> Give ear, O Shepherd of Israel.
> Stir up your might.
> Turn again, O God of hosts.
> Give us life, and we will call on your name. (Psalm 80)

Such prayer can have long-term impact on our whole way of being in the world.

Advent prayer is this kind of prayer. The call of this Sunday's liturgy, culminating in its reference to the final judgment that each of us will have to deal with, is a call to move forward in hope, to experience God who is continuously, eternally coming.

You may have heard the saying "Be patient. God isn't finished with me yet." That's another way of looking at the same experience, the experience of being human. God is not finished yet.

> He will also strengthen you to the end, so that you may be blameless on the day of our Lord Jesus Christ. God is faithful; by him you were called into fellowship with his Son, Jesus Christ our Lord. (1 Corinthians 1.8-9)

Wake-up Call

Second Sunday of Advent

Isaiah 40.1–5, 9–11
Psalm 85
2 Peter 3.8–15
Mark 1.1–8

Around this time several years ago, the *National Catholic Reporter* published a series of book reviews in its bookshelf column. If I remember correctly, the particular books in this group were designated "wake-up calls."

The reviewer began by recounting a "wake-up call" written by Flannery O'Connor in 1963, a short story entitled "Revelation." It's an odd, unlikely story, but it sure is a wake-up call! The story begins in a doctor's office. Mrs. Turpin and her husband are sitting on one side of the waiting room; a young, hippie-type woman by the name of Mary Grace sits on the other side. The Turpins are busily chatting. It's pretty clear from their conversation that they have the perfect family, the perfect car, the perfect house, the perfect children, and a perfect plan for the winter—going south, of course. Mrs. Turpin, however, isn't feeling very well and is concerned about feeling 100 per cent before setting off on their winter vacation. Mary Grace, on the opposite side of the room, is reading a book entitled *Human Development*. Tired of their talk, she hurls the book across the room, hitting Mrs. Turpin right on the head. "Go back to hell where you came from, you old warthog!" she shouts.

Imagine that happening in your doctor's office! Mrs. Turpin is getting some wake-up call: hit in the head with *Human Development* hurled at her by *Mary Grace*. O'Connor's symbolism is pretty clear.

Mrs. Turpin goes home with a headache and comes to realize that she is in hell—the hell of emptiness. That night she has a dream. There's a horde of people moving around in the starry skies of heaven, a horde of people, all shapes and sizes and colours. They're all singing Alleluias. They're being gathered into a procession. She and her husband are only more or less included. They're kind of dangling at the back, not singing Alleluias, but mumbling something undistinguishable under their breath.

We never learn what happened to Mrs. Turpin. We just know that something had to happen, hit over the head as she was by Mary Grace with *Human Development* and dreaming about her dangled mumbling. The story heralded the beginnings of something new for the Turpins, at least the possibility of new beginnings. It's pretty clear, at least in Flannery O'Connor's mind, that something new had to happen. Some changes would have to be made.

The beginning of the good news of Jesus Christ, the Son of God.

Mark's gospel, his own literary crafting of "the greatest story ever told," is designed to have the same effect. It is a wake-up call inviting us to participate in another kind of heavenly procession, to follow in the steps of Christ, who carries his cross into fullness of life. God's own plan and will for human development can be read in the person of Jesus. Mark's book is a call of grace.

Mark lays out the beginning of the good news in the life, death and resurrection of Jesus, but fully expects that this same transforming good news will be carried forward in the many and varied ways in which believers of every generation will take up where Jesus left off.

Did you notice Mark's robust and inclusive description of the scene at the river Jordan?

> John the Baptist appeared in the wilderness, proclaiming a baptism of repentance for the forgiveness of sins. And people from the *whole* Judean countryside and *all* the people of Jerusalem were going out to him, and were baptized by him in the river Jordan, confessing their sins. (Mark 1.4–5)

Quite a procession, isn't it? Picture it. People from the whole Judean countryside and all the people of Jerusalem coming out to the wilderness confessing their sins and going down into the waters of repentance.

John's message was clearly a wake-up call. He must have been hitting people right between the eyes. The ancient Israelites had passed through the Red Sea under Moses, and had passed through the Jordan under Joshua. Now they were being invited, not only to stand still for a moment to get their bearings, but to step back into the waters that gave birth to their nation. Confessing their sins, they were being born again. John's baptism for repentance was a big deal. The Greek word *metanoia*, which we translate as "repentance," is a very rich and broad concept involving not just minor adjustments, but a whole new way of living. It implied being reborn. Recognizing their sinfulness, the people chose to go back into the waters, not just for cleansing, but for rebirth in the faith and ideals that were their heritage. It's easy to understand how this kind of theology was incorporated into our understanding of Christian baptism.

It is this context that makes the text from the second letter of Peter so interesting. It really stands as a kind of homily about what Mark understands as the beginning of the good news—stretching out and continuing until the end of time, which may originally have been thought to be very near at hand, but turns out to be in the indefinite future. If, for example, you knew that you were going to die tomorrow, you'd probably have a pretty intense and busy day today.

Skeptics can scoff all they like about the myth of a final return, but that in no way compromises its inevitability for believers. My world is passing away—as is yours. The end is coming. "Prepare the way of the Lord, make his paths straight." The fact that the time, place and circumstances of my last day are unclear to me doesn't give me permission to enter into a Mrs. Turpin drift mode. The fact that the date for the end of the world is unknown and seems so far away doesn't give us permission to just let things go, whether it's the rights of the poor, the dignity of elders, or the condition of the ozone layer. Our judgments are to be made in light of the truth of our death and the truth of God's final judgment.

Perhaps this doesn't sound too Christmasy, but in fact, it is very much to the point. It would take another homily to deal with the fiery elements in verses 10 to 13, so let me read the text without them. The core meaning remains clear:

The day of the Lord will come …What sort of persons ought you to be in leading lives of holiness and godliness, waiting for and hastening the coming of the day of God?… In accordance with his promise, we wait for new heavens and a new earth, where righteousness is at home. (2 Peter 3.10-13)

In just a few weeks we'll all be singing one of my favourite Christmas hymns, "Hark! The Herald Angels Sing." Listen to the third verse:

Hail the heaven-born Prince of Peace!
Hail the Sun of righteousness!
Light and life to all he brings,
Risen with healing in his wings.
Mild he lays his glory by,
Born that we no more may die,
Born to raise us from the earth,
Born to give us second birth.

Can you sing those lines in anticipation of Christ's coming at our death or at the end of time with the same energy that we will find in our voices on Christmas Day? Can I?

That question may be kinder, gentler or subtler than the book Mary Grace whipped across the room at Mrs. Turpin, but it's just as disturbing. Still, we can be grateful that all of us probably have a good bit of time left before we have to deal with those eventualities first hand, for as 2 Peter says:

The Lord is not slow about his promise, as some think of slowness, but is patient with you, not wanting any to perish, but all to come to repentance.

'Tis the season. Seize the moment. Repent and believe the good news. Join the procession.

Come, Lord Jesus

Third Sunday of Advent

Isaiah 61. 1-2a, 10-11
Luke 1
1 Thessalonians 5.16-24
John 1.6-8, 19-28

About ten years ago now, Terry and Madeleine Anderson's book *Den of Lions* was published.[4] Terry Anderson, a good journalist, a good Catholic, engaged to be married—an overall remarkable man—was swept up in the violent conflict of a turbulent time in Lebanon. He lived in chains at the mercy of his Shiite Muslim captors for seven years. In one three-year period, he saw the light of day once. Imprisoned and beaten like an animal, he was tortured by grief, fatigue and hopelessness, but his spirit soared. Let me quote a few lines from his poem "Stigmata":

Seven years in chains
while love lies barren ...
Grim terrible years
in subterranean cells ...
passed from hand to hand ...
taped and bagged like
some dead meat, despised,
inedible, but useful in a trade.
Harsh and painful years
of darkness, damp, and dirt,
humiliations heaped in myriads ...
Wasted empty years? Not quite.
No years are empty in a life; and wasted—
that depends on what is made of them, and after.[5]

Not only was his own spirit remarkable over those seven years, but those who loved him—his sister, his fiancée, his daughter, his friends and colleagues—never gave up. That in itself was an overwhelming experience when he was finally reunited with them.

"I rarely ask God for freedom anymore," he wrote in 1988, half-way through his imprisonment. "He knows how much I want to go home. I've told him so often, He better know by now. I pray for patience, acceptance, strength. I give thanks for what I have. I'm not a saint or anything. But I'm sane. I think I am. I still rage. Sometimes I want to scream in frustration, but less often now. I am deeply unhappy and alone, but I know I can live. I'm just trying to be in touch with God. Not praying for freedom, but just trying to be in touch with God."[6]

Does it remind you of Paul's counsel from today's reading?

Rejoice always, pray without ceasing, give thanks in all circumstances; for this is the will of God in Christ Jesus for you. Do not quench the Spirit … May the God of peace himself sanctify you entirely. (1 Thessalonians 5.16-19, 23)

Terry Anderson lived those words. Although he was unable to "re-joice always," he was nevertheless able—really able—to remain faithful in prayer.

As we reach Advent's midpoint today, I suggest that all of us get in touch with our own life of personal faith and prayer.

"Come, Lord Jesus," we pray so often these days. "Come to be with me as I really am—in my situation today. Help me to embrace my life—whatever it may be today. Help me in the midst of the reality of my life to be filled with praise and thanksgiving. Help me to worship in spirit and in truth."

This kind of prayer is not just, or even primarily, a matter of asking God to change things around me. Prayer is openness to the possibility of change *within* me—change in how I see things, how I experience things, how I evaluate things in light of faith and hope. Sometimes these changes may be minor adjustments; at other times they may be very profound.

Faith and prayer are not lived in general but person by person. Individuals like you and me live out faith and prayer just as for centuries people like Isaiah, Mary, Paul and John the Baptist, all of whom are featured in today's liturgy, once lived.

We Catholics have the tradition of "hero worship"—the celebration and veneration of saints whose stories have come down to us from every time and place. In celebrating and venerating them, we recognize and affirm our very own possibilities. If God can work such marvels in them, what's stopping that same God from working marvels in me? If faith and prayer can sustain Isaiah, Mary and Paul—and, much more recently, Terry Anderson in a Lebanese jail cell—who's to say that I, too, will not be sustained in my own hope?

> Come, Lord Jesus: be *my* Lord—*my* guide and teacher.
> O come, Emmanuel: be God with *me*, God in *my* world.
> O come, thou Wisdom from on high:
> show the path of knowledge to *me*.
> O come, thou Dayspring from on high: cheer *me* by thy drawing nigh.
> O come, Desire of Nations: make *me* an instrument of peace and reconciliation.
> Maranatha. Come, Lord Jesus, come!

Let's let Paul continue his own reflection:

> Do not quench the Spirit. Do not despise the words of prophets, but test everything; hold fast to what is good; abstain from every form of evil. May the God of peace himself sanctify you entirely; and may your spirit and soul and body be kept sound and blameless at the coming of our Lord Jesus Christ. The one who calls you is faithful, and he will do this. (1 Thessalonians 5.19-24)

Let it be. Amen.
Maranatha. Come, Lord Jesus, come.

Unsettling David

Fourth Sunday of Advent

2 Samuel 7.1–5b, 8b–12, 14a, 16
Psalm 89
Romans 16.25–27
Luke 1.26–38

David was settled in his house. (2 Samuel 7.1)

David has big plans. Everything seems well under control. The Lord had, in the words of Second Samuel, given him rest from his enemies and now it's his turn to do something for God. David was living in a nice cedar house and, now that he has some free time, he thinks he'll build a house for God, a decent place for the ark of the covenant, which, until now, has been housed in a tent. Building a temple for his God would be an act of great piety, and a way of celebrating the peace and tranquility that he and the people are experiencing.

The word of God comes to Nathan who passes it on to David. God seems almost to be making fun of David's lofty plans. "Who do you think *you* are, making a house for *me*?" God seems to be asking. "I'm the one who is making a house for you. I am making you into a royal house."

Although temple building becomes a huge preoccupation with David's son Solomon just a generation later, at this stage God insists on remaining free, mobile and dynamic, unconfined to one place. Unlike his neighbours' gods, David's God wants no temple, needs no temple, and will approve of no temple.

No doubt you've heard this line quoted from John F. Kennedy's 1960 inaugural speech: "Ask not what your country can do for you. Ask what you can do for your country." Well, God is saying something quite different to David. "Ask not what you can do for me. Ask what you are ready to let me do for you."

Today's reading portrays God as giver of gifts, not the recipient of homage. David can do nothing for God. He can only be open to receive the gifts that come his way and respond. This kind of passivity goes against the grain, especially with men. The emphasis here is on what the living, moving God can do to unsettle David rather than what David can do to settle God.

> The Lord has taken David out of the fields to shepherd
> people instead of sheep.
> The Lord is building David a house.
> The Lord declares himself father to David.
> The Lord establishes David's throne and lineage forever.

There's a story told about a soldier who, at the end of a six-year career, had not received a single military paycheck since boot camp. It was later discovered that his records had been lost at his first duty station. Cannon never complained; he just didn't even notice, although he had missed 144 paychecks, totalling more than $103,000! Cannon lived in the barracks, ate in the mess hall, and set aside birthday and Christmas cheques from his family for special personal needs. He seemed to think that room and board were what the military offered for his services and thought he was being taken care of just fine. He was, after all, "in the service."

Is this ignorance or naïveté gone to seed or what? There is, however, something disarming about his simple trust in authority, in the system, and in the inherent value of what he was about. He was not only being given orders, but was also being given everything he needed to fulfill them as well as to sustain himself. He was "in the service."

This soldier's story blends Kennedy's line—"Ask not what your country can do for you. Ask what you can do for your country"—and God's line—"Ask not what you can do for me. Ask what you are ready to let me do for you." When a spirit bigger than your own gets under your skin, you find yourself ready to give more than could ordinarily be expected. Even what you can do for your country relies on a prior spirit of national pride, patriotism, generosity and sense of duty that was somehow given to you by your country, by its history, culture and ideals. None of us are real self-starters. Our batteries have been boosted by energies higher than or beyond our own.

David is asked to be in touch with that kind of paradoxical thinking. He's called to come to terms with the fact that as soon as he thinks he's running the show, as soon as he thinks he's a self-starter, he's in for a surprise and the surprise won't be funny.

Paul summarizes this theology of divine initiative and the primacy of grace in today's second reading.

> To *God who is able to strengthen you* according to … the revelation of the mystery … now disclosed … according to the command of the eternal God, *to bring about the obedience of faith*—to the only wise God, through Jesus Christ, to whom be the glory forever! Amen. (Romans 16)

Enter Mary, the Virgin Mary. Enter the angel Gabriel. The divine call and initiative taken with David, the shepherd boy of Bethlehem, is magnified in the divine call and initiative taken in the Virgin Mary of Nazareth.

Gabriel addresses Mary: "Greetings, favoured one! The Lord is with you," and assures her, "You have found favour with God." The Greek word *charis*, the root of our word "charism" or "charismatic," is here translated "favour," but could as well be translated "grace," as we do in the traditional form of the Hail Mary. "Hail Mary, full of grace"—full of divine favour. Hail Mary, gifted one. Mary is the object of God's special favour. Mary is the object of God's grace. Mary is the recipient of God's gifts.

Whatever motivated God to choose her, whatever prerequisites God may have noticed or discovered in her are not mentioned. Absolutely nothing is mentioned about Mary's faith, piety, virtue or family background. Luke identifies her simply as a young girl engaged to be married to a man named Joseph. More is said about Joseph, who is of the house of David. That gives him at least some qualification to be the father of the messiah, which, of course, it's clear will not be the case. Zechariah and Elizabeth are righteous and blameless, people who have kept God's commandments and prayed to God. They will be the parents of John the Baptist. Nothing of the kind is said of Mary. Absolutely no reason is given as to why God might have chosen her.

This is precisely the point. Nothing could have prepared her for this vocation. Nothing could have made anyone an appropriate choice for such a role in the ongoing story of God's love for the world.

After her dialogue with the angel, Mary makes a final response that is entirely consistent with this theological perspective.

"Here am I, the servant of the Lord; let it be with me according to your word." (Luke 1.38)

It's not even that she's embracing her vocation. She is resigned to it. "Let it be." There's no "Thank you very much." There's just "Let it be."

"Here am I, the servant of the Lord; let it be with me according to your word."

The Greek word *doulos*, translated here as "servant," literally means a slave.

"Here am I, a *slave* of the Lord; *let it be* with me according to your word."

Quite striking is the question of involuntary service deriving from an involuntary relationship to which Mary passively acquiesces.

God's instruction to David in the first reading—"Ask not what you can do for me. Ask what you're ready to let me do for you"—takes on new proportions when applied to Mary's response to the message of the angel. In our own circumstances and experience, it takes on new proportions again.

What are we ready to let God do with us and within us? How flexible are we? How open to possibilities? How ready to let go of what we think we are controlling in favour of something bigger? How ready are we to go beyond categories of worthiness and readiness when we think of our own future and that of others? What levels of faith and hope are operative in our lives? These might be very good questions to consider in preparation for our parish Advent Reconciliation service.

For now, let's just brace ourselves to say Amen—"Let it be"—at eucharist today.

The Christmas Initiative

Christmas Day

Isaiah 52.7-10
Psalm 98
Hebrews 1.1-6
John 1.1-18

And the Word became flesh and lived among us, and we have seen his glory, the glory as of a father's only son, full of grace and truth. (John 1.14)

This set of readings for the liturgy of Christmas Day tells no stories of Mary and Joseph; in fact, they are not even named. You may well have expected to hear about them this morning, to listen again to the familiar story of angels and shepherds, even to connect with the "lowing cattle" of the familiar carol.

In these texts, you find no angels, no shepherds, no baby Jesus, no sheep, no cattle, no Magi. You have, however, heard a story, a wonderful story: "In the beginning was the Word ... the Word became flesh and lived among us." Rather deep for a Christmas morning when gifts await unwrapping, and a turkey, roasting. Listen again to its main lines:

In the beginning was the Word, and the Word was with God, and the Word was God. He was in the beginning with God. All things came into being through him, and without him not one thing came into being. What has come into being in him was life, and the life was the light of all people. The light shines in the darkness, and the darkness did not overcome it.

And the Word became flesh and lived among us, and we have seen his glory, the glory as of a father's only son, full of grace and truth ... From his fullness we have all received, grace upon grace. (John 1.14, 16)

It is a wonderful story, a cosmic story that finds its beginnings in the creation of the universe, moves forward to the incarnation of the Word in Christ, his coming among us that we celebrate today, and moves forward again to our own connectedness with this fullness of grace and truth, and our potential to be beneficiaries of "grace upon grace."

The images and metaphors of this gospel invite us to enter into the familiar story of Jesus' birth through another door, to view it through another window. If we want, we can read the Jesus, Mary and Joseph stories as outsiders; we can stand back from them. They are, after all, about something that happened in a long distant past. John's telling of the story leaves no such option. It draws us in and offers important, clear options. It reaches forward, inviting people in every age to participate. Some accept him and some do not, but those who do "see his glory ... and receiv[e] from his fullness grace upon grace."

Let's spend a few moments with the central image of the story, the image of a "word taking flesh." How does your own word take flesh? The word is that by which we express ourselves. It begins in your mind, heart and soul, but takes concrete form "in flesh." Sometimes it takes flesh in language, sometimes in gesture, sometimes in a facial expression, perhaps even in a work of art.

A word or an idea cannot simply remain in our minds and hearts and expect another to receive it. To effect or create anything, it needs to be expressed. It can't do anything if it's bottled up in our interiority. It has to come out somehow. A clenched fist is a word made flesh. A smile is a word made flesh. A spoken word is an idea, a concept or a feeling made flesh. A blueprint for a building or a work of art is a word made flesh.

In the prologue to John's gospel, we read how the Word of God became flesh, how Jesus Christ himself is God's ultimate self-expression, God's greatest word.

The text begins with references to the book of Genesis, where God's creative self-expression is first found in light, and continues to develop throughout the creation process, culminating in humanity made in the image and likeness of God. This kind of language suggests that in a certain sense, God is already incarnate in human beings, but because we failed to live up to our full potential, God takes a new initiative— the Christmas initiative. God's selfexpression takes new and definitive form in the Word-made-flesh, the incarnate Word, the Light of the world, whom we recognize as Jesus Christ, the utter fullness of God's image and likeness, born on Christmas Day.

The wonderful mystery that is proclaimed in John's gospel and celebrated on Christmas Day is that God did not choose to limit his self-expression to creation, however wondrous and varied. Nor was God satisfied with expressing his will in commandments and covenants, however clear and specific. Instead Christmas announces that God's ultimate self-expression is found in the person of Jesus, the Word-made-flesh whom John's gospel will ultimately reveal as the Way, the Truth and the Life for all believers.

The Word-made-flesh!

Let's look a little more carefully at the consequences of this marvellous divine decision, this wonderful initiative.

Some Christians in the past and, I suspect, some today may be uncomfortable with the word "flesh" for various reasons. They may lean towards considering the world to be an evil place from which they must escape to more spiritual realms. For them salvation involves getting out of or beyond worldly matters and concerns. From this vantage point, redemption means freedom from the earthly, the historical, the sensual.

The Christmas gospel will have none of this. Salvation is the fulfillment, not the negation, of creation. If anything, it exalts the possibilities of human life lived fully and abundantly. "The Word became flesh and lived among us." He who "was in the beginning with God" and "without whom not one thing came into being" himself "becomes flesh." Jesus as Word-made-flesh does not come to rescue God's people from a dark and dangerous world, but to embrace that very world and to teach us how to embrace it in his spirit, to find abundant life in its abundant possibilities.

I came across a story about King Henry III of Bavaria, who lived in the eleventh century. Apparently he became tired of his earthly duties and responsibilities and felt a call to a simpler, more spiritual life. He made an application to Prior Richard to enter his monastery as a contemplative, finally free from worldly distractions to foster his spiritual life.

Prior Richard responded, "Your Majesty, do you understand that one of the vows here is that of obedience? That will be hard for you since you have been a king and are used to giving, not receiving, orders." "I understand," Henry said. "For the rest of my life I will be obedient to you, as Christ leads you."

"Then I will tell you what to do," Prior Richard responded. "Go back to your throne and serve faithfully and generously in the place where God has put you."

God's ultimate self-expression is about embracing the world with all of its complexities and challenges as God embraced the world in Christ. It is an invitation to enter ever more deeply into the concrete possibilities inherent in the "flesh," which, in Christ, God's very self shares with every human being. It is the Word-made-flesh who says, "Follow me" in a life that is self-giving, generous, gracious and authentic in the midst of the world.

It is the Word-made-flesh, the Jesus who is born on Christmas Day, who is grace upon grace and the best and fullest sign of our own possibilities as words made flesh in our own right—for we are created in the image and likeness of God. In the very person of Jesus, God reveals humankind's highest and most glorious possibilities, and invites us to discover our highest potential and destiny in Jesus.

As John's gospel unfolds, we see powerful examples of persons who came to terms with this revelation. They came to life in new ways and discovered God's own life and glory at work in their own flesh. Among others, we meet Nicodemus, who first came to Jesus under the cover of darkness and only gradually opened up to the possibility of rebirth in him. We meet an anonymous woman at the well, and an anonymous man born blind, who represent all of us in both our fragility and our deepest potential. We see and are invited to identify with the transformation that takes place in them.

Today the word of God is as true, as active and as creative as is our own capacity to listen. The word of God is as active as our readiness to receive its promptings. Jesus is as ready to be "grace upon grace" for us as we are ready to embrace him, follow him, live his way, and find life and glory in his transforming presence at work in our own history, in our own flesh. In Christ, God is as ready to embrace our flesh as we are ready to embrace his Spirit.

In a profoundly mysterious way, God takes the initiative in the incarnation. God enters into a new depth of holy communion with the whole of humanity, indeed with the whole of the created universe. We, for our part, are invited to respond with open hands, minds and hearts as we speak our eucharistic "Amen."

Seniors Say
the Darndest Things

Feast of the Holy Family

Genesis 15.1-6; 17.3b-5, 15-16; 21
Psalm 105
Hebrews 11.8, 11-12, 17-19
Luke 2.22-40

Simeon took him in his arms and praised God, saying, "Master, now you are dismissing your servant in peace, according to your word; for my eyes have seen your salvation, which you have prepared in the presence of all peoples, a light for revelation to the Gentiles and for glory to your people Israel." (Luke 2.28-32)

Do you find it strange that there is not one word in this story about any temple official being involved in the purification or presentation rituals? There is no mention whatsoever of a liturgical prayer or of a word of congratulations or admonition from a priest or other temple official. Instead it is Simeon and Anna, two faithful elders of the community, who speak up to acknowledge who Jesus is on the occasion of his presentation and his mother's purification. They offer both promise and warning. Although they are not ordained and have no official capacity, Luke recognizes the impeccable credentials that are to be found in their long life and consistent witness. Luke gives them the speaking parts.

Simeon, for his part, is "righteous and devout." For his whole life he has looked forward to the "consolation of Israel." The Holy Spirit is guiding his life, resting on him, telling him that he will live to see the Messiah, and directing him to the temple when the time arrives. For her part, Anna, who doesn't say as much, is always in the temple. "She never left the temple but worshipped there with fasting and prayer night and day."

From the vantage point of their whole life and their whole experience with God, they see and articulate what others who may have been present must have missed. Even with all their years behind them, their hope has kept them alert to the fulfillment of God's promises. These two astonishing figures announce to Mary, Joseph and anyone else who may have been within earshot that the infant Jesus is the key player in the huge drama of God's plan. He is the "consolation of Israel" and the "redemption of Jerusalem." Here, in the magnificence of the temple, they see in this child something even more magnificent. This child will transcend space and time. His significance will go beyond a place where ritual worship is offered. In his person, he will be a sign, however violently opposed, through which *interior worship* will be offered. In him "the *inner thoughts* of many will be revealed." In him the external rites of the temple will be transcended. Here, in the person of Jesus himself, the final sacrifice will be offered, Israel consoled, and Jerusalem redeemed—and a sword shall pierce his mother's heart. The temple experience of purification will continue into her whole experience of being this child's mother.

It is in this rich theological context that we recognize and celebrate the piety and faithful religious observance of the Holy Family. We can imagine Mary and Joseph making their way to the temple, perhaps taking turns carrying the child. We learn that they are of modest means, offering "a pair of turtledoves or two young pigeons" rather than a more costly sheep. While we can see in them a certain modelling of fidelity and religious piety that we can certainly imitate, Luke clearly has other insights that take us beyond the traditional sentimentality of this feast and place it in the context of the paschal climax of Jesus' life.

Even as we ponder the close-up of Mary and Joseph changing their coins, purchasing doves, and carrying out their religious duties, we need to see the big picture of the temple itself and of the city of Jerusalem in which it stood. In bringing Jesus to Jerusalem, and to the Jerusalem temple at the appropriate time for his presentation, Mary and Joseph are beginning a process that will come to its completion in his death and resurrection. They are setting the stage for a story that will reach its climax when Jesus will come back to Jerusalem and its temple for its purification and, paradoxically, its redemption for the consolation of Israel and the world.

Here are two of Luke's references to that climactic moment:

> When some were speaking about the temple, how it was adorned with beautiful stones and gifts dedicated to God, Jesus said, "as for these things that you see, the days will come when not one stone will be left upon another, all will be thrown down ..." (Luke 21.5-6)

> It was now about noon, and darkness came over the whole land until three in the afternoon, while the sun's light failed; and the curtain of the temple was torn in two. Then Jesus, crying with a loud voice, said, "Father, into your hands I commend my spirit." Having said this, he breathed his last. When the centurion saw what had taken place, he praised God ... (Luke 23.44-47)

"Presentation in the temple" indeed: Simeon was quite right in pointing to the truth that the consolation of Israel and the revelation of inner thoughts of the heart would not come without a price.

Over the years I've often been struck by the presence of grandparents and great-grandparents at the baptism of infants. I guess it's the experience we would have that corresponds most closely to the events of today's gospel.

Years ago, Art Linkletter hosted a TV show called *Kids Say the Darndest Things,* in which he interviewed children. Maybe it's only you grandparents who even know who Art Linkletter was—I guess that dates me, too. I'd like to suggest that *seniors say the darndest things.* It's not that people of a certain age are in the early stages of dementia, although some may be, but at a certain age people find a certain freedom to tell it exactly as they see it.

Our understanding of family and our commitment to family is a many-splendoured thing. The small, intimate picture of family life, however functional or dysfunctional, is set within the context of history and culture. Family values celebrated at Christmas extend far and wide.

Simeon and Anna knew this. They were among the first to proclaim it. They explicitly called the holy family beyond the event of the day to the universal significance of the Christ event itself. They set the story in its broadest possible context.

We are all part of a big world, a big family, in which each of us takes our place. We don't know for sure how Anna prayed, but Simeon's prayer has been at the centre of the church's night prayer for centuries—and not just at Christmas. The liturgy stretches it to its paschal limits, tying it with Jesus' last word from the cross. Simeon's spirituality is linked directly with the spirituality of Jesus himself.

"Father, into your hands I commend my spirit." (Luke 23.46)

"Master, now you are dismissing your servant in peace, according to your word; for my eyes have seen your salvation, which you have prepared in the presence of all peoples, a light for revelation to the Gentiles and for glory to your people Israel." (Luke 2.28-32)

"Father, into your hands I commend my spirit." (Luke 23.46)

Yes, indeed! The prophecies of Simeon and Anna were fulfilled!

The child grew and became strong, filled with wisdom; and the favour of God was upon him. (Luke 2.40)

Addressing God in the Diminutive

Solemnity of Mary, the Mother of God

Numbers 6.22-27
Psalm 67
Galatians 4.4-7
Luke 2.16-21

When the fullness of time had come, God sent his Son, born of a woman, born under the law, in order to redeem those who were under the law, so that we might receive adoption as children ..., God has sent the Spirit of his Son into our hearts, crying, "Abba! Father!" (Galatians 4.4-6)

Mary treasured all these words, and pondered them in her heart. (Luke 2.19)

New Year's Day is surely not an occasion for a long or complicated homily. Nobody's in shape for that. But here we are in church on the first day of a new year—a day that celebrates Mary, the mother of God and invites us to pray for peace. Surely this invites at least a medium-length homily!

When hearing that beautiful text from Luke, I have always liked to picture Mary treasuring and pondering. I like to picture Mary praying. Today I'd like to picture her praying over what Paul is writing to the Galatians. I don't imagine that she ever knew that text, but, who knows, she could have still been alive when it was written. It is highly unlikely that she would have prayed over that text itself, but in her own experience of the resurrection of Jesus, she surely prayed over the content, the subject matter of Paul's theological reflection on her mission and her own place in God's plan.

> When the fullness of time had come, God sent his Son, born of a woman, born under the law, in order to redeem those who were under the law, so that we might receive adoption as children ... God has sent the Spirit of his Son into our hearts, crying, "Abba! Father!"

Has it ever struck you how bold Paul's theology is here? Maybe New Year's Day is a good day to be "struck." That God exists isn't that big a stretch. Actually, there is all kinds of discussion among scientists linking certain aspects of physics with a divine mind, and with the utterly inconceivable probability that the universe in all its wonder and complexity exists "by chance."

Believe it or not, the radio program that awakened me this morning was discussing astronomy. Did you know that at this point over fifty million stars have been officially named? That's almost twice the population of Canada! Maybe I was half asleep and didn't get the numbers right, but that's my recollection—fifty million stars named! Imagine the immensity of what is yet to be discovered and remains unnamed in the huge expanse of the universe. Imagine, too, the "length and breadth and depth" of the God whom we name "creator of heaven and earth."

Another way of coming at the mystery of creation is to go not big, but small, to look not up into the heavens, but down the lens of a microscope at a single cell of matter. I remember as a teenager—I guess I was in Grade 10—looking at a slide through a microscope for the first time. I don't remember what I was looking at, but it was amazing! That tiny little thing was so complex and full of life: it had countless moving parts, I later learned, that we couldn't see even through our high school lab microscopes.

> When the fullness of time had come, God sent his Son, born of a woman, born under the law, in order to redeem those who were under the law, so that we might receive adoption as children ... God has sent the Spirit of his Son into our hearts, crying, "Abba! Father!"

The truth being proclaimed here is that the God of the stars and the God of the tiny cells teeming with life entered personally into time and space. God's Son, "God from God, light from light, true God from true God, begotten not made, one in being with the Father through whom all things were made" was born under the law, born of a woman, that *we might receive* adoption and call that creator of heaven and earth "Abba." I know that was a mouthful, but you get the point. Wonder of wonders: Mary's privileged role is to be the instrument of incarnation—the Mother of God.

This goes way beyond the mystery of creation. The creation of heaven and earth is one thing, but God entering into time and space, knowing me, adopting me, and letting me call him Abba, "Father," and its familiar diminutive form, the equivalent of "Daddy"—that's totally awesome. You don't just look into the heavens or through a microscope and call God "Dad."

It's wonderful to note here that even prior to the incarnation, this kind of theology was at work in Israel. Psalm 131 says, "I have calmed and quieted my soul, like a weaned child with its mother." Another translation reads: "As a child rests on his mother's knee, so I rest with you, my God."

Here, too, we find a diminutive form of the more formal "Mother." Yes, Israel was invited to call God "Mom." The God of the Bible is that close—as close as your mother's knee, as close as your mother's breast! We, too, are invited to address the Almighty in the diminutive. We're invited to be that confident and sure of ourselves in our relationship with God.

As we were discussing the mystery of vocation, one of my students last year commented that this kind of thinking is either "high arrogance or transforming grace." Let us pray in the ancient words of Aaron that it will be high grace for us all:

May the Lord bless us and keep us;
the Lord make his face to shine upon us,
and be gracious to us;
the Lord lift his countenance upon us,
and give us peace.

Brightest and Best
of the Sons of the Morning

Epiphany

Isaiah 60.1-6
Psalm 72
Ephesians 3.2-3a, 5-6
Matthew 2.1-12

Star of wonder, star of night,
Star with royal beauty bright,
Westward leading, still proceeding,
Guide us to thy perfect light.

Every year when this feast comes up I find myself fascinated by the star of Bethlehem, the star that invites and guides the wise to Jesus, the star that moves, that leads, that guides. When the star stops over the place where Jesus is, the wise will come to terms with Jesus himself as light of the world. As the star in heaven disappears, it will dawn on them that the real star is Jesus himself.

Star of wonder, star of night,
Star with royal beauty bright,
Westward leading, still proceeding,
Guide us to thy perfect light.

Most Catholics aren't all that familiar with my own favourite epiphany hymn, "Brightest and Best of the Sons of the Morning." Written by Reginald Heber, an evangelical missionary to India, it is sung to the wonderful tune MORNING STAR. This is its first verse, repeated also at the end.

Brightest and best of the sons of the morning,
Dawn on our darkness and lend us thine aid.

Star of the east, the horizon adorning,
Guide where our infant redeemer is laid.

In Heber's text the star takes on a prophetic personality. The star of Bethlehem is personified. He is the brightest and best *son* of the morning, reflecting in his own personality the brightness of the infant redeemer—the brightest and best of all.

The image of Jesus as light and warmth is one with which we can identify very easily. Children, for example, when examining the paschal candle at Easter, come very quickly to see how the light of the candle helps them to see with their eyes but that the light of Jesus is about seeing with their minds. They don't use the language of insight or inner vision, but they do know what it's all about. They can recognize, too, that as the candle warms their hands when they hold them over its flame, so Jesus warms their hearts if they let themselves get near enough to him.

It all seems so bright and warm and attractive, doesn't it? The reality is, however, that new or fresh insight is not always easy to receive. Many of us would rather be left in the dark about some things. "What you don't know can't hurt you." It's true, too, that if you get too close to the fire, you might get burned. We'll learn later that it's a refiner's fire that Jesus brings. His is transforming, purifying energy that may not be all that comfortable.

An epiphany meditation by Karl Rahner S.J., one of the pre-eminent Catholic theologians of the twentieth century, was published a while ago in the *Catholic New Times*. Rahner writes:

Sometimes we don't want our hearts stirred up. Sometimes we don't want to leave home. We don't want a star moving anywhere. We want to curl up like a cat for a snooze.[7]

King Herod was like that, only worse. The original wise ones, kings themselves in the familiar carol, were ready to risk new insight and transforming energy to meet a baby king whose nativity was being publicized by a heavenly light show. Instead, they first had to deal with his antitype, King Herod, who, in secret, tried to defeat the purposes of the star that was *made to appear*.

Do you notice the passive voice here? The star was "made to appear." Herod is not in charge of this epiphany and, in the night sky above his kingdom, the brightest son of the morning proceeds without his consultation or consent, and the wise continue to track it. For all of his own resistance to its rays, Herod cannot stop God's epiphany. He cannot put out the fire or snuff out the light of the world. We'll learn later of the extremes to which he went trying to do just that, but the star moves on and will continue to move on in spite of him and those like him in every age.

> [The star] stopped over the place where the child was. When [the magi] saw that the star had stopped, they were overwhelmed with joy. (Matthew 2.9b–10)

It is then, when the star stopped, that the wise entered the house and saw the child. They reacted as I suppose one should to an epiphany: they fell on their faces. They prostrated themselves in a position of reverence and homage from which, ironically, they wouldn't be able to see anything but the ground. Only then did they take out their gifts.

> The Lord will arise upon you,
> and his glory will appear over you.
> Nations shall come to your light,
> and kings to the brightness of your dawn …
> They shall bring gold and frankincense,
> and shall proclaim the praise of the Lord. (Isaiah 60.2b–3, 6b)

Rahner suggests that the kind of ardent restlessness that is the foundation of the Magi's stepping out after the star is not a comfortable impulse. Is there a star out there beckoning you? Is it big, bright and steady, or is it small and twinkling? How do you feel when you look at it?

Like it or not, there is a star out there for all of us. The light of Christ and the transforming warmth of his grace are for all people. The star is the good out there to be sought, the truth to be embraced. Even your regrets about your weaknesses and sinfulness which can sometimes stir your conscience could be that twinkling star. Don't let it frighten you. Don't create clouds to hide it from you. Don't pull out your sunglasses or your baseball cap to shield your eyes from its rays. Follow where it leads, and when it stops, go into the house, prostrate yourself, and offer your gifts—your heart's adoration, the prayers of your own poverty.

My Son, the Beloved

Baptism of the Lord

Isaiah 55.1-11
Isaiah 12
1 John 5.1-9
Mark 1.7-11

And just as he was coming up out of the water, he saw the heavens torn apart and the Spirit descending like a dove on him. And a voice came from heaven, "You are my Son, the Beloved; with you I am well pleased." (Mark 1.10-11)

Over the last couple of years, teaching sacramental theology to seminarians and working with them in developing their own pastoral and spiritual approaches to the celebration of the sacraments, I have come to appreciate even more the richness of biblical texts such as this one. At first sight, it appears to be just a two-verse description of a remarkable event in the life of Jesus, but, on closer examination, virtually every word in it reveals an aspect of his ultimate significance for us and for the whole world. The text also invites each of us personally to understand the significance of our own baptism as we contemplate his, to recognize something of our own vocation as he experiences his. Let's look at the text more carefully.

In *coming up out of the water,* Jesus is heralding a new creation. Genesis 1 reports that the earth was a formless void, that the spirit was hovering over the deep, and once the waters were ordered and "tamed," creation could continue. He is coming out of waters, out of the deep. He leaves chaos and death behind. The waters out of which he arises can also be reminiscent of the flood in Noah's time that destroyed evil while at the same time buoying up an ark of renewal for the world. They are the waters of the sea through which Moses led the people of Israel to freedom from bondage, the waters of the Jordan through which

Joshua led them to their promised home. Coming up out of the waters, Jesus is Adam, Noah, Moses and Joshua all at the same time. Coming up out of the waters, he brings with him the whole story of his people with its promise of re-creation, purification, liberation, freedom and the security of being at home.

He saw the *heavens torn apart.* In Mark's time it was popular to believe in a plurality of heavens, many layers beyond the earth. God would dwell in the farthest, most remote of these heavens. God was acting decisively in the heavens being torn apart. God was, as it were, escaping traditional boundaries and becoming present on earth in a new way. The tearing or splitting open of the heavens at Jesus' baptism matches the splitting or tearing of the temple's curtain at the moment of his death. In Jesus God is escaping traditional boundaries. God is now present and active in a new way—beyond the heavens, beyond the holy of holies. God is acting decisively in the life, death and resurrection of Jesus.

And he saw *the Spirit descending like a dove on him.* The Spirit appears as a dove. Noah's dove? Yes, and more. Genesis uses a kind of bird language in the creation story when the spirit (breath of God) is hovering over the deep. For Moses and the people, it was a "strong east wind all night" (breath or spirit of God) that opened the sea for their deliverance. Once again, this time over Jesus, the descending spirit is creativity, purification and liberation, God at work in a new way.

And a voice came from heaven, "You are my Son, the Beloved; with you I am well pleased. It is noteworthy in all of this that *Jesus saw* and *Jesus heard.* There is no indication that anyone else saw or heard anything at the time. Of course, Mark's readers see and hear everything. We know from the "beginning" of the good news that this Jesus is the Son of God. Here, at the outset of the gospel, Mark describes how Jesus, in the fullness of his humanity, experiences the call of God to which he will respond in stages throughout his life. The experience of his baptism sets him on the right path. In his baptism he gets off on the right foot.

Just who he is, the "messianic secret," will be revealed in the gospel only in stages. It will first be revealed to an intimate core group of his disciples at the transfiguration, with Moses and Elijah as witnesses, when the voice from the clouds again proclaims Jesus "my Son, the Beloved" (Mark 9.7). They, as we know, will misinterpret the message.

Jesus himself will acknowledge the truth of this revelation at the time of his trial when he will affirmatively answer the question of the high priest, "Are you the Messiah, the Son of the Blessed One?" (Mark 14.61-62). The priest, of course, will reject and mock his answer.

What was revealed to Jesus at his baptism comes out to the world only at the cross, where there will be no further possibility of misunderstanding its meaning and consequences. Only then will the secret be out.

> And the curtain of the temple was torn in two, from top to bottom. Now when the centurion, who stood facing him, saw that in this way he breathed his last, he said, "Truly this man was God's Son!" (Mark 15.38-39)

The word is out. At the cross Jesus is most definitively recognized and affirmed for what he really is. No mistakes or misunderstandings are possible anymore. God is well pleased.

You are my Son, *the Beloved*. We haven't said anything yet about the "Beloved." Could it be that this word links God and Jesus with Abraham and Isaac? Isaac is the son, the only son, the beloved son of Abraham through whom a people will arise whose members will outnumber the sands on the shore or the stars in the heavens. Is there already in this scene a foreshadowing of the Father's readiness to sacrifice his son, his only son, the beloved, out of whose death will arise a new people? Is Jesus here being designated as a new Isaac for a reconfiguration of God's people beyond traditional racial and cultural lines? Can we discern here the implied promise of a new covenant, inclusive of the likes of us? Such would surely be consistent, wouldn't it, with the heavens being torn open and the temple curtain split.

Is it any wonder that our theology of Christian baptism arises out of these very symbols and images, and finds its roots in this scene? In its "secret message" that we are still gradually coming to terms with in our own life of faith? The baptism of Jesus is the beginning. Its direction, energy and significance continue in us who have been baptized into his name—"The Son, the Beloved."

As we celebrate baptism today, and whenever we do so, we will hear all of these themes re-echoed in the blessing of the baptismal waters out of which two infants will arise, reborn in him.

Father, look with love upon your church and unseal for it the fountain of baptism. By the power of the Holy Spirit give to this water the grace of your Son, so that in the sacrament of baptism all those whom you have created in your likeness may be cleansed from sin and rise to a new birth of innocence by water and the Holy Spirit. We ask you, Father, with your Son to send the Holy Spirit upon the waters of this font. May all who are buried with Christ in the death of baptism rise also with him to newness of life.

What a plunge these two little ones will take! Baptized into the death and resurrection of Christ they will take their place with us as instruments for the re-creation of the world in his image, for purification and liberation—what a plunge!

Are we ready?

Come and See

Second Sunday in Ordinary Time

1 Samuel 3.3b-10, 19
Psalm 40
1 Corinthians 6.13c-15a, 17-20
John 1.35-42

Getting to know you, getting to know all about you,
Getting to like you, getting to hope you like me...

I'm sure you all recognize these lyrics from Rodgers and Hammerstein's *The King and I*. Anna, the teacher from far away, is making her way into the lives of the children of the King of Siam. Gradually they need to learn how to be at home with each other.

Introductions are also happening in today's passage from the very first chapter of John's gospel. The first disciples are getting used to the presence of this new figure and to what being at home with him will involve for them. Let's take a closer look at the text to see how really intense and compact it is.

"Look, here is the *Lamb of God!*"
"*Rabbi,* where are you staying?"
"We have found the *Messiah.*"

"You are Simon son of John. You are to be called *Cephas*"
(which is translated Peter).

Lamb of God, Teacher, Messiah—all titles given to Jesus. How did they really see all that in him—and so quickly? Astonishing!

Cephas-Peter-Rock—a name or title given to Simon. How could Jesus really see that kind of potential in Simon, so early in their relationship?

Notice, too, some of the key verbs in the text.

"*Look,*" John said.

Jesus turned. "What are you *looking for?*"

"*Come* and *see.*"

They *came* and *saw* and *remained.*

What's happening here is clearly more than comings and goings motivated by curiosity. There is looking, there is searching, there is probing, there is a relationship developing where people can look into each other's hearts and see what is invisible. There is depth perception; there is spiritual recognition; there is faith. "Getting to know you" is a very big deal—it's life-changing!

This kind of developing faith recognition—these titles and searching verbs—are even more interesting when we see how John places this scene on the second of three consecutive days at the beginning of his gospel.

On the third day   does that make you expect something special? he went to Cana, to a wedding feast, where water used for footwashing was transformed into the finest wine. On the third day, in this sign, Jesus *revealed* his glory. They *saw* and *believed* in him. There will be another third day on which they will see and believe in a new way, a day on which his glory will be revealed, the day when his "hour" will come.

Every year, it seems, Jesus makes front-page headlines. A few years ago, in the weeks just before Christmas, he was on the front page of the *Ottawa Citizen* twice, and made it to the cover of *Time* magazine as well. In all three cases, the journalists were dealing with questions of what really happened: exactly who Jesus was, what he thought of himself and his mission, what exactly was the content of his preaching, and what his contemporaries would have thought of him.

As interesting as this discussion might be for some, and as disturbing as it might be for others, it invites us to take a close look at the nature of the gospel accounts. Clearly they are trying to communicate more than historical facts. Although based on historical experience with Jesus of Nazareth, they are crafted to invite faith and decision. The sequence of events in today's gospel is a case in point. More important to the author than the details of the events of three days is his intention to bring the reader into the action, to draw us beneath the surface into the mystery of the story itself.

Let's look at the three titles found in the story.

Lamb of God: Clearly, the evangelist believed that Jesus is the ultimate sacrifice. Rooted in the Jewish sacrificial traditions, the event of his death on Good Friday has been interpreted in sacrificial terms. Volumes have been written analyzing these connections. But how is Jesus becoming the Lamb of God for those first disciples who accepted John the Baptist's challenge to "look"? More important are these questions to us: How do you see Jesus as the Lamb of God? In what way does he take away the sins of the world? How do you see and experience that? How does his sacrificial life and death purify you? The answers to questions like these are clearly beyond the evangelist's reporting of the events of those first three days. From its roots in the historical Jesus, a theology of sacrifice takes off. What happens to believers as they get to know him as the Lamb of God?

Rabbi: Jesus is teacher. That Jesus was actually engaged with his contemporaries in the classical Jewish forms of debate and discussion is clear. The gospels disclose something of his style and his slant on the tradition. But what happens to people who, as they get to know him, become disciples? What do they see in his teaching? How are they formed and changed by the vision he shares with them? Perhaps more importantly, in what way is he your teacher, my teacher? Can you picture yourself at home with him, sitting at his feet? From their roots in the historical Jesus, his teachings take off. What happens to believers in the process of getting to know him as Rabbi?

Messiah: Let's explore just one aspect of this rich title. What was the liberating power of Jesus? How do the New Testament writers understand this aspect of his life and ministry? What did his way of being liberator accomplish? Volumes have been written analyzing various approaches to christology (the theological interpretation of the nature of Christ) and soteriology (theology dealing with his work of salvation). For the evangelist, however, the dominant issue is this: What kind of freedom, safety or liberation did those first disciples experience? How were they saved? What difference did it make to them? Perhaps more importantly, how does Jesus free you? How does he save *you*? From what forms of slavery are you being drawn away? From its roots in the historical Jesus, his liberating power "takes off." What happens to believers in the process of getting to know him as Messiah?

Could you or I be living testimony to the power of his death, the truth of his teaching, the freedom of his salvation? From our roots in the historical Jesus, can our day-to-day living of the gospel witness to the power of his sacrifice, the integrity of his teaching, the hope of his messianic death and resurrection? From their roots in the historical Jesus, do our own faith, hope and love take off? How do getting to know him and learning to be at home with him make a difference?

Huub Oosterhuis was a prominent Dutch priest, poet and university chaplain. I've adapted his own vision of Jesus that he used to share with his students as he prepared to lead them into the action of the eucharist.[8] Originally it was set to music and used as a communion song.

> Like all other people, he was called by a name when he was born far from here and in a distant past. He was named Yeshua, Jesus, son of Joseph, son of David, son of Jesse, son of Judah, son of Jacob, son of Abraham, son of Adam, son of man…
>
> He was also called Son of God, saviour, vision of peace, light of the world, living bread, saving cup…
>
> Like so many other people, he was loved, but misunderstood. He was preserved in memory and story. In his flesh he was companion, teacher, healer, comforter, challenger, confronter— but servant, who gave up his life for his friends, who was betrayed by a friend, who was tortured on the cross, who prayed for his enemies, who died like a criminal…
>
> Unlike anyone else, arising he rises. Arising he remains alive in word and sign handed down for the safety and forgiveness of all who name him and bear his name. Arising he lives as a name in my memory, a voice in my conscience. I remember him and name him, as arising again in my living—and my dying—I recognize him as bread and wine broken and poured out for life and communion, as bread to be eaten and wine to be passed, he becomes human again in me and my countless companions.
>
> I am mindful of him here, I name him and commend him to you. Look! Come and see!

Second Fiddle

Third Sunday in Ordinary Time

Jonah 3.1-5, 10
Psalm 25
1 Corinthians 7.29-31
Mark 1.14-20

"And they lived happily ever after." Remember that line? It was the last line of countless tales that you were probably told as children getting ready for bed so that you would have "sweet dreams."

Biblical stories, even those that seem to have happy endings, are more complex. They lead to dreams all right, but dreams that have a bittersweet quality to them. The story of Jonah is a case in point: the wonderful, ironic, even humorous story of a reluctant prophet. God called him with a mission to go to Nineveh, which was the last place in the world Jonah cared to go. Thinking he could escape even God, he got passage on a ship to Tarshish, but when a storm broke out, threatening his life and everybody else's, he knew that God had caught up with him. He jumped ship, was swallowed by a giant fish and was spit up on the shores of, you guessed it, Nineveh. How's that for a bedtime story?

The reluctant prophet got to Nineveh in spite of himself, and in spite of himself he did God's work with phenomenal success. The people repented: even the animals were in sackcloth and ashes, and God "changed his mind about the calamity that he had said he would bring upon them; and he did not do it." Was Jonah thrilled? Was he happy and relieved? Not on your life. Here's the ending of the story:

This was very displeasing to Jonah, and he became angry. He prayed to the Lord and said, "O Lord! Is not this what I said while I was still in my own country? That is why I fled to Tarshish at the beginning; for I knew that you are a gracious

God and merciful, slow to anger, and abounding in steadfast love, and ready to relent from punishing. And now, O Lord, please take my life from me, for it is better for me to die than to live." And the Lord said, "Is it right for you to be angry?" Then Jonah went out of the city and sat down east of the city, and made a booth for himself there. He sat under it in the shade, waiting to see what would become of the city. The Lord God appointed a bush, and made it come up over Jonah, to give shade over his head, to save him from his discomfort; so Jonah was very happy about the bush. But when dawn came up the next day, God appointed a worm that attacked the bush, so that it withered. When the sun rose, God prepared a sultry east wind, and the sun beat down on the head of Jonah so that he was faint and asked that he might die. He said, "It is better for me to die than to live." But God said to Jonah, "Is it right for you to be angry about the bush?" And he said, "Yes, angry enough to die." Then the Lord said, "You are concerned about the bush, for which you did not labour and which you did not grow; it came into being in a night and perished in a night. And should I not be concerned about Nineveh, that great city, in which there are more than a hundred and twenty thousand persons who do not know their right hand from their left, and also many animals?" (Jonah 4.1-11)

God has the last word. It's a happy ending, but an open-ended ending. We can only guess what a sequel would look like ... but then, we don't have a sequel to the Book of Jonah.

On the other hand, when Jesus calls Simon, Andrew, James and John in today's gospel, there appears to be no reluctance at all. "Immediately they left their nets and followed him." "Immediately he called them; and they left their father Zebedee in the boat with the hired men, and followed him." (Mark 1.18, 20) Only as they come to realize the cost of following Jesus does reluctance develop. The radical nature of Jesus' call is clear from the beginning. The call is "to follow."

Leonard Bernstein, the famous composer and conductor, was once asked: "What is the hardest instrument to play?" Without hesitation he replied, "Second fiddle." He had no trouble at all finding musicians who thought they were first violinists, or thought themselves capable of sitting in the first chair of a section, but—second fiddle?

Peter is the first to be called, and his primacy will develop as Mark's telling of the story unfolds, but as it unfolds, Peter seems less sure that he wants to be a follower. Giving up his profession is one thing, but he finds himself reluctant to let go at other levels. Jesus redefines their profession as fishers of people, but he'll be the one to set the pace. Peter and his brother Andrew will have to learn to play "second fiddle" in Jesus' "royal water music."

The second pair of brothers owned a boat and worked with their father. They were small family business people. They left their father with the hired men. They were called to exchange their biological family for kinship with the "Son of God," whom they would only gradually come to recognize, and the consequences of which they would accept only with reluctance.

In the wonderfully imaginative narrative of the Book of Jonah, the reluctant prophet only slowly begins to figure out what playing second fiddle feels like, and we're not all that sure he got the message even at the end of the story. In the true-life story of Peter, Andrew, James and John, we know that their initial enthusiasm for following the new beat that Jesus was setting went through any number of reluctant stages.

The Book of Jonah has no sequel, but "the beginning of the gospel according to Mark" does have a sequel in which we all have a part. Following Jesus, playing second fiddle to him, is for all of us an ongoing process of getting into the swing of things *his* way. For most of us, the ultimate resolution, the final chord, the happy ending may be any number of pages ahead. Our response will be ongoing. We might as well get used to the challenge, and enjoy it!

Prophetic Words

Fourth Sunday in Ordinary Time

Deuteronomy 18.15–20
Psalm 95
1 Corinthians 7.17, 32–35
Mark 1.21–28

"I will put my words in the mouth of the prophet, who shall speak to them everything that I command." (Deuteronomy 18.18b)

He taught them as one having authority, and not as the scribes … "He commands even the unclean spirits, and they obey him." (Mark 1.22, 27b)

The text from Deuteronomy has Moses sharing a promise that he himself has received from the Almighty. "I will raise up for them a prophet … I will put my words in the mouth of the prophet." This is framed by the overall context in which Moses authorizes and establishes various leadership roles within the community, specifically judges and priests. These leadership roles are to guide and guard Israel when it finally comes into the land of promise. The judges will deal with day-to-day matters, encouraging, even supervising and mandating structures of justice among the people and ways of communicating with and dealing with the outside world. Priests will be responsible for the pattern and structures of ritual and prayer. There is something distinctive, however, in the role and responsibilities of the prophet. His is a ministry of the word—the very word of God. His is a ministry that keeps alive and brings to bear the will of God, the high ideals of God's covenant love into which limited human beings and human institutions have been invited.

As hard as judges might try and as sincere and conscientious as they might be in fulfilling their responsibilities, the perfection of justice in the concrete will elude them. As holy and faithful as priests might be, the worship they lead will never be worthy of God, will never be perfect. Their prayer and ritual activity will never express the fullness of what is appropriate as a community of faith stands before God.

The word, however, has the potential for a wonderful fullness and purity. The word can express the vision, the ideal, the dream in a way that will always elude concrete situations. It keeps the covenant story and dream alive in the limitations of particular times and circumstances. It's true in a sense that actions speak louder than words, but it's also true that the word can penetrate to places in the heart in ways that no particular "for instance" can accomplish.

Here are some examples.

> I, Mary Ellen, take you, James, to be my husband. I promise to
> be true to you in good times and bad, in sickness and in health.
> I will love you and honour you all the days of my life.

This is clearly a prophetic word. It's a word that, when spoken, reaches deep into the heart and soul of the person speaking, reflecting more than she can understand and more than she can perfectly or adequately accomplish. It's a word of faith and hope and love that will always transcend the concreteness of her experience, however carefully she may try to "judge" situations and however faithfully she "prays." It's a huge word. Those of you who are married know exactly what I mean.

> Are you resolved as a sign of your interior dedication to Christ,
> to remain celibate for the sake of the kingdom and in lifelong
> service to God and humankind?

> Are you resolved to carry out your office with humility and
> love?

> Are you resolved to hold the mystery of faith with a clear
> conscience, and to proclaim the faith in word and action?

> Are you resolved to maintain and deepen a spirit of prayer
> appropriate to your way of life?

Are you resolved to shape your way of life always according to the example of Christ, whose body and blood you will give to the people?

I am, with the help of God.

I can surely testify to the flawed way in which my life reflects that huge prophetic word which I spoke in a seminary chapel long ago.

This is not even to take account of statistics relative to marriage breakdown, or to public scandals in the church's ministry.

Marriage is a covenant: a divinely ordained expression of God's love for humanity, a sacrament of Christ's love for the church. Ordained ministry is a covenant, a divinely established way in which Christ continues to shepherd his people. Marriage and ordained ministry are ways of being in relationship with God's ongoing presence to community, intimacy and creativity.

The word is always somehow more elevated than its lived experience. The prophet in whose mouth God will place his word is vital for ongoing discernment, even judgment, as well as for strengthening and keeping visions, dreams and ideals alive in a faith community.

Mark portrays Jesus' ministry, from its earliest days, as coming out of the prophetic tradition. Jesus speaks for God, both in what he says and what he does. In him there is perfect consistency between word and the action. He speaks "as one having authority," not as the scribes.

The contrast here is especially noteworthy. The scribes were regarded with great respect as bearers of their heritage. They were trustworthy and reliable to the extent that they were consistent with the tradition. Mark speaks of Jesus as teaching with another kind of authority. The Greek word *exousia* expresses the concept of authority in an interesting way. It is formed from *ex,* meaning "out of," and *ousia,* meaning "being." Jesus teaches out of his own being. His teaching is not derivative nor does it merely explain something that has gone before. In Mark's theology, Jesus is the one from whose mouth God's word is spoken, with whom God's word is, in fact, identified.

Today's text points to just how powerful this prophetic word really is. What does it do? It casts out an unclean spirit. And what is the response of the onlookers?

They were all amazed, and they kept on asking one another, "What is this? A new teaching—with authority! He commands even the unclean spirits, and they obey him." (Mark 1.27)

Strange? In what way is the casting out of an unclean spirit teaching? And with authority? How is this command linked up with teaching?

In today's example, the unclean spirit bursts into the synagogue. The man who is afflicted with the unclean spirit is not the story. He comes on stage simply as the carrier of the unclean spirit. Nothing is said about him, his background, his faith or lack thereof. We're not even sure how it is that such a person was admitted to the building! After the exorcism there is no word of thanks or mention of the rejoicing of family and friends at his restoration to spiritual wholeness. The response of witnesses to the cure is not about the man and what happened to him later, but curiosity and amazement at what happened and what it means. It is clearly "a new teaching—with authority."

The question is: What is this authority by which it happened? The ultimate question is: Who is this Holy One of God whose word carries such authority and power?

In her wonderful book *Preaching Mark*, Bonnie Thurston suggests that the contact point for our own entry into the story, our own asking of those questions, is the "exclusionary" effect of possession as we might know and experience it.[9] She notes as well that the use of the Greek word *phimotheti*, which our translation renders "Be silent," is actually more colourful in the original. It means literally "Be muzzled." It's what you would do to a dangerous dog to stop both his bark and his bite. That's what the word of Jesus does to the unclean spirit. He speaks with that kind of authority. He says, "Shut up, you!" in no uncertain terms.

What are the unclean spirits that are speaking up even now, that are striving to get your attention, that are working even now at "excluding you" from authentic worship? In this place of learning and prayer, in this "synagogue" today, what are the spirits working against your own full "inclusion" in the prophetic mystery of your marriage, or for me of my ordination? What unclean spirits are at work in our lives that inhibit our reaching towards our best ideals and dreams in our personal and professional lives? What are the demons that are in the way of our own full participation in the life of the gospel, that covenanted life with God in Christ that we share and to which we adhere in faith? What are these spirits saying and how can they be silenced?

I'd suggest that, if truth be told, the point of all this is that none of us is completely without the presence and influence of unclean spirits that test and compromise even our best efforts and visions. Perhaps we need to let the Holy One of God whom we encounter today in word and sacrament say, "Be silent. Come out of them." We need to believe that indeed they can be muzzled by the authority of the living Christ whom we encounter today in word and sacrament.

The First Deacon

Fifth Sunday in Ordinary Time

Job 7.1-4, 6-7
Psalm 147
1 Corinthians 9.16-19, 22-23
Mark 1.29-39

Today's gospel story spans two days. Although we're still only in chapter 1, Mark's text, entitled "The beginning of the good news (gospel) of Jesus Christ, the Son of God," is moving forward decisively.

In a very important and interesting way, the days match and balance each other. The first day actually began in last Sunday's text, when Jesus muzzled the unclean spirit in such a clear and authoritative way. After leaving the synagogue at Capernaum, he went with James and John to the house of Simon and Andrew. The two sets of brothers were clearly witnesses to Jesus' teaching, authority and power. That Simon had a mother-in-law implies, of course, that he was married. That the house belonged to him and Andrew implies that they lived in an extended family dwelling typical of first-century Palestine.

A few years ago, over forty of us from the parish travelled to the Holy Land and visited Capernaum. We celebrated the Eucharist in a church built on stilts over excavations of "Peter's house." The excavations show that it was actually a house, and a rather large one that could well have housed an extended family. The association of this house with Peter and Andrew goes back to the fourth century. There are graffiti, little carved Christian symbols on the site, that are even older. Given the ways in which memory of place was treasured in the ancient world, we all believed that we were standing, singing and praying above the very spot about which Mark writes.

That Simon's mother-in-law was in bed with a fever and that they told him to come "at once" certainly signals urgency.

Jesus came and took her by the hand and lifted her up. (Mark 1.31a)

Last Sunday we were in touch with how he spoke, with the kind of authority that his word—unlike that of the scribes—exercised. Today we are in touch with the authority of his touch that reaches out in a new way, again unlike that of the scribes. That on the Sabbath Jesus would "work," that he would reach out and touch a woman—and a sick woman at that—raising her up, would clearly have been legally, culturally and ritually unacceptable, well beyond anything the world of the scribes could have countenanced.

As a woman, Bonnie Thurston is particularly sensitive to women and to their appearance in the text.

The fever left her, and she began to serve them. (Mark 1.31b)

Poor thing. She got up off her sick bed and began immediately to serve—presumably the men: Peter, Andrew, James, John and Jesus. Yes, that's what happened, but the real power, force and dignity of the text goes far beyond. As Thurston did last Sunday, she again gives us a little Greek lesson to help us understand what Mark is really saying.[10]

First, the word *soma,* used to express healing, is the same word used for salvation. More than being physically healed, she is being saved. It's both/and. She's being called beyond her sickness to something more.

Second, the word *diekonei* for "served" is the root word of the English word "deacon." That Simon's mother-in-law served makes her, in a sense, the first deacon. She took her place among the disciples in what mattered most—service. The standard pattern in Mark's miracle stories is that those who are healed (saved) move immediately to following or serving. That's what the healing is for. That's what the experience of salvation is all about. Simon's anonymous mother-in-law is the first such instance, the first to understand when it comes to discipleship.

Third, the language about her fever is more colourful than can be rendered in English. Literally her fever was "fire in the bones." There is a sense in which the fever didn't as much leave her as become something else, another kind of fever. Her healing gave her a new and transformed way of having "fire in the bones."

Can you see what Mark's getting at? He's doing a lot more than reporting a story; he's giving a concrete object lesson in discipleship. He's giving us a "for instance" that invites our participation in the action. Is what's happening to Simon's mother-in-law happening to us?

Mark then mentions evening and sundown, a redundancy that makes it clear that the Sabbath is over and that the sick and possessed could now legally be brought to Jesus. The whole city was gathered at the door. His ministry is extending beyond the synagogue and beyond the intimacy of a family home to the world, to the "whole city." He healed many and cast out many demons. Jesus had a very busy day.

On the next day, he got up in the darkness of very early morning and went to a deserted place to pray. Jesus prays in the darkness of the very early morning. What is that saying about his ongoing sense of need for direction and focus in his ministry?

Simon and his companions "hunted for him." What an expression! It's the same expression used for hunting an animal or for hunting down a criminal. In fact, the same expression will be used when the enemies of Jesus hunt him out for execution. Jesus then sets out from prayer to preaching and casting out demons in neighbouring towns. His mission is expanding.

I've been stressing Mark's use of language quite a lot today, not so much to give you a scripture lesson, but to show how masterfully he is trying the invite the imaginations of his hearers and readers into the story. Even in the first days of Jesus' ministry, it is clear that what is being described is not so much a story that took place way back then or way out there, but a story that continues to happen. Jesus' mission expands to neighbouring towns and cities—including our own. There, unclean spirits—including our own—are still muzzled; sickness—including our own—is transformed into opportunities for service; and those who are alienated—including us—are drawn to communion.

Mark's first chapter summarizes and tells the whole story. In these two days Jesus' authority is clear. Unclean spirits, disease and alienation are turned around by his word. Fortified by prayer, he resists the distractions and temptations even of well-intentioned friends to hunt for him. He's already bracing himself for the climactic confrontation with evil in the cross, which he will embrace with integrity and courage.

71

These two remarkable days may even be a remote preparation for a great third day, when the real truth of his ultimate authority over sin and death will be available in a new and definitive way.

Jesus lives: muzzlings and fire in the bones and cleansing reunions happen. They really do. Prayer fortifies and expands horizons. It really does. Let all of that be true for you.

Throw Deep

Sixth Sunday in Ordinary Time

Leviticus 13.1-2, 45-46
Psalm 32
1 Corinthians 10.23–11.1
Mark 1.40-45

"'Unclean, unclean.' A person shall remain unclean as long as the disease persists; and being unclean, that person shall live alone with a dwelling outside the camp." (Leviticus 13.45b–46)

A man with leprosy came to Jesus begging him, and kneeling said to Jesus, "If you choose, you can make me clean." (Mark 1.40)

"Go, show yourself to the priest." (Mark 1.44)

We're spending our fourth Sunday in chapter 1 of Mark and are now meeting the third remarkable instance of Jesus' authority over anything that keeps people down. We already met the unclean spirit who inhabited a nameless man, and Simon's mother-in-law, herself nameless. Today we meet an anonymous leper. What authority Jesus has in every case! Could it be that all three individuals are nameless because they have universal significance? Could their very namelessness invite us to see them as much more than isolated examples of Jesus' exercise of divine power?

I remember visiting and caring pastorally for a man with AIDS some years ago. His parents stopped me at the back of church and asked me to visit him in the hospital. At that time there was such fear surrounding the disease and such a stigma attached to its victims. This man had long been alienated from the church, and was quite amazed that I was ready not only to listen to him and hear his confession, but physically hold him—to help him to prop himself up in his bed so that he could receive holy communion. Having felt so rejected by the church, he was amazed at my response to his condition and his need. The depth of his amazement troubled me. It made me feel that the church needed to be reconciled with him as much as he needed to be reconciled with the church.

"If you choose, you can make me clean; if you choose, you can reach out and touch me." In the name of Jesus and in his spirit, we need to be ready to make such choices.

Not only did leprosy involve great fear of contagion, but the rotting away of one's body symbolized for many an interior rot that manifested itself in such a disease. It was closely associated with sin, and anyone coming into contact with such a person would become ritually impure.

That the likes of Jesus would reach out to him is remarkable. It corresponds to his muzzling of the unclean spirit and raising Simon's mother-in-law back to service on the Sabbath. Jesus has authority—beyond concern with ritual purity—a new teaching, not like the scribes.

That Jesus is "moved with pity," as our text read, could equally well have been translated "moved with anger." Literally, it means having your intestines turn. It's as if you're so moved you feel like throwing up. It's not very polite to talk about that sort of thing in church, but that's what the text implies. In coming in contact with this leper, seeing his plight and hearing his "If you choose," Jesus was profoundly moved. He felt something at the pit of his stomach; he was shaken to the very depths of his being.

One wonders what the tone of his voice must have been as he said, "I do choose." Jesus speaks out of those very depths of his being as he stretches out his hand. I wonder if his hand was trembling. His word and his outstretched hand signal an unequivocal connection with the leper's plight, but what follows is perhaps even more important:

> After sternly warning him Jesus sent him away at once, saying to him, "…go, show yourself to the priest, and offer for your cleansing what Moses commanded, as a testimony to them." (Mark 1.43b-44)

The man was not just cleansed, but sent back into the very middle of things, charged with wasting no time in getting back to a productive, functional role in a worshipping and serving community. He was to reconnect with life in all its facets. Like the muzzling of the unclean spirit and the transformation of the burning in the bones of Simon's mother-in-law, the leper's cleansing and transformation are for a purpose. In spite of Jesus' stern warning to be silent and go about his business, the leper cannot help himself. He spreads the word everywhere; he becomes a herald of good news.

There was once a newspaper sports journalist who happened to visit the Jack London Historical Park in the Sonoma Valley of California.

Jack London, who lived from 1876 to 1916, grew up among the factories and waterfront dives of West Oakland, but became one of the best-known short story writers and novelists of his time. I remember reading some of his work, *The Call of the Wild* in particular, when I was a teenager.

This particular journalist was struck by the vitality of London's prose, a few fragments of which were in the park's guidebook. The first fragment described the place itself and the kind of energy that he found and derived from his environment.

> The grapes on a score of rolling hills are red with autumn flame. Across Sonoma Mountain wisps of sea fog are stealing. The afternoon sun smolders in the drowsy sky. I have everything to make me glad I am alive. I am filled with dreams and mysteries. I am all sun and air and sparkle. I am vitalized, organic.

Filled with dreams and mysteries, sun, air and sparkle, "vitalized, organic"—that's what you call living!

The sportscaster was even more struck by the next quote:

I would rather be ashes than dust!
I would rather that my spark
should burn out in a brilliant blaze
than it should be stifled by dry rot.
I would rather be a superb meteor,
every atom of me in magnificent glow,
than a sleepy and permanent planet.
The proper function of a man is to live, not to exist.
I shall not waste my days trying to prolong them.
I shall use my time.

Not having a lot of confidence in the sensitivity of football players, he read it anyway to the Los Angeles Raiders in their locker room the next time he was covering one of their games. "What do you think that means?" he asked. Quarterback Ken Stabler surprised him with his answer. "Throw deep," he said.

Throw deep, indeed!

In reading Mark's first chapter, which concludes today, it strikes me that this is the kind of life towards which Jesus' teaching is pointing, the kind of life that his authority is encouraging. Jesus throws deep. He speaks clearly and stretches far in muzzling unclean spirits, turning fevers around, and cleansing people from alienating fear.

In terms just of today's gospel, can Jesus' spirit be as contagious as leprosy ever was?

Become ashes, not dust. Let your life burn in a brilliant blaze.

Throw deep.

Being at Home

Seventh Sunday in Ordinary Time

Isaiah 43.18-19, 20-22, 24-25
Psalm 41
2 Corinthians 1.18-22
Mark 2.1-12

There's no future in that.

Get a life!

Did you hear those sayings, perhaps those clichés, coming out of the scriptures today?

"Do not remember the former things, or consider the things of old. I am about to do a new thing…" (Isaiah 43.18-19a)

"Son, your sins are forgiven … I say to you, stand up, take your mat and go to your home." (Mark 2.5b, 11)

Journalist Tom Harpur published a series of his *Toronto Star* columns about ten years ago now. I find one of these to be right on target for today. Commenting on some of the cultural or moral movements of the time, he named, for example, the New Age phenomenon, feminism, holistic medicine, the peace movement, and the green or environmental movement. As he was writing, he asked himself whether these movements might have something in common, whether they might represent a common set of questions, or root need. The commonality he found was not just the desire, but the real need, for wholeness. He discovered an expressed need in all these movements for a healing word, a healing vision that would lead to wholeness in persons, in groups, and in the world.[11]

When we think of the New Age phenomenon as a religious or quasi-religious movement, we find people who are striving for a central source of energy or a centre of motivation that can "get it together" for them: one they can't find either in the consumer culture or even within the cultures of established religions, which such people feel are stuck in competing doctrinal systems or ideologies. Whether by searching for their alleged past lives or reading tarot cards, New Agers are seeking a personal centre of gravity that will bring wholeness and a sense of direction to their lives.

At a profound level, Harpur discovers the same urge behind the struggle of women for liberation and empowerment over the last twenty years or so. There's something missing, crippled or limping in systems or society in which women are not equal partners with men. Societies need to be made whole. Women need to be at home in them.

Holistic medicine is something else. Do you just take an aspirin and go to bed, or is there a lot more required for good health—diet, exercise, even meditation? There's more to good health than what surgery and drugs can provide. Health as wholeness has almost become a byword.

The peace movement certainly has taken a turn since the war on terror has been declared, but it should be even more evident now that escalating violence is not the way to victory over the root causes of terrorist movements in the world. The alienation caused by deeply rooted conflicts and tensions among peoples and nations cannot be healed by violence. Reconciliation will come by another way.

Harpur also cites the green movement as an example. The word "ecology" comes from the classical Greek word meaning "house," "home" or "household." The underlying claim of the green movement is that the planet is home, not just to humans, but to every living thing. Humans are part of a bigger household. If one member of the household is suffering, the whole family is off balance and suffering.

When it comes right down to it, any solid religious tradition is ultimately about all of these things. It's about healing the rift between humans and the Almighty, healing relationships with others and coming to a deeper sense of at-homeness with self, to personal integrity.

Becoming whole at every level is life's biggest and most important project and goal. Sin is that which divides and tears apart. Grace is that which pulls together and draws to serenity and communion.

The Bible never tires of proclaiming these possibilities. Isaiah speaks of a "new thing," a new intervention of the Almighty in the lives of the community and the nation. God's judgment on the past becomes a promise for the future; exile becomes homecoming; alienation becomes reconciliation; death becomes life; the dry, parched land will becomes a well-watered garden where all can be at home.

In the gospel, all of this is taking place on a smaller scale in the life of an individual. In Jesus, the Almighty intervenes for the overall well-being of the person on the stretcher that is being lowered through the roof. The forgiveness of sins and restoration of health are clearly linked; moral and spiritual wholeness are clearly linked with physical well-being. We know ourselves that sometimes our "dragging ourselves around" has nothing to do with physical tiredness or a bum leg. It's our soul that's dragging, and even our face and eyes reflect the sickness.

The story is really quite extraordinary. It begins by alluding to the practical and persistent caring shown by the paralyzed man's friends in getting him into the place where Jesus was "at home." It must have been a typical house of the period; its flat roof made of sticks and mud could be reached by outside stairs. For Jesus, the removal of part of the roof was not an act of vandalism but an act of faith, and when the man is lowered down, he is already at home, already in a context of wholeness. Jesus uses tender, familial language to assure him of his wholeness and at-homeness with God: "Son, your sins are forgiven."

This saying sets Jesus up for the controversy that follows about just how sin and paralysis are connected and who has power over what. It's clear that Jesus continues to exercise his unique authority when, moving from his proclamation of forgiveness, he commands the man to take up his mat and go to his "home." Jesus is putting the whole person back together again and sending him home.

The name Mickey Mantle probably conjures up memories of booming home runs, tremendous speed, and the enormous natural ability that he showed during his Yankee days. A different Mickey Mantle presented himself to the world towards the end of his life. Just a month after receiving a liver transplant made necessary by years of alcohol abuse, he was able to face squarely that while he may have been a superstar on the field, his personal life was not one to hold out to others for emulation. If I remember correctly, his liver transplant was not successful, but with humility, humour and without self-pity, he went public with his story. His final days were marked with a great outpouring, not so much of adulation for Mickey the Yankee, but of love and respect for Mickey the human being. Virtually overnight, organ donations increased all across the continent, making physical wholeness possible for others in a way that had become impossible for Mantle at this stage of his life. He had, however, found something more. He was genuinely at home with himself.

In the midst of controversy, Jesus announces that the "Son of Man has authority to forgive sins," and that this authority is as certain as the fact that this man was brought to physical wholeness by his command to pick up his mat and go home. They were amazed, as well they should have been. "We have never seen anything like this!"

Can all of us who are at home with Jesus and with each other in this household of faith not recognize and respond to his power at work in our midst? Can we in this eucharist be called to deeper personal integrity, greater personal wholeness, and a deeper sense of bondedness and holy communion with all that is?

Think of it. We're eating and drinking together. What does that say? And—it's the Body and Blood of Christ that is our food and drink at this table. What does that say? Let's all be "at home" here.

Prophetic Destabilization

Eighth Sunday in Ordinary Time

Hosea 2.14, 15, 19–20
Psalm 103
2 Corinthians 3.1–6
Mark 2.18–22

A wonderful story that dates from the 1950s is still told about the late Cardinal Spellman of New York. Tired and frustrated with the questions being posed at a surprise interview, he finally pointed up to a mounted fish on the wall behind his desk. A brass engraving attached to it read: "If I had kept my mouth shut, I wouldn't be here." I don't know very much about Cardinal Spellman and can certainly not judge how prophetic he may have been in his life and ministry, but he clearly knew that what you say can get you into as much trouble as what you do, and had an open-mouthed fish on his wall to prove it.

Prophecy is a dangerous occupation. To claim that you see something that others are missing can get you into a lot of trouble.

Prophets have been described in any number of ways. One of the more colourful and descriptive that I've come upon lately is that a prophet is the "midwife of new consciousness." Dreams are buried deep in the consciousness; high ethical standards are buried deep in the conscience. God himself has planted them there in the very act of creating us as human beings with an amazing capacity for restless probing and searching. The prophet names this restlessness and coaches us as we bring it before our eyes, nourish it and deal with it.

Another way of describing the prophet is that he or she is destabilizing. We're all into certain systems of thought and action. Certain social symbols such as flags, anthems, health care systems and school boards are presumed to have a certain legitimacy. They order and define our sense of who we are, what we believe, and how we will care for ourselves and the next generation. Managers and benefactors within these systems tend to know what is good for us, and tend to absolutize their point of view, even fighting any attempt to propose alternatives to what is—just because it is.

Within the biblical tradition, a prophet's voice claims that alternatives are possible. The immediate impetus for such a person coming forward can be corruption in a system that's long presumed to be "just fine." Another impetus would be the presence of a powerless or disenfranchised group within the fabric of society that is being ignored. Prophetic voices claim that changes to the status quo are not only thinkable, but may be necessary; they may even be God's will. Recently, prophetic voices, horrified at the collapse of Enron that left so many people's savings and pensions in a shambles, have been wondering about a high government official who pronounced that "the system" (Western capitalism) is sound and will fix itself. Is it acceptable that so many fall between the cracks? Are you so sure that the system as we have it is sound?[12] Such prophetic questioning, to say nothing of prophetic proposals for reform, destabilizes a lot of people who would rather not examine these issues.

Mark's gospel offers perhaps the most radical depiction of Jesus as a herald of good news within this prophetic tradition. His words and deeds are destabilizing and, for those who allow him to enter into their lives, he becomes a midwife of new ways of thinking and behaving that lie deep within their beings. Let's take a close look at how that's played out in the metaphors he uses in dealing with the question posed to him in today's gospel. Imagine: it's about fasting!

> "Why do John's disciples and the disciples of the Pharisees fast, but your disciples do not fast?" (Mark 2.18b)

> "The wedding guests cannot fast while the bridegroom is with them ... [but] when the bridegroom is taken away ..." (Mark 2.19a, 20a)

Weddings were big events in Palestinian villages. People lived together in large extended families. Their strongly felt sense of community and interdependence extended even beyond blood relatives. Everybody had a stake in everybody else's life. They were all related. Wedding parties went on for days. There's something very attractive in that way of life, but in our cultural context, most of us would rather not be that close. Am I right?

A wedding celebrated not only the kind of felt communion and intercommunion of marriage, but also the future. Consciously or not, the young couple was making an act of faith and hope in the future. The family would live on. The village would live on. A marriage celebration both gathered and highlighted the community's stories and traditions, and brought on its future.

That such an event, such a celebration, had religious, even mystical, overtones is not surprising. Our text today from Hosea uses the marriage metaphor to describe God's communion with Israel and God's hope for their common future. In spite of any past shakiness in Israel's fidelity to her vows, God makes clear his personal desire for and commitment to renewal.

> "I will take you for my wife in righteousness and in justice, in steadfast love, and in mercy. I will take you for my wife in faithfulness; and you shall know the Lord." (Hosea 2.19-20)

Expectations surrounding the coming of the messiah included a great feast at which the covenant, this marriage with the Almighty, would be renewed. Israel, the bride of the Almighty, would be lifted up in all her glory.

In dealing with the people's objection that his disciples did not fast, Jesus contextualizes his answer in the marriage metaphor and applies it to his own person, mission and destiny. He is clearly alluding to something beyond an ordinary wedding. He wasn't getting married that weekend, but a wedding feast was underway.

> "The wedding guests cannot fast while the bridegroom is with them, can they? As long as they have the bridegroom with them, they cannot fast. The days will come when the bridegroom is taken away from them, and then they will fast on that day." (Mark 2.19-20)

Mark's readers already know that Jesus is the Son of God, the Messiah—the bridegroom. That was announced in chapter 1, verse 1, but at this early stage there's no way Jesus' contemporaries would have discerned that, which makes his immediate move to the wedding meta-phor all the more striking. Even more telling and poignant is his refer-ence to the *taking away* of the bridegroom. Usually the groom and his bride would leave at their discretion; they would not be *taken away.*

Here Jesus is pointing to the kind of messiah, the kind of bride-groom, he is and will become as his life and destiny unfold. He will be *taken away.* Violence is implied. The cross is already in the picture. Jesus is destabilizing the going vision of what God is about. Jesus is already exercising his mission as midwife of another understanding of what it might mean to be messiah.

He continues his prophetic word with two other metaphors, little parables drawn from domestic life. One of them would probably have been more familiar to the women of his time, the other to the men. He speaks of sewing and winemaking, and in doing so makes it clear that old can't just blend in with the new, that they will not be able to harmonize their traditional ways of thinking with the good news he is offering them. Once again the language of tearing and bursting refer-ences his passion. The cross is on the horizon.

The prophetic newness to which he points doesn't come out of nowhere. Remember: he silenced the demon; he raised Simon's mother-in-law; he cleansed the leper; he forgave and liberated the paralyzed man; he called a tax collector to conversion and dined with his friends at his home. These are prophetic actions. His whole life is destabilizing midwifery. He is Son of God/Messiah, and this is what being Son of God/Messiah is all about. It's good news—or is it?

For some, it was clearly not good news. Destabilization and bring-ing new life into the world are not always and everywhere "good news," which is the whole point of the proclamation of this gospel in our own church today.

Is it good news for us? Can we receive it?

In the midst of a war on terror and economic destabilization, can we be open to even part of a prophetic solution? Can we envision a suffering bridegroom as messiah, the fabrication of a whole new cloak, a whole new set of wineskins?

Paradoxically, the Archbishop of Wales, Rowan Williams (who in July 2002 was named Archbishop of Canterbury, the spiritual head of 70 million Anglicans, and is in the position to crown the next king), signed an open letter to the British government questioning "knee jerk" military action against terror, insisting that "eradicating the dangers posed by malevolent dictators and terrorists can only be achieved by tackling the root causes of the disputes." Standing in the tradition of Jesus, he insists that "Any Christian pastor or priest is going to have to ask awkward questions."

> "Why do John's disciples and the disciples of the Pharisees fast, but your disciples do not fast?" (Mark 2.18b)

That's the awkward question presented to Jesus. What is so remarkable is that his response itself comes down to us as an awkward question, one with which we are struggling to this very day.

Lord of the Sabbath

Ninth Sunday in Ordinary Time

Deuteronomy 5.12-15
Psalm 81
2 Corinthians 4.6-11
Mark 2.23–3.6

The Lord says this: "Observe the sabbath day and keep it holy, as the Lord your God commanded you. Six days you shall labour and do all your work. But the seventh day is a sabbath to the Lord your God; you shall not do any work." (Deuteronomy 5.12-13)

Jesus said to [the Pharisees], "The sabbath was made for people, and not people for the sabbath; so the Son of Man is lord even of the sabbath." (Mark 2.27)

Before the beginning of the Sabbath, the lady of the house kindles the Sabbath lights. She then spreads out her hands between her eyes and the lights and recites the following blessing: "Blessed be you, God our God, King of the Universe, Who has sanctified us by Your commandments and commanded us to kindle the Sabbath light." (from the *Siddur*)

At the time of Jesus, the Sabbath was a wonderful institution; it continues to be so.

Created in the image and likeness of God, the first human couple would observe the Sabbath as God, their Creator, did. As God's companions, human beings were invited to be contemplative, to wonder at and rejoice in the world around them, and at their place in that world.

On the other six days of the week, they would exercise their role as co-creators with God, but on the Sabbath they would rest and wonder. They would recognize in prayer and contemplation that the whole of creation and their role in it is gift. They would learn to celebrate in joy and thanksgiving their ongoing dependence upon God.

The first reading from today's liturgy reminds us of the second dimension of Sabbath faith and practice.

"Remember that you were a slave in the land of Egypt, and the Lord your God brought you out from there with a mighty hand and an outstretched arm; therefore the Lord your God commanded you to keep the sabbath day." (Deuteronomy 5.15)

Along with creation, Sabbath celebrates liberation. It celebrates freedom. Work is not the be-all and end-all of life. We are more than what we make or what we do. Remembering God's action of creation and liberation, the Sabbath offers a privileged opportunity to contemplate and celebrate human dignity on a day of rest; given the compulsive nature of so many of us humans, its observance became law.

For the Pharisees, concern for the Sabbath was not a matter of petty legalism. The Sabbath observance, a consistent reminder of God's place in their lives, lay at the heart of their identity as faithful Jews. As a particular way of making the Torah visible and concrete, it helped them resist pressures to conform to the broader society. It was an ordering feature of their life, a visible sign of their faith and observance, providing stability and an identifiable mark of holiness, not to mention the social and personal benefits of a day off.

For the most part, they were not evil people or narrow-minded legalists. Of particular interest to them as lay people, not priests or nobles, was that this was "their day." Ordinary families celebrated it, not in the temple, but in the home. It did not require the presence or services of priests.

Beyond the context of family, the Sabbath also offered them the occasion to gather, once again not in the temple, but in their local synagogues, to discuss their scriptures and to deepen their sense of community. They were deeply religious Jews who treasured these traditional and legal structures that enabled all people, wherever they might be—not just the priests in the temple—to take their religious duties seriously. In doing so they could maintain their distinctive status as a special people called by God who were responding very concretely to that call.

For the Pharisees, there is a sense in which "people are made for the sabbath." There's a sense in which the Sabbath stands over and above the ordinary, commonsense requirements of life. The Sabbath calls people beyond themselves to see and celebrate themselves as God sees them. The Sabbath deserves protection—careful, even scrupulous protection. It's that valuable. It's that important.

That Jesus would claim authority even over the Sabbath was clearly "over the top." It's certainly no wonder that such a claim generated a lot of hostility. In insisting that "The sabbath is made for people, not the people for the sabbath" he is starting down a slippery slope. He insists that the Sabbath is a gift from God to enrich our experience of being human. It is not another way of burdening us, another subtle form of slavery.

Jesus went beyond the procedures of his contemporaries in discussing appropriate ways of observing the Sabbath. He even dismissed such rulings and traditions, some passed down for generations, as too often prone to obscuring or frustrating the original intention for which the Sabbath commandments were given. He appealed to God's mind, to God's original intention, bypassing the "traditions of the elders," insisting that the Sabbath is most worthily kept when God's purposes are fulfilled. Bold or what?!

"The Son of Man is lord even of the sabbath" is a bold saying indeed. It's interesting that the title "Son of Man" will not be found again in Mark until Jesus' first prediction of his passion. He himself is on a slippery slope. In the turbulent social and political circumstances of his day, fooling with and destabilizing the traditions of the elders was thought to be just too risky. His approach is too scary—in the establishment it will contribute to the buildup of hostility that will lead to the cross.

As noble and conscientious as most of the Pharisees must have been, Bonnie Thurston's commentary, to which I've referred before, suggests that we take a good look at the way the particular group of Pharisees is presented in today's passage. She wonders:

> How did they know that Jesus and the disciples were going through the fields on the Sabbath day? How did they know that they were plucking grain? Were they in the fields

themselves? Did they station themselves out there to spy, or what? Is that any way to keep the Sabbath?

They were in the synagogue with a man with a withered hand. Fine. But they were there "to watch so that they might accuse him." Literally, according to the Greek original, the word translated watch means "to lie in wait." Pretty strong! Was the presence in the synagogue of the man with the withered hand a "set up"? Pretty sick! Is this any way to observe the Sabbath?[13]

Jesus looks beyond specific Sabbath expectations and regulations to the most fundamental ethical and religious question of all.

"Is it lawful to do good or to do harm on the sabbath, to save life or to kill?" (Mark 3.4)

In a subtle way, Jesus may even have been accusing these particular Pharisees who had so distorted their own tradition of counter-sabbath activities and plans even in his own regard. Were they already plotting his death?

That he was grieved at their hardness of heart is particularly telling. The heart was not understood to be just the seat of emotion, but of understanding and will. It was the core of the whole person. That these people would be in the synagogue with hard hearts, and on the Sabbath besides, borders on the sacrilegious.

That these same people, furthermore, who, with their lay and egalitarian bias, had no use for the Jerusalem establishment, would now plot with Herodians to destroy Jesus gives us even more indication of the depth of their hostility.

I've dealt with this text in more detail than usual because it gives us an opportunity to discover how Mark's presentation of Jesus is "shaping up," and at the same time challenges our own "hearts" in terms of our readiness to receive him and his word. It's clear that what is at stake is more than ceremonial or ritual detail around a privileged day of the week. The gospel offers a purifying word, a healing word, an energizing word, even a galvanizing word that makes it possible for people who are ready to enter into Jesus' own world. Jesus' words and deeds work together to provide what one writer has called an "invasion" of the ordinary by the reign of God, the "invasion" of a world view and ethic based upon a clear and radical sense of God's own purpose and will.

What's left in all of this is to ask ourselves just where and how we stand. Where are we in our own structures of faith, religious practice and ethical standards? Where would we be in Mark's chapter 2? How would we describe or classify our own loyalty to, practice of and, yes, critical stance towards our own faith tradition?

As for myself, I was quite struck by the journalist Tom Harpur's questioning of himself: "Am I a Christian?" When asked to label himself, he would say, "A radical-liberal-conservative-evangelical-Christian-humanist." He explains:

> By "radical" I mean concerned with the roots (from the Latin *radix*) or fundamentals of any given spiritual or religious question. By "liberal" I refer to a commitment to openness and to the use of reason wherever appropriate and possible. By "conservative" I mean concerned to preserve and maintain the essential truths of the Judeo-Christian inheritance. By "evangelical" I mean the conviction that there is indeed Good News to be shared and made known. By "Christian" I mean committed to following the teachings of Christ. Finally, by using the word "humanist" I want to assert my belief that any true religion worthy of the name has as its highest aim the celebration and the enhancement of what it truly means to be a human being in God's world.[14]

Do you think that Mark's Gospel is pushing us in this kind of direction? I do.

Out of His Mind

Tenth Sunday in Ordinary Time

Genesis 3.8-15
Psalm 130
2 Corinthians 4.13–5.1
Mark 3.20-35

Jesus went home, and the crowd came together again, so that they could not even eat. When his family heard it, they went out to restrain him, for people were saying, "He has gone out of his mind." (Mark 3.20-21)

In the 1930s, Istvan Sinka (1897–1967) achieved literary recognition in his native Hungary for his commitments as one of the "writers of the folk." During the Soviet occupation, his passionate belief in the rights and freedoms of ordinary folk to think and write earned him the designation "non-person," whose very name became unlawful to mention. In his poem "Jesus Leaves Home," he seems to find some affinity with the kind of alienation Jesus himself experienced. Let me quote a few lines:

In the inner courtyard
bearded folks were sitting
stubborn, unappeasable, none of them weeping;
vineyard workers, hewers of skillets, sellers of oddments,
sons of the Law each one;
loitering among the roses
waiting for "The Raving One,"
"The Astounding One," the carpenter
with the lightening eyes
who swirls in mirrors of skies and seas,
dreams dreams and sits among—the others ...

Oh, it was because of him that the family
became targets of gossip in
Nazareth, but he must leave now
like the wind which rises on the Hermon,
on this cool golden ladder,
and comes and sweeps through Galilee
and then is no more, is gone forever ...
And Jesus came—
and stepped out the gate.
And music rose from every zither on earth
And long dead flowers burst to bloom anew,
birds trilled, and every bird
and every wanderer was called—to Capernaum ...
Where will there be a bench or a bank
for him in this world, room enough?
They looked at each other ...
their earthly values, weighed with reality and facts;
they looked after him and were watching with amazement
the otherworldly radiance of Jesus.[15]

It's clear from Sinka's poetic imaginings of the day Jesus left home that Jesus is doing more than changing residences. He's leaving home, going beyond the village where he was raised in ways that are deeply personal and spiritual. He's stepping out in ways that are clearly beyond the physical. Sinka imagines mixed reactions, mixed feelings, mixed emotions. Parents can certainly identify with that. Sometimes kids take off in directions that are pretty scary. You're proud of them, sort of—but?

Today's text takes up the story at a point somewhere down the road. After his initial leave-taking, Jesus is now at home in a new place, but what a place to be at home! He's not at home at all, so surrounded and pressed by the crowds that he cannot even find time to eat. He had passed his first thirty years among the common places of an ordinary life. How could his neighbours and kinsmen suddenly accept the fact that he whom they had known at such close quarters was going around the countryside making exorbitant claims for himself: proclaiming forgiveness of sins, which is God's prerogative; correcting the law and such venerable institutions as the Sabbath? "Has he gone out of his mind?" people were asking. Literally, "Is he beside himself?" The family is concerned, deeply concerned.

It's time for a family intervention. We all know what those are, and some of us have been part of one or more such interventions. Perhaps it's in regard to an aging parent who adamantly refuses to give up his driver's licence, or refuses even to think about giving up her own apartment, even though the time has come. It could be an alcoholic uncle who's just about hit bottom, and whose career is in jeopardy. The family gangs up, sometimes at the urging of a doctor or other professional who knows how desperate the situation has become, but is not in the position to exert any more pressure. It takes family. In this case, we can assume that his relatives have Jesus' best interests in mind. They know what's best. It's time for him to turn around and come back home. Mark says that it is actually their intention to "restrain him." It's that bad! As far as they're concerned, he's clearly gone off the deep end.

The story goes on. The scribes come down from Jerusalem with a rescue mission of their own. In their case they are trying to rescue themselves and their traditions from all this craziness that might even be demonic. It's a family intervention of another kind. The whole house of Israel is in danger and needs to be rescued from the likes of this Jesus. Who's to say that this man Jesus is not possessed himself, a part of the devil's extremely sophisticated trickery? Maybe he's possessed by the prince of demons, who gives him the power to order other, lesser demons around.

Jesus' response to both groups is revolutionary:

> "Truly I tell you, people will be forgiven for their sins and whatever blasphemies they utter; but whoever blasphemes against the Holy Spirit can never have forgiveness, but is guilty of an eternal sin"—for they had said, "He has an unclean spirit." (Mark 3.28-30)

Jesus affirms in no uncertain terms that he is on the side of God. To attribute his ministry to the devil is to be closed to the spirit; to place oneself and one's home over and above the unfolding of God's own providence and will is to insult and abuse the Spirit, to be closed off to God's future. It is blasphemy—the ultimate sin.

In Mark's gospel the life and ministry of Jesus involves a public critique of the numbness of his social context. Even in our own time, empires live by numbness. Empires, in their militarism, hope for numbness concerning the human cost of war. Corporate economies depend upon blindness to the price of profit in terms of personal and natural resources. Governments and societies of domination go to great lengths to keep people at home in their numbness. Jesus was ultimately crucified because he couldn't be at home in such a world. His way of proclaiming the presence of the spirit, of the nearness of the reign of God, was an intolerable challenge to the lifestyle of the guardians of such village boundaries.

> And Jesus replied, "Who are my mother and my brothers?" And looking at those who sat around him, he said, "Here are my mother and my brothers! Whoever does the will of God is my brother and sister and mother." (Mark 3.33 35a)

To his family who thought he was "beside himself," Jesus proclaims a new way of being family. He ventures beyond "the fence, the latticed slats, the inner courtyard where bearded folks were sitting stubborn, unappeasable, none of them weeping; sons of the Law each one, loitering among the roses waiting for 'The Raving One,' 'The Astounding One,' the carpenter with the lightening eyes who swirls in mirrors of skies and seas, dreams dreams and sits among—*the others* ..."

> "Whoever does the will of God is my brother and sister and mother."

Remember the story of Jesus' baptism, with the spirit hovering over the waters from which Jesus arises: a new creation, a new Adam, the beloved Son in whom the eternal Father is well pleased. His baptism is already heralding the rebirth of humanity, a new way of being family that transcends nationality and culture, whose criterion for membership is openness to the spirit, openness to the reign of God, doing the "will of God" as Jesus himself does that will—that same Jesus who is "'The Raving One,' 'The Astounding One', the carpenter with the lightening eyes who swirls in mirrors of skies and seas, dreams dreams and sits among—*the others*..."

Almighty and eternal God, words cannot measure the boundaries of love for those born to new life in Christ Jesus. Raise us beyond the limits this world imposes, so that we may be free to love as Christ teaches and find our joy in your glory revealed in him.

May this prayer with which we began this celebration be our prayer for the whole week.

Cross-shaped Ashes

Ash Wednesday

Joel 2.12-18
Psalm 51
2 Corinthians 5.20–6.2
Matthew 6.1-6, 16-18

Remember Jack London's words about ashes, which I quoted a few weeks ago?

I would rather be ashes than dust!
I would rather that my spark
should burn out in a brilliant blaze
than it should be stifled by dry rot.
I would rather be a superb meteor,
every atom of me in magnificent glow,
than a sleepy and permanent planet.
The proper function of man is to live, not to exist.
I shall not waste my days trying to prolong them.
I shall use my time.

Those wonderful images reflect a powerful preference for energy over inertia, for life over death!

Our ritual books speak of the "imposition" of ashes. Isn't that an interesting description of what we do with them?

We impose them.
Like it or not, they're in your face.
Ashes, not dust, will be imposed.
They will be rubbed into your forehead
in the form of a cross.
Be in touch with the ashes.
Be in touch with the mystery of the cross.
Let the cross-shaped ashes penetrate your being.

Discernment and Temptation

First Sunday of Lent

Genesis 9.8–15
Psalm 25
1 Peter 3.18–22
Mark 1.12–15

He was tempted by Satan. Sounds ominous, doesn't it?

After Jesus was baptized, the Spirit drove him out into the wilderness. He was in the wilderness forty days, tempted by Satan; and he was with the wild beasts; and the angels waited on him. Mark 1.12-13)

For all of its brevity and seeming lack of detail, there's clearly a lot going on in Mark's brief account of the temptation of Jesus. There may be no conversations with the devil, or trips to temple towers or high mountains, but much is happening.

Mark fully expects that the number forty will remind his hearers of the forty years of wilderness testing in the stories of the Hebrew people, as well as Moses' forty days on the mountain and Elijah's famous trip to Horeb. In all of it there was testing, temptation and discernment. Thus it's no accident that both Moses and Elijah will appear with Jesus on the Mount of Transfiguration next Sunday.

As for the wild beasts, if, as is generally assumed, Mark's gospel was originally directed to an early Roman audience, the presence of the wild beasts would remind them of the horrors of Nero's persecution and the temptations to which they themselves have been subjected.

After experiencing God's call in his baptism, Jesus is driven by the Spirit into a place of quiet isolation, a place conducive to reflection and discernment, a place where temptation would be inevitable. Before beginning his public ministry, before actively beginning to live out the consequences of his designation as Beloved Son, Jesus is driven by the Spirit into the wilderness to be in touch with what is most basic: to pray, to confront Satan, to be with the wild beasts and, yes, to be served by angels.

Like those who went before him and those who follow after, Jesus will enter into the experience of discernment and temptation.

Reflection is the kind of inaction that alone makes action meaningful and focused on what is really good. Neither reflection nor discernment carries any of the glamour of achieving greatness or pursuing success in whatever the project might be, however noble. In the process of reflection or discernment there will be inevitable tensions that tear at a person's soul.

Perhaps Mark's temptation account is so short because he understood the whole of Jesus' life to be fraught with temptation. Temptation isn't something you experience once and for all, and then put behind you. Likewise, discernment isn't something that you use to come to important decisions and then simply move forward. Discernment and its accompanying tensions and temptations are perennial features in any serious person's life experience.

Discernment includes learning to listen to our own innermost being—the voice of the divine mystery within and allowing that voice to stand up to competing pressures and tensions. Discernment may also involve the very experience of being in the wilderness. The wilderness may itself be a source of revelation. There's a wisdom to be found in being in the middle of nowhere; there's wisdom to be found in seeking out a spring of water, in confronting a mountain that's older and bigger than you are, even in the flight and squawking of a crow.

Tom Harpur has some pretty tough things to say about the kinds of temptations we face in our culture. We need to be careful not simply to be taken in by its values and assumptions. We may all need to look at ways of simplifying our lifestyle and deepening our sense of purpose. We may need to take a close and critical look at our way of life to make sure that it reflects our true priorities and deepest aspirations. Lent provides us with just such an opportunity.

Harpur recognizes that there are some ethical advertisers and that there is a place for making known a product's function in a positive and helpful way, but he suggests that much of the advertising that we experience in the Western world is wittingly or unwittingly engaged in the propagation of lies:

> Much of current marketing research is involved in the sophisticated exploration of where it is that people may feel an "itch" or be encouraged to feel an "itch." The challenge then is to come up with cleverly packaged and marketed products to scratch that itch. The temptation to pander and pimp on behalf of every weakness—from covetousness or envy to insecurity about one's personal image or fears about one's health—has been too seductive for many of us to resist.

> But there is a more malignant twist as well. In addition to sniffing out more existing itches, like ferrets in a rabbit warren, there is a vast, high powered endeavour aimed at constantly creating new itches hitherto unfelt and unknown—undreamed of, in fact. They thus beget false needs (wants) and then trumpet the glad news that their client just happens to have the product to satisfy them.

> Bluntly put, this is immoral. It not only ensures that our wasteful consumption of planetary resources—no matter how many "green" slogans we are sold—will keep growing apace, it also flies directly in the face of the basic laws of human happiness and fulfillment. The message is: The more you buy, possess, consume, or enjoy, the happier you'll be.[16]

It's a lie.

Listen to the first words of Jesus as he comes out of the wilderness and addresses his own age. As he comes out of his Spirit-driven experience of discernment and temptation, this is what he says:

> "The time is fulfilled, and the kingdom of God has come near; repent, and believe in the good news." (Mark 1.15)

"Repent and believe in the good news." That's what I said as I rubbed ashes in the shape of a cross into your forehead just this past Wednesday.

There's good news in all this. Repent and believe in it. The time is fulfilled. This is the time. The promise of Lent, the promise of Mark's gospel, is that the wilderness discernment and victory over temptation in the life of Jesus continues in our own lives. His readiness to be driven by the Spirit can continue in our own lives.

Repent and believe the good news ... and don't worry ... there will be angels to minister to you as well.

Come to the Mountain

Second Sunday of Lent

Genesis 22.1-2, 9-13, 15-18
Psalm 116
Romans 8.31b-35, 37
Mark 9.2-10

I didn't watch the *Dobie Gillis* TV series in the 1960s regularly, but an episode was airing on one of those specialty channels while I was channel-surfing last August in a motel room on my way back from a vacation in Upper Michigan. It really was pretty good. One of the central characters was Maynard, a beatnik with beads, sandals and a goatee. Among other things, he avoided work at all costs. In this particular episode he was planning to do what his favourite rock star of the time had done. He was going to go on pilgrimage to the Far East to consult with a guru on the meaning of life. Maynard was doing his best to justify his adventuresome plans to Dobie, to explain just why he thought it was so important that he seek out an ancient wise man to find out who he really was. Dobie finally said to him, "Maynard, you'll never *find yourself* on a mountain in Tibet." "Why not?" Maynard asked with his typical goofy look. Dobie replied, "Because you didn't *lose yourself* on a mountain in Tibet. That's why not."

Today we find ourselves on a holy mountain, where, paradoxically enough, the agenda is losing and finding ourselves. Mark invites us to join the three chosen companions of Jesus as witnesses of his transfiguration.

At this point these disciples are unable to come to terms with just how deep this losing and finding will be. At this stage they have no clarity about any of this, only many hints. We readers, who have already been let in on Mark's messianic secret, that Jesus is the Son of God, are nevertheless invited to enter into the story with them. We are invited to join with them in reading the hints as a way of making our own faith and understanding more explicit, and of heightening our sense of participation in the mystery of Christ. Let's begin by observing some of the symbols and allusions that Mark uses in offering these hints.

First, the location itself is a high mountain traditionally associated with the special presence of God. The dazzling whiteness in Jesus' appearance associates him with heavenly beings. The presence of two monumental figures from the past heightens his importance in God's plan. There's a cloud such as led ancient Israel through the desert, and the suggestion that tents be constructed. A voice from the cloud reveals him as Son and Beloved. Finally there is discussion and puzzlement about what rising from the dead might mean.

Dobie wasn't at all convinced that Maynard would have gone very far in finding himself on a high mountain in Tibet, but as Mark invites us to the mountain of transfiguration, he clearly anticipates that we will find ourselves. His use of so many symbols and allusions, and his way of weaving them together, point to the depth of the story's significance and its life-giving possibilities.

Let's take the presence of Moses and Elijah with Jesus, and probe one of any number of ways in which their presence with him might be interpreted. What does the presence of Moses and Elijah have to contribute to the discussion of what death and rising from the dead might mean as Jesus and the disciples come down the mountain?

You'll remember that Elijah had a kind of resurrection in his own life—actually, more an assumption. Elijah never tasted death. He had close calls, but he always stayed one step ahead of death's grasp. He was taken into heaven in a fiery chariot. Did you sing this song as kids?

> A wheel within a wheel a turnin',
> way in the middle of the air.
> Elijah's in those wheels a turnin',
> way in the middle of the air.
> The big wheel runs by faith,
> and the little wheel runs by the grace of God.
> A wheel within a wheel a turnin'
> way in the middle of the air.

Actually, the song mixes up the Elijah story with Ezekiel's vision in chapter 1 of his prophecy. Ezekiel saw the wheel within the wheel, but no matter. Elijah went up in a fiery chariot and it surely must have been faith and the grace of God that made those wheels go round, too.

Let's look at Moses. I wonder if, from the Mount of the Transfiguration, Jesus and the disciples would have been able to see across the Jordan to Mount Nebo. The scripture says that Moses died there, but that no one knows where they laid him. The scriptures also testify that his eyes were yet undimmed and his vigour undaunted. Somehow or other Moses seems to have had perpetual youth. The process of death and dying was different for Moses than it was for the rest of us mortals. It seems as though Moses just fell asleep in the midst of his power, though a very old man.

It is Moses and Elijah—these figures who had such a privileged intimacy with God, however challenging that intimacy may have been for them—who appear with the transfigured Jesus. Both Moses and Elijah had a special relationship with death. Wouldn't it be logical to expect that the transfigured Jesus, declared Beloved Son, would have some kind of privileged relationship with death that would transcend that of these two monumental figures from Israel's past? The answer is yes, but ...

> A cloud overshadowed them, and from the cloud there came a voice, "This is my Son, the Beloved; listen to him!" Suddenly when they looked around, they saw no one with them any more, but only Jesus. (Mark 9.7-8)

Moses and Elijah are gone. Their ways of being raised up as prophets and leaders are past. Their ways of being guided and protected by God are past. Their ways of intimacy and communion with the Almighty are past. What we have is the Son, the Beloved, no longer transfigured but on his way down from the mountain, not to fall asleep in the strength of his vigour or rise to the heavens in a fiery chariot, but to embrace the cross. The wheels of faith and grace are turning indeed, but in a new direction.

The transfigured Jesus is no longer visible; we see only the Son of Man, who in no way would bypass death or experience anything of the human condition in a mitigated or softened way. Unlike Moses and Elijah, the clarity of Jesus' vision and the character of his vigour will be demonstrated in the way he embraces the cross. His resurrection into glory will arise out of that same experience.

The disciples needed to come to understand that Jesus is both *Son of God,* powerful agent of healing and subject of dazzling glory, and the *Son of Man,* who will be betrayed, persecuted and crucified. The disciples, like the first projected audience of Mark and all subsequent readers, need to know that glory cannot be separated from the commitment out of which it arises. Life is found in the midst of death. Over and over again Mark lifts up both aspects of Jesus' identity, relentlessly recalling that suffering will ultimately yield to triumph, but that any triumph apart from suffering is cheap and empty.

Still today we are discussing and experiencing for ourselves what this rising from the dead might mean. It would probably have been a pretty big step for beatnik Maynard with his beads, sandals and goatee to enter into this discussion, but, hey—why not? We're part of it. Why not Maynard, too? Come to the mountain.

Reading Between the Lines

Third Sunday of Lent

Exodus 20.1–17
Psalm 19
1 Corinthians 1.18, 22–25
John 2.13–25

The *Baltimore Sun* last summer had a picture of a young man standing in front of a granite monument in a public park in Frederick, Maryland. The park had originally been a cemetery where some of the early residents were buried. Now, while still including the gravesites, it has become a multi-purpose public space. This particular monument, not much larger than the headstone of a prominent family buried nearby, was placed there years ago by a service organization. It has blended into the landscape of Maryland's second largest city for decades, but now it's getting the kind of notice that could mean its demise. The commotion started when this same young man, then a high school senior, completed an essay assignment and, finally, sent it as a letter to city officials. It seems that a similar monument was taken down in Indiana. On the monument are inscribed the words of the Ten Commandments; its presence on public property may be a constitutional violation of the separation of church and state.

It would be hard to overestimate the influence of the Ten Commandments on culture and civilization. Yes, of course, the foundations of the Jewish and subsequent religious traditions and organizations are found there, notably in the first three commandments. Foundational religious truths such as the unity and transcendence of God, the need to respect the name of God and to acknowledge the presence and activity of God in a regular and disciplined way are present, but there's so much more that simply reflects good order. Basic values of morality and subsequent civil law—respect for parents and family, respect for human life, reputation and personal property—are enshrined there.

Even the foundations of good mental health can be discerned in the last two commandments: Do not covet the lives and goods of others; rather, live your own life and your own relationships to the full.

Who knows whether the stone will have to be removed, perhaps to the front lawn of a church or synagogue. I'm not sure it really belongs in a cemetery: the Ten Commandments are a challenge to the living, not a commentary on the dead. People standing in a graveyard and reading them may experience a special power and unique feeling, but that's not the point of these commandments.

The Ten Commandments were read today as part of our liturgy of the word in connection with texts from 1 Corinthians and John 2, which clearly transcend those commandments.

> God's foolishness is wiser than human wisdom, and God's weakness is stronger than human strength. (1 Corinthians 1.25)

> "Destroy this temple, and in three days I will raise it up" ...
> Jesus was speaking of the temple of his body. (John 2.19, 21)

Clearly, more than commandment-keeping lies behind these texts. As much as we would love to think of a world in which the commandments were engraved on the hearts and souls of all people, the scriptures draw us beyond even that dream.

I read somewhere that the reign of God is a passionate commitment to reading between the lines of the commandments and understanding that the relationship between humanity and God cannot be captured in words or prescriptions. The truth of such high and passionate commitment to letting God reign calls for ongoing personal and communal discernment. What lies between the lines of the commandments calls for generosity and self-sacrifice that clearly go beyond their prescriptions.

To use the language of the scriptures, God calls people beyond commandment-keeping into covenant. In dealing with the theme of covenant, I always find myself going back to marriage, which is probably the most familiar covenant into which people enter, and one which people find so challenging. I would even dare to say that persons whose marriages have not been sustainable for whatever reasons would be the first to say that marriages don't succeed or fail because the partners keep something that can be written down in a contract or presented as the "ten commandments of a good marriage." Rather, a depth of spirit and energy goes beyond commitments that can be formulated in words, however noble or sensible they may sound. Paul's experience with the "foolishness of God" and Jesus' passionate commitment to his Father's house are good examples of passionate covenant commitments that go far beyond clear and specific expectations.

Relative to our text from Exodus about Moses and the Ten Commandments, there's a charming Jewish traditional story that both "reads between the lines" of the original and "fills in the blanks."

As we know, Moses was wandering in the desert with the people for forty years, during the course of which they camped at Mount Sinai. Moses left the people at the bottom of the mountain in their camp while he went to the top for a meeting with God. After forty days of fasting and prayer, he came back with two stone tablets under his arms.

As he reached the camp, he noticed that, far from being faithful to God, the people had built an idol, a golden calf around which they were dancing and singing. In a fit of anger, Moses smashed the tablets and subsequently had to go back to the mountain to get another set.

The "between the lines" or "fill in the blanks" question is this: If Moses, under God's direction, had chiseled out the commandments, surely he should have been able to remember them. After all that time and trouble, surely he could have reconstructed them. Why didn't he just write them again? Why did he have to go back to the mountain?

This was the answer: The first tablets were blank. How could a covenant be described? The future is open-ended. Who can say just what is going to be required for fidelity to God as the years pass? The tablets were signs of a mysterious future with God that in faith and hope could be solid as a rock.

Moses, on seeing the golden calf and the people's antics, smashed the tablets and went back to God. "Hey, God," he said, "You've just got to be more specific." And so we have the Ten Commandments.

I think that's a wonderful story. We can be very grateful for the commandments, but it is precisely in their concreteness that their limitations lie. Maybe I'm exaggerating, but can it not be said that our relationship with God and, in fact, all of our really significant relationships, as rock solid as we think they are, are mysterious, open-ended blanks?

As helpful as the commandments are in organizing our thinking and our values, as prominently as we might wish to see them displayed, we all know from experience that God's law sometimes bubbles up in the silence of our consciences in ways that transcend the words of the commandments. Sometimes, far beyond the prescriptions of the commandments, we find ourselves called to foolishly passionate connectedness with what is truly right.

Do You Have a Personal Relationship with Jesus?

Fourth Sunday of Lent

2 Chronicles 36.14-17a, 19-23
Psalm 137
Ephesians 2.4-10
John 3.14-21

Jesus said to Nicodemus: "Just as Moses lifted up the serpent in the wilderness, so must the Son of Man be lifted up, that whoever believes in him may have eternal life. For God so loved the world that he gave his only Son, so that everyone who believes in him may not perish but may have eternal life. Indeed, God did not send the Son into the world to condemn the world, but in order that the world might be saved through him." (John 3.14-17)

"For God so loved the world" (John 3.16)—the most oft-quoted text of the whole New Testament? The most often "bannered" or billboarded? Probably. When you're driving through the bible belt, you'll see it painted on barn roofs, or stretched word by word over smaller signs attached to fence posts. It's probably distracting for the driver, but as a kid I remember having fun with such signs that advertised just about anything.

"Come to me all you who labour ..." or "God is love and he who abides in love ..." may be a close second. What do you think?

Deciding what sayings like these mean, and what they mean for each of us, is a lot more difficult than reading them on progressive signs at high speed. For today, let's just stick to John 3.16.

"For God so loved the world that he gave his only Son, so that everyone who believes in him may not perish but may have eternal life."

Experiencing God's love in his gift of Jesus to save: What does that mean? What does believing that feel like? How does it work? To "perish": What does that mean? "Eternal life": What's that? Can we be sure everybody wants it? I've known people—psychologically healthy people—who come to a point in life when, because of sickness or advanced age, they feel they've been around long enough, thank you. Some of these people have no expectations of an afterlife, either.

Originally, Jesus spoke these words to Nicodemus, a leader among the Jewish people who came to Jesus at night. That says something about his dispositions. He and Jesus have quite an involved conversation about the kingdom of God, about being born from above, about entering your mother's womb for a second time, about water and spirit, and wind blowing where it chooses. Today's text is the first part of Jesus' longest and final response to Nicodemus. It goes on to speak about light and darkness—about learning to love the light and coming out of the darkness into truth and goodness. I wish we had read the whole thing. It's only a few more verses.

After Jesus' crucifixion, it was this same Nicodemus who found the courage to accompany Joseph of Arimathea to prepare the body of Jesus for a dignified burial. Surely something must have gone on in his own inner core. That's the point of this whole text. It has to do with inner core stuff.

As we pass through Lent and move closer to the Triduum, I encourage all of you to do what Nicodemus did, even under cover of darkness. Let's ask ourselves core questions about what it really means to be alive and be born again at many levels; about water that cleanses and refreshes; about spirit and wind that breathe and energize; about light and darkness—about real life-and-death issues. Where is Jesus? Where and how do you experience him as saving gift? Where and how do you experience the Lord Jesus as your personal saviour? Lest you think that experience is reserved to Protestants, consider this.

Martin Luther, the great Protestant reformer, is reported to have had a profound and transforming spiritual awakening before a large crucifix—a very large crucifix, like those found near the front and to the side of many of our older churches. As a monk and priest he had been struggling with his life and with his quest for salvation and for perfection in keeping the commandments and being faithful to his vows. He fasted, he prayed, he went to confession all the time, but just couldn't make his grade. As I heard the story, one day while he was praying before the crucifix, he came to great peace. It was as if a huge burden had been lifted off the shoulders of his soul. It's not that he hadn't been trying, but he finally realized that he couldn't save himself; he couldn't perfect himself; he couldn't earn his salvation; he couldn't merit his way to heaven, however hard he might have tried or would try in the future. Before that crucifix he felt saved; he felt within himself that salvation was a gift. He couldn't earn it, he could only believe in it. Faith saves, not works. It's as if he woke up to the truth of today's gospel as well as the second reading from the liturgy.

> "For God so loved the world that he gave his only Son, so that everyone who believes in him may not perish but may have eternal life." (John 3.16)

> For by grace you have been saved through faith, and this is not your doing; it is the gift of God. This is not the result of works, so that no one may boast. For we are what he has made us, created in Christ Jesus for good works, which God prepared beforehand to be our way of life. (Ephesians 2.8-10)

This is surely not just a Protestant experience. Ignatius of Loyola, one of the great figures of the Counter Reformation, has this eloquently stirring prayer to Jesus as a foreword to his Spiritual Exercises. It was taught to me as the *Prayer Before a Crucifix*.

> Soul of Christ, sanctify me
> Body of Christ, save me
> Blood of Christ, inebriate me
> Water from the side of Christ, wash me
> Passion of Christ, strengthen me
> O Good Jesus, hear me
> Within thy wounds hide me
> Permit me not to be separated from thee

From the wicked foe defend me
At the hour of my death call me
And bid me come to thee
That with thy saints I may praise thee
For all eternity.
Amen.

Can you pray that way? I wonder if, in his experience of the passion, death and resurrection of Jesus, Nicodemus had reached that point of utter surrender.

What is the shape and quality of your personal relationship with Jesus? A personally felt connectedness with the mystery is surely an essential aspect of our faith.

At Lent's midpoint today, both readings from the New Testament concern deeply rooted, personally appropriated experiences of faith. Even the historical text from Chronicles is accompanied by a response that reflects a deeply personal appropriation of the story: "Let *my* tongue be silenced, if *I* ever forget you."

The children in one of the parish schools offered another way to look at this personal relationship. The other day they were singing a little song:

Peace before me
Peace behind me
Peace under my feet
Peace beside me
Peace over me
Let all around me be peace.

It didn't dawn on me at the time, but the little song is an adaptation of this prayer attributed to Saint Patrick:

Christ with me, Christ before me, Christ behind me, Christ in me, Christ beneath me, Christ above me, Christ on my right, Christ on my left, Christ when I lie down, Christ when I sit down, Christ when I arise, Christ in the heart of everyone who thinks of me, Christ in the mouth of everyone who speaks of me, Christ in every eye that sees me, Christ in every ear that hears me.

At a religious education conference I attended, a feisty young woman named Linda told another story of a personal relationship with Jesus. Linda was traveling from somewhere in Alberta to the Yukon. The highway was rugged, but she was even more so and set out in her little Toyota. She stopped one night at a motel high in the mountain range through which she was passing. When she heard the 5 a.m. wake-up call, she saw the mountaintops shrouded in early morning fog. There was no one in the breakfast room except two burly truck drivers. "Where are you headed?" one of them asked. "Whitehorse," she responded. The other driver couldn't believe it and said, "No way are you heading out today." "That's what you think," Linda said with a sort of reverse machismo. "If you go, we'll 'hug' you," one of them said. "Forget it," she replied, not ready to be hugged by the likes of them. No way. They laughed. "We'll put one truck ahead of you and the other behind. We'll get you through the mountains. We'll hug you. That's what we mean." And so all morning long, until the fog lifted, she followed the two little red dots of the truck ahead of her as the other big escort followed her two little red dots that were ahead of him. She was being hugged all the way to safety.

"That's what Jesus does for me all the time. He hugs me," she shared with the rest of us who were with her at that conference.

Christ before me
Christ behind me
Christ under my feet
Christ beside me
Christ over me
Let all around me be Christ

Linda would love St. Patrick's hymn and the kids' song.

Let's join Nicodemus, Martin Luther, Ignatius of Loyola, the kids at school, Saint Patrick and Linda in getting in touch with the form and quality of our own personal relationship with Jesus. With them, let's be open to the extraordinary gift that he is for us, coming straight from the heart of God.

Lifted Up

Fifth Sunday of Lent

Jeremiah 31.31–34
Psalm 51
Hebrews 5.7–9
John 12.20–33

Among those who went up to worship at the festival were some Greeks. They came to Philip, who was from Bethsaida in Galilee, and said to him, "Sir, we wish to see Jesus." Philip went and told Andrew; then Andrew and Philip went and told Jesus. (John 12.20–22)

Isn't it striking that we get no indication whatsoever if those Greeks ever got to see Jesus. Instead of offering to set up an appointment with the Greeks, Jesus answered:

"The hour has come for the Son of Man to be glorified. Very truly, I tell you, unless a grain of wheat falls into the earth and dies, it remains just a single grain; but if it dies, it bears much fruit. Those who love their life lose it, and those who hate their life in this world will keep it for eternal life. Whoever serves me must follow me, and where I am, there will my servant be also. Whoever serves me, the Father will honour." (John 12.23–26)

Isn't that strange? Some interested Greeks want to see him, to make an appointment, but instead of any openness or readiness to receive and welcome them, Jesus gets heavy—very heavy.

It's not a matter of making an appointment or of seeing Jesus. It's a matter of being with Jesus, of following him, of being planted in the earth oneself, of losing one's life in order to keep it.

It's interesting to look at the details of what set Jesus up for this weighty pronouncement. Philip and Andrew are the only ones among the apostles who had Greek names. The text notes that Philip came from Bethsaida, which was a commercial centre. He would surely have contact with Greeks. He would have experience with them and their way of thinking about things. He must have even spoken their language. Philip may have been pretty pleased, even proud that he had some hot prospects for the RCIA! He went and got Andrew to join him and went to Jesus with the news. Maybe the two of them could be the sponsors!

I'm delighted, by the way, that with us at this liturgy are catechumens who will be baptized at the Easter Vigil in just two weeks. Candidates for full communion will also be confirmed and received at that same celebration. From my experience with them at our Sunday evening gatherings, I can assure you that they have come to know personally that there's a lot more to the Christian life than making an appointment to see Jesus. The whole experience of Lent has underscored for all of us what real faith and commitment require. We have to see with more than our eyes. Like young infants, we have to take in everything.

Whether the Greeks ever got to see Jesus, we don't know. But we do know for sure that Philip and Andrew eventually took it all in or, better still, were "taken in" by the power of his Spirit.

Towards the end of the second century, the bishop of Ephesus reported that Philip died as a missionary to the Greek-speaking people in Asia Minor. In the *Ecclesiastical History of Eusebius,* Andrew is also named as having been a missionary to the Greeks. Tradition has it that both of them were martyred, giving the ultimate witness to what they had come to see in Jesus, how they had been taken in by it, and how it had transformed their lives.

We can be sure that many Greeks got to see and meet Jesus through their ministry. "Come along, we'll show you Jesus," the apostles said by their very way of being. Through their word and way of life they could most powerfully and credibly invite others into the mystery. They would re-incarnate his truth in their own stories and invite others to do the same. The Risen Jesus would be present to others in and through them.

"Unless a grain of wheat falls into the earth and dies, it remains just a single grain; but if it dies, it bears much fruit. Those who love their life lose it, and those who hate their life in this world will keep it for eternal life. Whoever serves me must follow me, and where I am, there will my servant be also."

The passage goes on:

"Father, glorify your name," Jesus' troubled soul implores.

"I have glorified it and I will glorify it again," a heavenly voice responds.

It sounded like thunder!

"This voice has come for your sake, not for mine …

I, when I am lifted up from the earth, will draw all people to myself."

Jesus said this to indicate the kind of death he was to die. (John 12.28, 30, 32 33)

To "the kind of death he was to die" I would add *and the kind of resurrection he was going to live*. In seeing Jesus, in allowing our inner vision of his glory to expand in our minds and hearts, it's not so much a matter of seeing, even of "taking it all in," but of being "taken in."

"Lifted up, I will draw all people to myself."

Lifted into the mystery of Christ's own death and resurrection, Philip and Andrew became credible signs of his glory. The Risen Christ is lifted up once again in their own stories, drawing more and more people to a share in his sacrificial death, his way of finding life by losing it.

From the very beginning, our eucharistic theology has stated that in remembering the story of the death and rising of Jesus, we enter into it.

We remember Jesus. We remember Philip and Andrew. Seeing and hearing their stories again invite our participation in their meaning, in their mystery. We ourselves are drawn in—drawn to communion with them.

In just a few moments, this is what I'll be proclaiming as I lead the eucharistic prayer with words so familiar that they may pass us by rather than take us in:

> Father, *calling to mind* the death your Son endured for our salvation, his glorious resurrection and ascension into heaven, and ready to greet him when he comes again, *we offer you in thanksgiving this holy and living sacrifice.* Look with favour on your church's offering, and see the victim whose death has reconciled us to yourself. *Grant that we, who are nourished by his body and blood, may be filled with his Holy Spirit, and become one body, one spirit in Christ.* May he make us an everlasting gift to you and enable us to *share in the inheritance of the saints,* with Mary, the virgin mother of God—*with the apostles Philip and Andrew* ...

"Lifted up from the earth, I will draw all people"—I am drawing all people.

Come and see.

Take me in. Let me take you in.

Truly This Is God's Son

Passion (Palm) Sunday

Isaiah 50.4-7
Psalm 22
Philippians 2.6-11
Mark 14.1–15.47

There are three great epiphanies in the Gospel of Mark, and the passion is the third and greatest.

We're not used to using or hearing the word *epiphany* at this time of year. It's usually restricted to January and refers to wise men and such, but in my reading of Mark it's here on Passion Sunday that it finds its climactic home.

Epiphany is about manifestation. Where and how is Jesus manifested for who he truly is? Where and how are his true nature and purpose revealed?

There are three major epiphany moments in Mark. The first is the baptism of Jesus in the river Jordan, where Jesus descends into sacred waters, in which he himself experiences the voice of divine election calling out to him.

The second is his transfiguration on a holy mountain with heavenly assistants and luminescent robes. The same divine voice heard at his baptism discloses his identity, this time to his most intimate companions and disciples, even though they miss the point of it entirely.

In this third and greatest epiphany, the passion story, the point is clear. Today Jesus is manifested as he truly is—for all to see. There is no missing the point, however unlikely the locale or circumstances.

I'd like to suggest that today's great epiphany begins in the mocking of Jesus, when the Roman cohort of soldiers dresses him in a preposterous parody of royal regalia and offers this object of their scorn their royal salute and act of homage.

"Hail, King of the Jews."
They knelt down in homage to him. (Mark 15.18b, 19b)

This mocking homage of the soldiers finally leads beyond itself to the declaration of their superior officer. The centurion "stood facing him, and saw the way in which he breathed his last." It is the centurion who, however inadvertently, now beyond any possibility of mocking or ridicule, makes the words of divine revelation his own. "Truly this was God's son."

Mark's book is quickly drawing to a close. Mark's book entitled "the beginning of the Gospel of Jesus Christ, the Son of God" is in its final movement. The beginning is coming to an end in the centurion's remarkable affirmation.

There's only one thing wrong with the centurion's remarkable affirmation. It's the verb.

"Truly this man *was* God's son."

No.

"Truly this *is* God's son."

And God's Son continues to live in the hearts of all who feel his rising in their own depths and who see his rising in the mysterious faith and hope witnessed by others who bear his name. Let the word go out. This is God's son. Let the story continue.

The presence of the Lord remains indeed mysterious, perhaps as yet largely undiscovered. Mark teaches us, however, how and where to look for him. Huub Oosterhuis captures this in one of his poems. It's really an epiphany hymn, but is strangely appropriate on this Passion Sunday.

Lest the word be far from us,
God prepared his coming.
One who longed to share our fate
made with us his dwelling.
There among you is one you do not know.

Who is everywhere at hand
who is wholly human,
one who goes unrecognized,
silent, never spoken.
There among you is one you do not know.

God from God and Light from Light,
guarding all creation,
one with us in flesh and blood,
calls to every nation.
There among you is one you do not know.

Then let patience be your guide,
walk in ways of justice;
show each other at all times
every kind of goodness.
There among you is one you do not know.

Now be carefree, full of joy:
God, who knows and calls us,
brushes by us every day,
makes a home among us.
There among you is one you do not know.[17]

The Easter Triduum

Beautiful Feet

Evening Mass of the Lord's Supper
Holy Thursday

Exodus 12.1-8, 11-14
Psalm 116
1 Corinthians 11.23-26
John 13.1-15

How beautiful upon the mountains
are the feet of the messenger who announces peace,
who brings good news,
who announces salvation,
who says to Zion, "Your God reigns." (Isaiah 52.7)

"Lord, are you going to wash my feet?"
"You do not know now what I am doing,
but later you will understand....
Unless I wash you, you have no share with me."
(John 13. 6-8)

How beautiful the feet—indeed!

In the chapter of John's gospel that precedes the story of Jesus washing of the feet of the disciples at table, we find the equally wonderful story of Mary of Bethany, sister of Martha and Lazarus, anointing the feet of Jesus at the table in their home.

Centuries earlier, not far from there, Samuel the priest had anointed the head of David, the shepherd king, as a sign of divine election. This priestly anointing set David on the road to the destiny God had preordained for him.

Mary's anointing of Jesus' feet is equally priestly. In her own way and in her own time, she is anointing a king. Samuel empties the horn of oil on David's head. Mary breaks off the long neck of her jar, designed to make it easy to measure out small quantities of precious ointment. No measuring here. She empties the whole jar on Jesus' feet. The whole house is filled with the fragrance of the oil poured out in extravagant affection, tenderness and hope. She anoints his feet for the road to Jerusalem, the city of David. She anoints them for a march to the temple mount and beyond. She anoints his feet for a path to glory, to royal enthronement on Golgatha, the "place of the skull." She anoints his royal feet for death, burial and resurrection—all of it glorious.

And what about the feet of Peter and the others? These feet have to be cleansed, purified and refreshed for a walk whose meaning and consequences elude them. These feet have to be baptized so as to participate in the royal procession through death to life. These feet need to be made ready for the road to glory. Jesus washes these feet. The servant king takes off his garments, wraps himself in a towel, and kneels down before them. Like Mary of Bethany, Jesus pours himself out in extravagant affection, tenderness and hope.

"You do not know now what I am doing, but later you will understand ... Unless I wash you, you have no share with me." In other words: If I wash your feet, you'll be able to walk with me in confidence. You'll be able to fit into my footsteps. You'll be able to set your feet on a path to glory. And furthermore: "If I, your Lord and Teacher, have washed your feet, you also ought to wash each other's feet. For I have set you an example, that you also should do as I have done to you." (John 13.14-15)

Tonight, as we enter into the Triduum, it is in Jesus' name and in his spirit that we wash each other's feet. Obedient to the royal servant son, and true to his example, we kneel before each other in extravagant affection, tenderness and hope, with a basin and pitcher in our hands and a towel around our waist.

We affirm our faith in Jesus as Lord and Teacher. We affirm our faith, perhaps in trembling humility, that his road is ours; his glory is ours; his feet are ours.

Treading in Relays

Celebration of the Lord's Passion
Good Friday

Isaiah 52.13–53.12
Psalm 31
Hebrews 4.14-16; 5.7-9
John 18.1–19.42

Carrying the cross by himself, he went out to what is called The Place of the Skull. (John 19.17)

These will be last steps for royal feet, anointed for the journey. The king approaches his throne. Love incarnate steps through death to life. "The royal banners forward go, the cross shines out in mystic glow."[18]

In just a few moments we will all be invited to join his procession. We will be invited to step out and to move towards the cross, to come forward to embrace Love's mystic glow. Our own feet will bear the weight of our bodies as we move to the sanctuary. Our hearts and minds will bear the weight of our memories and our dreams as we approach the throne of grace.

"This is the wood of the cross,
on which hung the Saviour of the world."
"Come let us worship."

We who have crowded into this church today embody the vastness of humanity. The centre aisle of this church is the road to The Place of the Skull. Bearing our own life stories, we will hang them on his cross—with a bow, with a loving touch, with a kiss.

"Men and women tread in relays the way of the cross."[19] This procession, this movement forward, both heralds and models the life that we are all invited to embrace and to share. In solidarity we stand; in relays we run the race.

124

The following wonderful invitation offered in the Letter to the Hebrews is particularly striking today as we prepare to join this great procession.

> Therefore, my friends, since we have confidence to enter the sanctuary by the blood of Jesus, by the new and living way that he opened for us through the curtain (that is, through his flesh), and since we have a great priest over the house of God, *let us approach* with a true heart in full assurance of faith, with our hearts sprinkled clean from an evil conscience and our bodies washed with pure water. Let us hold fast to the confession of our hope without wavering, for he who has promised is faithful. And let us consider how to provoke one another to love and good deeds, not neglecting to meet together, as is the habit of some, but encouraging one another, and all the more as you see the Day approaching. (Hebrews 10.19-25)

There is not even a fraction of our sufferings that the Lord Jesus has not already lived and transformed. "As Christ's cup of suffering overflows, and we suffer with him, so also through Christ our consolation overflows." (2 Corinthians 1.5, NEB)

So come forward with confidence to the cross, his royal throne. Come forward in your relays. Come forth in confident procession. Bear your whole lives on your shoulders as you walk. Let them be drawn into communion with the life of him who walks before you. Let your lives and his melt together. Let Incarnate Love embrace and include you.

It is the depth and wonder of this kind of "holy communion" that is so beautifully expressed in a poem by the English Jesuit poet, Gerard Manley Hopkins.

> I say more: the just man justices;
> Keeps grace: that keeps all his goings graces;
> Acts in God's eye what in God's eye he is—
> Christ—for Christ prays in ten thousand places,
> Lovely in limbs, and lovely in eyes not his
> To the Father through the features of men's faces.[20]

Believe that Jesus lives:"lovely in limbs not his"—your own;"lovely in eyes not his"—your own ... lovely in the features of your own faces. Step forward and know that you do not walk alone.

Going Ahead of You

Easter Vigil
Holy Saturday

Genesis 1.1–2.2
Psalm 104 or 33
Genesis 22.1-18
Psalm 16
Exodus 14.15-31; 15.20, 1
Exodus 15
Isaiah 54.5-14
Psalm 30
Isaiah 55.1-11
Isaiah 12
Baruch 3.9-15, 32–4.4
Psalm 19
Ezekiel 36.16-17a, 18-28
Psalm 42 or 51
Romans 6.3-11
Psalm 118
Mark 16.1-8

"Do not be alarmed … He has been raised … He is going ahead of you" … So they went out and fled from the tomb, for terror and amazement had seized them, and they said nothing to anyone, for they were afraid. (Mark 16.6-8)

Here endeth the lesson. This, the end of Mark's gospel? What an ending! What happens next? How does the word finally get out? Do the women get over their speechless fear, their paralyzing anxieties? They must have, because the news got out somehow. At any rate, it leaves a lot of questions unanswered. That everybody lived "happily ever after" is neither apparent nor likely in such an abrupt and ambiguous ending. It's something of a "cliffhanger."[21]

Scholars suggest that this unending ending may well be purposeful. Maybe it's not supposed to be an ending at all. Maybe it's designed to suggest that the story has no ending.

Let's check the gospel's first line. It reads: "The beginning of the good news of Jesus Christ, the Son of God."

It's been suggested that this first line is a sort of title for the whole book, that the whole book is a beginning, that its sixteen chapters actually comprise chapter 1 of an ongoing story yet to be told. Subsequent chapters continue to be written in the lives of those who have taken this beginning of the good news to heart and carry it forward in word and deed.

It is at the "end of the beginning" of the good news that faithful women are being called out of the tomb by a mysterious young man who is clothed in white. This Easter, as we see white robes hanging ready for those who will be baptized, we might wonder if there is any connection. At any rate, the women came out of the tomb, but they didn't follow his instructions to tell the disciples and Peter that Jesus was going ahead of them to Galilee. Instead, it was in terror and amazement that they fled into the radiance of Easter morning, saying "nothing to anyone, for they were afraid."

There is an endearingly awkward realism in their response to the call to be heralds of risen life, as throughout the gospel we have witnessed the slowness of disciples to see and respond to Christ. I think that Mark is inviting us to recognize our own fear and awkwardness in the experience of these struggling first-generation believers. The story doesn't tell us how, but somehow they must have gotten over their terror. They must have found a way beyond fear to commitment, beyond amazement to proclamation. Otherwise the memory of Jesus and his call beyond the grave would have been lost in the shadows of history. There would have been just an empty tomb. Somehow or other, they finally got it right; we can, too. The good news can continue to be heard, lived and shared—even by the likes of you and me.

Mysteriously, Jesus went before his first disciples, and mysteriously they met him and came to faith. Mysteriously the Risen Lord has been going before men and women for the almost two thousand years since that first Easter, otherwise the good news could never have never reached into our own times. Mark's gospel is just the beginning. The risen Lord continues to go before disciples of every age.

> By the tender mercy of our God,
> the dawn from on high will break upon us,
> to give light to those who sit in darkness
> and in the shadow of death,
> to guide our feet into the way of peace. (Luke 1.78-79)[22]

It is the Risen Lord himself who leads women and men beyond terrified stumbling in a sure-footed procession into the way of peace.

In just a few moments, we will celebrate our solidarity with that great procession. As we move towards the baptistery, we will be chanting the Litany of Saints, and in our song we will be including the two Marys of tonight's gospel story, along with Peter and the disciples to whom they were sent. Numbered in a marvellously varied list of witnesses, we will be inviting them to be with us as the good news moves forward yet again to transform the lives of the men, women and children right here in the first pew who will be going down into the waters of Christ's death. We will imagine ourselves in procession with them, in the solidarity of their witness and prayer.

The good news moves into the future as together with the whole church we are drawn forward and upward to tell it with our lives.

Look Up!

Easter Sunday

Acts 10.34a, 36–43
Psalm 118
Colossians 3.1–4
John 20.1–18

If you have been raised with Christ, seek the things that are above … Set your minds on things that are above, not on things that are on earth. (Colossians 3.1–2)

In the passage from John that we just heard, we learned that, on the first Easter Sunday, Mary Magdalene went out to the tomb while it was still dark.

There's something very human and powerful about that picture, which may in fact be in sharp contrast to the verse from Paul's letter to the Colossians that talks of "looking up."

Imagine the shadowy figure of a woman moving quietly, almost surreptitiously, to Jesus' gravesite. Does she not want anyone to know of her early morning outing? Is she afraid? Or does she just want some time of privacy with her own thoughts? Perhaps she is just coming out for a time of private grieving, beginning the slow, painful process of coming to grips with her personal loss. At any rate, she is looking down, not up.

In this setting of a private early morning visit to the cemetery, her response of frustration and anger when she discovers that "they have taken the Lord out of the tomb" is altogether reasonable. To desecrate the body of Jesus would be the ultimate degradation. Any other possibility does not seem to have dawned on her. Even her encounter with the two angels provided her with no clarity about the truth of what had taken place. Her vision was so clouded that even when she saw Jesus, and first heard his voice, she was sure that he was someone else, likely the gardener. It was only when he called her name that she "turned" and said to him in Hebrew, "Rabbouni," which means "teacher."

She turned.
Isn't this what conversion is? A kind of turning?
There was a conversion.
She saw.
The light had come on.
The sun had come up.

The light of the world had risen and was once again her teacher, but in a new way.

Her turning was a conversion of heart.

Her perspective and indeed her whole experience of that dark morning had been transformed.

She listened to the teacher.
She knew that she had to learn to look up, not down.

"Do not hold on to me," the risen Jesus insisted, "because I have not yet ascended to the Father. But go to my brothers and say to them, 'I am ascending to my Father and your Father, to my God and your God.'" (John 20.17) Jesus had risen and was still "rising."

There's surely something more going on here than just rising from the dead, as remarkable as such a phenomenon might be in itself. This upward movement about which Jesus speaks is clearly more than physical.

Even the sky's not the limit for the rising and ascending Lord.

Nobody was taking his corpse anywhere; he was rising and ascending to his God and to Mary's God. His words to her and their profound significance echo through the ages: "Don't cling to me."

Raise your eyes. Lift up your heart. Be with me in this glorious movement. Let your mind be on things of heaven. Leave your mourning behind; leave this place of the dead. Move forward and outward. Tell my disciples and friends that I am ascending to my Father and your Father, to my God and your God.

That's the message, the enduring message of the resurrection of Jesus. That's our message for today. Being caught up in the spirit of Easter means being caught in an ascending whirlwind, a vigorous upward spiritual movement that pulls us into its ascending energy, a pattern of dying and rising that draws a community of faith to eternity after the pattern of Jesus himself.

The resurrection of Jesus invites and inspires hope and confidence in believers who no longer allow themselves to be pinned down, who can no longer stand still, and whose whole life is about "getting a life."

> If you have been raised with Christ, seek the things that are above … Set your minds on things that are above, not on things that are on earth …

The spatial metaphors of rising and ascending are clearly directional, but transcend physical or geographical directions. They are directional in a personal and spiritual way. Consistent with this spatial imagery, I like to think of our participation in the paschal mystery and our communion with one another in the risen Christ as a kind of launching pad.

> Open your arms in prayer.
> Lift up your hearts.
> Ready! Set! Go!

Right now I'm wondering if our Easter celebrations may be just too conventional. They may be just too dignified and solemn to express the mystery. Perhaps they make it all look too easy. It's as if we knew where we were going.

> Maybe we need to fasten our seatbelts.
> Maybe Easter bonnets need to be redesigned.
> Maybe it's madness to wear straw and velvet hats to church;
> we should be wearing crash helmets.

The ushers ought to be issuing life preservers and signal flares at the doors of the church on Easter morning, for the sleeping Messiah has awakened, and the waking Messiah is calling out, seeking companions for his ongoing adventure.[23]

He's asking Mary not to cling to him, but to lift up her eyes. The same invitational challenge is being offered to us who gather here this Easter day.

Nobody needs to tell you that it's not always easy to keep your eyes raised. It's not always easy to keep your imaginations and your dreams lofty and elevated. It's not always easy to be growing all the time, to be rising to new occasions, to be stretched. It's not easy to rise above cynicism, doubt and fear. Rising doesn't come naturally. Spiritual, moral and psychological gravity is a mighty force.

The weight of past pain and suffering and the wear and tear of life experience may well tempt us into believing that being stuck in the mud is more realistic, even more comfortable than thoughts and plans of fastening our seatbelts for a lifetime resurrection adventure, but it's just not so. Easter faith declares and proclaims: *"It's just not so."*

For his part, Christ is risen; he has defied death, which includes the laws of moral and spiritual gravity; he has left the tomb.

The sun came up for Mary Magdalene as the sun can come up for all of us.

She—and we with her—can be "converted."

We, too, even in whatever darkness we may be experiencing, can turn around and see the risen Jesus. We, too, can recognize him as our own "rabbouni," the teacher of teachers, the light of the world.

If you have been raised in Christ, seek the things that are above.
Set your minds on things that are above.
Nobody can hold you down unless you let them.
Lift up your hearts.
Fasten your seatbelts.
Sense paschal excitement.
Sense the Easter mystery.

Listen again to the ancient prayer that opened this morning's liturgy. Hear beyond its formal and traditional language to the paschal excitement to which it invites us.

God our Father,
by raising Christ your Son

you conquered the power of death
and opened for us the way to eternal life.
Let our celebration today
raise us up and renew our lives
by the Spirit that is within us.

Bearers of Peace

Second Sunday of Easter

Acts 4.32-35
Psalm 118
1 John 5.1-6
John 20.19-31

The doors of the house where the disciples had met were locked for fear of the Jewish authorities. Jesus came and stood among them and said, "Peace be with you." After he said this, he showed them his hands and his side. Then the disciples rejoiced when they saw the Lord. (John 20.19-20)

Peace be with *you*!

The resurrection and subsequent appearances of Jesus are more about the disciples to whom he appears than about Jesus himself. The resurrection is for them. It's more about influencing and changing their future than it is about vindicating the words and actions of Jesus' past or about explicitly proving anything particular about his life or mission. Does that surprise you?

Did it ever strike you that Jesus should have gone into the chambers of the high priests? "Look at me, you poor, misguided people, and repent of your ways," he could have said. "I am right. You are wrong. I am the Son of God. Now do you get it?"

Or why not go to the judgment seat where Pilate sat? "'What is truth?' you say. Here it is. 'Behold the man,' you said. Behold indeed. Don't just sit there with your mouth open. I've come back from the dead. Take a picture and send it back to your emperor."

No, Jesus does nothing of the kind. The resurrection is not about himself or for his own personal prestige or vindication. Instead of focusing on trying to prove anything, he comes through locked doors to greet and to challenge his shuddering, fearful and defensive disciples.

Jesus breaks into the company of bewildered and anxious people to offer them a new sense of meaning and purpose. These are the people who, in such a touching way, he called friends on the night before he died, and to a man they let him down. At this point they have lost any dimension of their sense of mission that they might have had or any sense of their being a living community with a clear sense of purpose and direction. All that binds them is fear.

They're not huddled in that room as athletes sometimes huddle to make plans for the next play or the next offensive, but simply to be huddled. Their huddling is for the sake of huddling. "Peace be with you," Jesus says to them, and suddenly a new spirit enters into that locked, shaded room; a new sense of energy and purpose enters into their closed and frightened presence.

The appearance of Jesus on that evening of the first day of the week is less about the past than about the future that will arise out of the light and power and peace of his Easter presence. It is less about evening and more about morning. The resurrection is about the future of those fearful disciples and about the future of the world they will begin to build in the power of his spirit. It is the intrusion of the risen Jesus into their frightened little circle that breaks them out of their inward-looking huddle and turns them around. Jesus turns their circle inside out. His presence and greeting of peace is a call to conversion—a real spiritual turnaround.

More than merely bringing peace to his frightened followers, he charges them to move into the future as heralds and bearers of that same peace. They themselves will take on his peace-making mission and bring it forward. His appearances do more than simply vindicate his personal integrity or prove the validity of his life and ministry; they evoke and provoke transformation among his disciples. In his appearances the risen Jesus confronts them with their own possibilities.

> Jesus said to them again, "Peace be *with you*. As the Father has sent me, so I *send you*." When he had said this, he breathed on them and said to them, "Receive the Holy Spirit. If you forgive the sins of any, they are forgiven them; if you retain the sins of any, they are retained." (John 20.21-23)

Many of us Catholics have learned to see in this text the roots of the Sacrament of Reconciliation. We have been taught to see the power of the keys here, as well as the need for discernment and right judgment in confessors, and the need for honesty and integrity in penitents. However important those traditions and values might be, I wonder if the meaning of the text is not actually much broader, much more inclusive. These frightened disciples are being presented with an important, even fundamental, choice about the basic stance they will take before the world.

> Jesus said to them again, "Peace be *with you*. As the Father has sent me, so I *send you*." When he had said this, he breathed on them and said to them, "Receive the Holy Spirit. If you forgive the sins of any, they are forgiven them; if you retain the sins of any, they are retained."

The peace is offered. The commission is given; the energy of the Spirit's breath is poured out from the very soul of the risen Christ, but the "Ifs" loom large, very large. A choice remains here—a big choice. They will have to make a decision that will give shape and direction to their whole future.

Would we be stretching the text, even stretching our imaginations to suggest how large and deep that choice really is? The choice is about being locked up in a huddle or being freed to become messengers of liberation and reconciliation. The choice is about staying in the upper room in self-righteous isolation, or moving to the ground floor. Take your pick.

You can look backwards and point fingers at the chief priests and Pilates in your own life who have hurt you, even at the Peters and the Thomases with their betrayals and doubts, or you can choose to move into God's future and go out to these same persons with a message of peace and healing. In the peace of Christ and in the power of his spirit you can believe in the possibilities of forgiveness and reconciliation or, with one eye looking backward, you can proceed with your own carefully controlled steps and plans and projects, guided by nothing more than your own limited vision and carefully contrived pragmatism.

Is it too much to say that this is the fundamental choice Jesus offers as he breathes on his first disciples and messengers of good news?

On the first page of the Bible, God is breathing. We encounter there a breathing God, a spirit-sharing creator. The spirit is hovering over the depths, over the formless void. God's breath, God's life, God's wind, God's energy, God's Spirit, hovering over the deep. The very inner being of God hovering over the deep, bringing life out of death, order out of chaos, harmony out of dissonance. Can we see and recognize that same Spirit-breathing God in the risen Jesus?

It is on the first day of a new week that Jesus breathes on his disciples. His resurrection day is the first day of a new creation. He personally is hovering over the chaos of the void, the dark empty deep of the earth. In his breathing God is breathing again.

In the book of Exodus, as Moses and the people are moving to freedom, the east wind dries up the sea before them. The east wind: the breath of God arising from the place where the sun itself arises? Arising from the future? Can we see and recognize a spirit-breathing God, a liberating east wind in the breath of the risen Christ?

Jesus has risen from the east like the rising sun itself and breathes on his huddled disciples. His breath is a breath of freedom, this time for an even greater movement to freedom, an even fuller liberation. "He breathed on them and said to them, 'Receive the Holy Spirit. If you forgive the sins of any, they are forgiven them; if you retain the sins of any, they are retained.'"

Our hymns and prayers throughout the Easter season speak of new creation and new exodus, the end of life as a formless void, the end of hostility, alienation and any form of sin that could contain and enslave people in their inward-looking huddles.

"Breathe on me, Breath of God."

In our own fears and limitations, can we muster the spirit to respond to the presence of Christ among us today with such a song? As was the case last Sunday, maybe we need to fasten our seatbelts to respond to the presence of his spirit, to breathe in the whirlwind.

Breathe on me, Breath of God,
fill me with life anew:
that I may love what thou dost love,
and do what thou wouldst do.

Breathe on me, Breath of God,
till I am wholly thine,
till all this earthly part of me glows
with thy fire divine.

Edwin Hatch (1835–1899)

Too Close for Comfort?

Third Sunday of Easter

Acts 3.13-15, 17-19
Psalm 4
1 John 2.1-5
Luke 24.35-48

"Why are you frightened, and why do doubts arise in your hearts? Look at my hands and my feet …" In their joy they were disbelieving and still wondering. (Luke 24.38-39, 41)

For believers of any age, Easter faith is clearly problematic. The Risen Lord is mysterious. He walks through closed doors and lets people touch his wounds. He talks for a good while with the two men along the road to Emmaus, is not recognized until he breaks bread with them and then promptly disappears. The first experience of the early disciples with the Risen Lord is not joy, or even pride in his vindication. It is fear and uncertainty. He cooks and they eat, he is present to them and they touch him, but they clearly cannot grasp the reality of this tremendous event.

What would their immediate and spontaneous feelings have been? If he is risen, what would that have meant to them? What would such an experience have been like for Peter, who betrayed him, for the apostles and disciples who fled the scene, and for so many others who, without knowing what they were doing, had some complicity in his suffering and death?

It doesn't matter that Luke's account of the passion has Jesus praying from his deathbed for their forgiveness. At this stage I can't imagine that that would have been much consolation. Instead I imagine the disciples to be very embarrassed at their poor performance under pressure. Embarrassed, guilty, full of shame and fear. How would you have felt?

From the very beginning, Easter's victory has had to be accepted and interpreted by and among people who are guilty, afraid, sometimes joyful, often disappointed. The women of the first Easter, the disciples along the road, the eleven and their companions and all believers since will never be immune from fear and doubt as they face the truth about themselves and stand in the presence of Christ.

Although life will move on for the two disciples who met him on the road, they will never be able to forget the one who broke bread for them and opened their eyes, nor will the eleven and their companions ever forget the risen one who, in his sharing of the broiled fish he gave them, drew them beyond their disbelief and wonderment.

The nineteenth-century French poet Paul Verlaine was a very interesting character. His early life was notoriously dissolute and his early poetry reflects his wild mood swings. He was even imprisoned for a time for having impulsively shot at his companion and fellow poet Rimbaud. While in prison he had some kind of conversion experience. His prayers written from that time of imprisonment are very moving. The following might easily reflect sentiments the first disciples may have had as they came to Christ, or rather as he came to them.

> Lord, I'm afraid. My soul is all aquiver
> I know I ought to love you, but how could
> a poor thing, like myself, God, be your lover,
> O Justice feared by the virtuous and the good.
>
> Yes, how? Beneath this troubled canopy
> Where my heart's been digging out its tomb
> And where I feel the heavens flow toward me
> I ask you, by what road you'd have me come.
>
> Stretch forth your hand to me, so I can raise
> This sickened spirit and this flesh that cowers.
> But shall I have the blessed accolade?
>
> Is it possible to find one of these days,
> In your breast, on your heart, what once was ours,
> The place where the apostle's head was laid?

Paul Verlaine (1844–1896), translated by C.F. MacIntyre.[24]

I have a feeling that there is no suffering greater than that caused by the doubts and anxieties of those who want to believe and draw close to God. Who of us is ready to lean our head against the heart of Christ? Perhaps this is the wrong question. It is the heart of Christ that reaches out to us, not the other way around. It is the risen Jesus who stands among terrified folks with a word of life: "Peace be with you."

To Paul Verlaine Jesus says: "It is not you who must come to me; it is I who have chosen to come to you. Look at my hands stretched out to you. Here, eat; be nourished. Let your mind be opened to understand."

Verlaine had to get used to the sense that he was loved by Christ before he could get over being "all aquiver." There will always be those among us who will hesitate to get "too close for comfort."

Such uneasiness before the glorified Christ may not only be understandable, but healthy. It takes time for all of us to come to terms with the truth of the scriptures that real salvation comes out of suffering, that real life comes out of death.

It takes time to develop the courage to accept that truth as our own, to proclaim it, and to witness it. The truth of the matter is that the church is a community of people who know not the joy that comes from strength, consistency and courage, but the joy that comes from grace and forgiveness. There is a way of being graced by Christ's presence that we can come to only gradually. There is a way of being summoned by the utter gratuity of God's gift rather than being repelled by its generosity. We people have to get used to being loved and forgiven. That's what it's all about.

> If we say that we have no sin, we deceive ourselves, and the truth is not in us. (1 John 1.8)

> God proves his love for us in that while we still were sinners Christ died for us. (Romans 5.8)

The summons of the risen Christ is to grow beyond fear to joy, beyond embarrassment to serenity. It takes some time for most of us to accept the gift of peace, the gift of serenity, the gift of joy that is the sure sign of God's presence and power at work in us. Ironically and paradoxically, it's hard for us to accept anything "free."

A wonderful response to Verlaine's uneasiness, and our own, comes in the beautiful text of "I Heard the Voice of Jesus," another favourite hymn of mine.

> I heard the voice of Jesus say,
> "Come unto Me and rest;
> Lay down, thou weary one, lay down
> Thy head upon My breast."
> I came to Jesus as I was,
> weary and worn and sad;
> I found in Him a resting place,
> and He has made me glad.
>
> I heard the voice of Jesus say,
> "I am this dark world's light;
> Look unto Me, thy morn shall rise,
> and all thy day be bright."
> I looked to Jesus, and I found
> in Him my star, my sun;
> And in that light of life I'll walk,
> till traveling days are done.

Horatius Bonar (1808–1889)

Flock and Shepherd: One with the Father

Fourth Sunday of Easter

Acts 4.7–12
Psalm 118
1 John 3.1-2
John 10.11-18

"I am the good shepherd. I know my own and my own know me." (John 10.14)

I'm sure you've all heard plenty of Good Shepherd Sunday ser mons or homilies that begin by noting how unfamiliar all of us really are with the whole business of sheep and shepherds. Few of us are really at home in the reality of the Scottish highlands or in the east of New Zealand.

As far as animals go, most of us are probably more familiar with dogs and cats. I've had both and can attest that my dog did know my voice and respond to his name when I called him. I'm not sure, how-ever, how he would have responded to being part of a "flock" of dogs. I have a feeling that he would have been a little frustrated. As for the cat, I found that she was quite happy that I recognized her voice and was never quite sure that she recognized mine. The dog was my dog. As for the cat, I was hers. Nothing to do, mind you, with the gender of the animals. It just happens that the dog was male and the cat female.

All of that notwithstanding, the images of sheep and shepherds continue to carry extraordinary weight in the consciousness of both Jews and Christians. In spite of our lack of direct contact with the lived experience of sheep and shepherds, the image or metaphor succeeds in creating a strong sense of comfort and security. Psalm 23, for example, "The Lord is my shepherd," is almost universally chosen as an element in sacramental events as diverse as baptism, first confession, first communion, anointing of the sick, viaticum, and funeral liturgies. In these sacramental events a certain vulnerability and need for guidance and protection is close to the surface of the participants' consciousness and sense of need.

The way in which Jesus uses the image in John 10, however, adds two dimensions not found in the familiar psalm. Let's listen again.

> "I am the good shepherd. I know my own and my own know me, just as the Father knows me and I know the Father. And I lay down my life for the sheep. I have other sheep that do not belong to this fold. I must bring them also, and they will listen to my voice. So there will be one flock, one shepherd." (John 10.14–16)

First of all he says: "I know my sheep as the Father knows me and I know the Father." We're not talking dogs and cats here. Nor are we talking about dependent relationships or about co-dependencies, to plug into modern psychological terminology. We're talking about mutuality. No dog or cat has ever called me "Father." Only real live *people* like yourselves have ever called me "Father," which, if nothing else, means that you consider me a member of the same species.

Fathers and mothers, and their daughters and sons, share what the ancient philosophers called the same nature, and so are fundamentally one. If the way the shepherd knows the sheep is the way a father knows his son, there is clearly more than a barnyard or a pastoral hillside in the picture.

"I lay down my life for the sheep." However the ancient world may have functioned in relationship to a shepherd's dedication to his or her flock, it's clear here that the metaphor is being stretched into human relationships, stretched to its limits. If you're a parent and you have ever experienced your child being threatened, you know about readiness to lay down your life. If you're a parent or grandparent who has suffered the loss of a child, you know first-hand of your readiness to propose that God substitute your life for that of your offspring. That Jesus moves so quickly from the animal kingdom to parent–child relationships is quite remarkable, even stunning.

We're not really talking about distant Australian or Scottish sheep and shepherds, or dogs and cats and their masters or owners about which we think we know something. We're talking here about human beings and God: about each other and the Almighty, as Jesus describes the relationship—about how Jesus says that he's one with the Father in the same kind of way as he's one with us. He knows us and we know him in the same way in which God knows him and he knows God. He can't possibly be talking about sheep. The metaphor is just his entrée into the "real stuff" of his teaching and witness.

"I know my own and my own know me, just as the Father knows me and I know the Father."

That's not all. Fasten your seatbelts and keep reading.

"I have other sheep that do not belong to this fold. I must bring them also, and they will listen to my voice. So there will be one flock, one shepherd."

It's not just about us who know and honour the Lord Jesus, but about those outside the flock—beyond our knowledge, beyond our ken, beyond our race or nationality. The flock is not fixed, but open-ended.

In another passage, Jesus looks out over the nameless crowds of people and takes pity on them because they seem to be scattered, to be like sheep without a shepherd. He saw clearly how people, all people, belong together, but as he and the Father are one? That really is stretching it!

We Christians have always believed that his vision is salvific. We have always said that Jesus saves, and that Jesus is our holy communion, and that we are one body in him, but we have not always been convincing. Father Joseph Donders, who served for years as a student chaplain in Kenya, reminds us how

two 'prophets' moved beyond us because of what they saw and experienced among us. Mohammed almost fourteen hundred years ago started a new "jamaa," a new human family, because the Christians he lived with would not accept or associate with him and his people. More than a hundred years ago, Karl

Marx started his new "commune" because he doubted whether Christians with their talk of faith could do it.[25]

The image of the Good Shepherd as John presents it to us today is not for children or for the fragile and vulnerable, but for the strong and courageous.

> "For this reason the Father loves me, because I lay down my life in order to take it up again. No one takes it from me, but I lay it down of my own accord. I have power to lay it down, and I have power to take it up again. I have received this command from my Father." (John 10.17–18)

It's pretty clear here that Jesus is both the Good Shepherd and the Lamb of God—at the same time. Both metaphors are invitations into holy communion to which we are invited to give our wholehearted assent: Amen.

Is God Bugging You?

Fifth Sunday of Easter

Acts 9.26–31
Psalm 22
1 John 3.18–24
John 15.1–8

When Saul had come to Jerusalem, he attempted to join the disciples; and they were all afraid of him. (Acts 9.26)

… and rightly so!

As many of you know, I'm a firm believer in celebrating first communion and confirmation with our young people on the Sundays of Easter. The sacraments of initiation belong within the context of Easter's great Fifty Days. All of Lent refers to Christian initiation and renewal. All of Easter celebrates that wonderful reality.

During one of the years when I was pastor out at Saint Patrick's, Fallowfield, Bishop Beahen came for confirmation on the Fifth Sunday of Easter, Year B. We heard these same texts from the scriptures, and he took off, as only he could, on this verse from Acts 9. Those of you who knew him will remember that his preaching had a certain oratorical flourish, and although some might have thought his biblical interpretation fanciful at times, it was always interesting. This particular rendition was no exception.

He started by recounting Saul's history, how he was a fierce persecutor of the church and that, of course, the church at Jerusalem would be wary of him. What the bishop did, however, was to relate the conversion of Saul, later Saint Paul, to a verse from the second reading about our "hearts condemning us at times and how God is greater than our hearts, and how God knows everything." He was suggesting that for all his determination and bravado there was something in the background that was troubling Saul along the road. He was suggesting that the human heart has its ways of stirring stuff up within us, issues and questions that we may rather not deal with. This stirring up might itself be an invitation from God to conversion. After all, God knows our hearts: God knows our full potential and wills our full potential.

With this in mind he tried to imagine what was going through Saul's mind along the road to Damascus before his dramatic confrontation with Jesus, before his sudden experience of conversion. He was trying to imagine what Paul was thinking as he was going along on that road to Damascus just before he was struck to the ground and heard the voice of Jesus saying: "Saul, Saul, why are you persecuting me?"

In the bishop's imagination, Saul was thinking about Stephen. It was the memory of Stephen that was bothering him, bugging him. Remember how Acts describes the scene of Stephen's martyrdom:

> Filled with the Holy Spirit, [Stephen] gazed into heaven and saw the glory of God and Jesus standing at the right hand of God. "Look," he said, "I see the heavens opened and the Son of Man standing at the right hand of God!" But [the people] covered their ears, and with a loud shout all rushed together against him. Then they dragged him out of the city and began to stone him; and the witnesses laid their coats at the foot of a young man named Saul. While they were stoning Stephen, he prayed, "Lord Jesus, receive my spirit." Then he knelt down and cried out in a loud voice, "Lord, do not hold this sin against them." When he had said this, he died. And Saul approved of their killing him. (Acts 7.55–8.1)

Saul, the bishop said, had met Jesus before, but didn't know it. He had heard his voice before, but didn't recognize it. He had seen and heard Jesus himself in the witness of Stephen, the first martyr for the faith. As he watched and approved of Stephen's stoning, he was watching an image of Jesus Christ himself. On the road to Damascus, it was the memory of Stephen—in other words, the spirit of the Lord Jesus himself—that was haunting him. He was picturing the rocks flying through the air and all those coats at his feet. He was possessed by Stephen's spirit and his memory, and thus it was through Stephen's words about forgiveness and Stephen's prayers that Jesus finally broke through and knocked Saul to the ground.

Fanciful? Maybe to a point, but the bishop was surely right in that spiritual and religious growth or conversion don't come out of the sky. Change doesn't come out of nowhere. It doesn't just happen. There's a background. There's an unsteady conscience or a question mark after some cherished positions; something is out of sync, off balance; there's a lack of equilibrium, otherwise, why change? People learn only when they're ready. People change only when they're ready.

Conversion doesn't come like a bolt of lightning from the sky, but from something inside that's already bugging us. In Saul's case, at least according to Bishop Beahen, it was the memory of Stephen and Saul's own complicity in his death. It was the depth and clarity of Stephen's vision and response to that vision. It was the extraordinary grace in Stephen's last prayer. Saul had been off balance ever since and it was just a matter of time before the Lord Jesus would break through. It was only a matter of time that in and through Stephen's witness and intercession, Saul would meet Jesus for himself and be transformed into Paul the Apostle.

Nobody knows for sure what Saul was thinking along that road, but the bishop's fundamental insight is a very important one. Conversion, growth and change don't happen out of a vacuum. They come out of something that's unsettled, something that's a little bit unbalanced, something we've learned, from our life or experience, that hasn't worked out the way we thought it should, something we discover in ourselves that's not as pure or as wholesome or as generous or as mature as we would like it to be or as we imagine ourselves to be. And dealing with this can be an invitation, a moment for growth and change. We reassure our hearts before God when our hearts condemn us, knowing that God is greater than our hearts, that God knows everything. God knows our full potential. God knows what we can be. Perhaps most especially when our hearts are troubling us about something are we in a position to hear God's voice. Our consciences aren't there for nothing. The conscience is God's way of inviting growth and new possibility.

To use the images of the gospel, the conscience is one of God's ways of pruning the vine and abiding in our personal depths.

The beautiful Psalm 139 begins:

O Lord, you have searched me and known me,
you know when I sit down and when I rise up;
You discern my thoughts from far away.

That whole psalm can be very reassuring and comforting, but it can also bug us. God can be kind of a nuisance, poking at us all the time, inviting us to move, to shift, knocking us a little bit off balance, making us aware of the possibilities that we haven't even really considered for ourselves.

Bishop Beahen imagined Saul on the road, remembering the innocent Stephen and his complicity in his martyrdom. His conscience was bothering him. He was being touched by Stephen's innocence and purity of heart. Saul was knocked off balance only so that he could learn to walk anew. He was blinded only so that he might learn to see anew.

It's that kind of dynamic and potential that lies in the depth of our own souls. Let yourself be bugged. Who knows the grace it will bring?

Abiding in Love

Sixth Sunday of Easter

Acts 10.25-26, 34-35, 44-48
Psalm 98
1 John 4.7-10
John 15.9-17

I'm sure you can't help noticing how positive and uplifting the scriptures have been throughout the Easter season—so much life and invitation and possibility so freely offered.

In the first reading today, for example, Peter, the chief of the apostles, insists that the Roman centurion Cornelius get off his knees. "Stand up," Peter orders, "I am only a mortal." The centurion is used to quite another system where there are insiders and outsiders, classes and classifications, and all the bowing and scraping that go with such established orders. Not so anymore. According to Peter, the fact that we are all mortals makes us one.

He goes on to describe what he himself has learned about this new state of affairs. "I truly understand that God shows not partiality, but in every nation anyone who fears him and does what is right is acceptable to him." (Acts 10.34-35) Even while he speaks, the Holy Spirit falls upon all who hear his liberating word. The old order has come to an end. Beyond distinctions of class and category, beyond racial and cultural boundaries, mortals now face new potential, new challenge.

The text from 1 John paints with even broader strokes to demonstrate what really and fundamentally unites us.

God's love was revealed among us in this way: God sent his only Son into the world so that we might live through him. In this is love, not that we loved God but that he loved us and sent his Son to be the atoning sacrifice for our sins. (1 John 4.9-10)

The love of God works among us and within us, not because we are of a certain class or because we are Jews or Gentiles, not even because we have taken any initiative of our own to reach out in love to God. God reaches out in love to us because God *is* love. To love is not even a decision that God takes, because God *is* love.

Jesus is the revelation of the amazing and overpowering reality of God's love. He delights in sharing his intimate knowledge and experience of the Father with his disciples. He does so at the table on the night before he died. "As the Father has loved me, so I have loved you; abide in my love." Jesus is the revelation of the Father's love. Only when that is clear is there any word about our response. Any response in love that we mortals are able to make flows out of the sense that we have been loved first. The initiative is God's. The movement begins with God and moves out to us through Jesus in the power of his Spirit.

> "If you keep my commandments, you will abide in my love, just as I have kept my Father's commandments and abide in his love. I have said these things to you so that my joy may be in you, and that your joy may be complete. This is my commandment, that you love one another as I have loved you. No one has greater love than this, to lay down one's life for one's friends. You are my friends if you do what I command you. I do not call you servants any longer, because the servant does not know what the master is doing; but I have called you friends, because I have made known to you everything that I have heard from my Father." (John 15.10-15)

Jesus passes on to his friends what he has learned, what he has experienced personally of the very nature of God. His word to them and to us is an open and expansive invitation to love each other, founded in energy flowing from the very being of God. It's not about being in a particular class or category of persons. It's not about narrowly defined religious orthodoxy, or about practising this or that spiritual discipline. It's about very basic human stuff: the readiness of real people not only to carry on with their lives, but to embrace them confidently, secure in their faith and confident in the God who is love and who is at the heart of their own deepest and best interests.

I remember attending a preaching/teaching workshop years ago where the presenter urged us to take this positive approach. She was basing her remarks on her own personal experience of being led in the ways of the Lord. I wish I could remember her name to give her proper credit for the point of view that she highlighted so effectively. She suggested that whether we realize it or not, a lot of our moral and ethical teaching highlights the "thou shalt not" side of life. Taking our cue from seven of the Ten Commandments, we focus on the negative and on the inevitable consequences of negative action—hellfire or at least long years in purgatory. She wondered aloud about preachers and smugly devout people who think that God can hardly wait to catch us doing something wrong so that he can send us to hell. She wondered aloud whether anyone could learn from a teacher if they thought that he enjoyed flunking people more than encouraging them, boosting them, and leading them forward. She wondered what the operative image of God was in the hearts and experience of people and how we as preachers and teachers could do better at imaging or reflecting the God who is love.

Instead of telling people that God disapproves of this or that, why not try reminding them how God longs for their happiness and well being? Why not ask them what they want for themselves—deep down? Can the love of God for them be discovered in their own longing? Ask them about integrity, about human dignity, about self-respect, about generosity, about community. Tell them stories; ask them about good and generous people who found their way through life knowing that they were touched and embraced by Love, who learned how to abide in love. Isn't that what the chanting of the Litany of Saints was all about as we prepared to receive new members into the church at the Easter Vigil?

It's a wonderful coincidence that we have in the congregation to-day a couple celebrating their 50th wedding anniversary. In a few moments we'll hear them renew their vows. Praying and celebrating with them is so much more inspiring and life-giving than treating ourselves to a diatribe or a harangue about the collapse of family values or something like that.

How do we see our own best possibilities as human beings and how can we talk about them? How can we share them? What can move and inspire us not just to avoid evil, but to be our best? How can we learn better to abide in love, the love of God "in whom we live and move and have our being"?

It seems to me that these are the right questions: Easter questions seeking Easter answers, which Jesus himself answers for us.

"You did not choose me but I chose you."

"Abide in my love as I abide in the Father's love."

"Go and bear fruit, fruit that will last."

Deep down, you'll know if you're on the right track. Jesus is risen. The Spirit is given—to you!

Bilocation

Ascension of the Lord

Acts 1.1-11
Psalm 47
Ephesians 4.1-13
Mark 16.15-20

"Men of Galilee, why do you stand looking up toward heaven? This Jesus, who has been taken up from you into heaven, will come in the same way as you saw him go into heaven." (Acts 1.11)

I don't doubt for one minute that virtually all of us heard the spatial language of the ascension account read from the Acts of Apostles without a whole lot of questions. We were expecting it. Resurrection means coming back from the dead. Ascension means going up to heaven. It's that simple, right? Only when we stop and think more deeply does it dawn on us that there's more going on here than a change of physical location.

Paul uses spatial language, too, but in his letter to the Ephesians it's much more complex and nuanced:

Therefore it is said, "When he ascended on high he made captivity itself a captive; he gave gifts to his people." When it says, "He ascended," what does it mean but that he had also descended into the lower parts of the earth? He who descended is the same one who ascended far above all the heavens, so that he might fill all things. (Ephesians 4.8-10)

It would be good for all of us to look again at the biblical stories and review their original context, as well as re-examine the language used and the presuppositions that arise from that language. Sounds like a big project—and indeed it is, but even looking at one or the other seeming oddity in the original language can be instructive, illuminating and even revelatory.

As I have often pointed out, our culture and our way of understanding our lives and our destiny is so far removed in time and space from the sources of sacred scripture that sometimes it is difficult for us to really be a part of what is being said when these scriptures are proclaimed. Even the ancient languages in which the content of our traditional faith and revelation is proclaimed sometimes express meanings or presuppositions that just can't be captured in translation, which means that there's simply no way for a modern reader to understand without explanations or commentaries.

When I was in Jerusalem a few years ago on sabbatical, I came across a very interesting slant on the Hebrew name of the city itself: *Jerusheleim.* It took a while for me to understand, so please bear with me. I learned that the Hebrew language has two ways of understanding and expressing opposites. There are opposites that are genuinely opposite and there are opposites that are merely balancing opposites. Good and bad, for example, are genuine opposites. Left and right, however, are balancing opposites. Left and right do not stand over and against each other in the same way as good and bad stand over and against each other.

Eyes come in pairs: left and right. Ears come in pairs: left and right. Hands and feet come in pairs: left and right. The two are opposite one another, but not in opposition. They are friends and partners, not true opposites. They are balancing opposites.

The way Hebrew deals with these kinds of pairs is quite interesting. In English we add an "s" to ear and get "ears." We can say that Jeremy has large ears. In saying that he has ears we all know that he has two, not five, yet the word "ears" does not tell us that.

Hebrew has a suffix, *eim*, which clarifies that eyes and ears come in opposing, but complementary, pairs. The suffix *eim* at the end of a word denotes a balanced and balancing pair working together for the good of the whole. Isn't it true that we need both our eyes and both our ears for fully dimensional sight and sound? The suffix *eim* makes it clear not only that there are two ears, but that they complement and balance each other.

In this regard, the brain is particularly interesting. It has a left and a right side. We have learned that the left brain deals more with the scientific side of life, with the mathematical, with what can be measured, counted and analyzed. The right side of the brain deals more with art and poetry. The left brain deals with rational and scientific material, the right brain with aspects of life that are more ephemeral, even mystical. We need both sides to be well-balanced people and to have a full appreciation of life, just as we need both eyes and both ears for full appreciation of the sights and sounds that come our way.

We can get lopsided in our thinking and our overall appreciation of life if one or the other side of our self is not activated. In the balanced person, the whole person, both the left and the right sides of the brain are functioning. Obviously, some of us are stronger on one side than on the other, but we try to keep some kind of balance so that we are not mentally or spiritually limping, tripping over ourselves or falling over.

Why am I making such a big deal of all this? It's because Jerusalem, Jerushel*eim,* is that kind of plural. The word itself, meaning city of peace, is plural—a balancing opposite kind of plural. Jerushel*eim* is plural as eyes and ears are plural. There's an earthly city and a heavenly city; there's a real Jerusalem and an ideal Jerusalem; there's a practical project and a dream... all in a special kind of balance.

In other words, in our ascension language, "up" and "down" are not really opposites. Heaven and earth are not opposites. They're not separate places, but two complementary realities in which we are invited to live.

Heaven and earth need to be considered not as opposing one another, but as *balancing* one another. The risen Christ, glorious wounds and all, ascends to the Father, and from the Father's right hand, the Spirit is poured forth. This kind of spatial language is not trying to divide heaven and earth, but unite them. Past and present are one; heaven and earth are one; Jesus, in his humanity and divinity, is one; Jerusalem in its earthly and heavenly forms is one.

What really strikes me in all this is how intimately connected social justice, real-life stuff and religious faith and hope thus have to be. They are like two eyes, two ears, two hands, two feet. The language of the Bible, as well as the images and poetry of our rituals and sacraments, invites us to be in two places at once: in heaven and on earth. We are called to be fully in the midst of the world, shaping it and reshaping it, fussing about the Jerusalem where we stand as we look forward to being drawn by a returning Jesus into the heavenly Jerusalem.

The English poet and engraver William Blake (1757–1827) had a wonderful and highly personal view of a world thoroughly penetrated by the divine. He consistently deals both with metaphysical questions about the place of humanity and our history in the universe, and with very specific social questions about the concrete nature of human responsibility. I find this particularly striking in his *Songs of Innocence and Experience*, which is subtitled *Shewing the Two Contrary States of the Human Soul*. Of particular interest for the Solemnity of Ascension is his poem "And Did Those Feet":

> And did those feet in ancient time
> Walk upon England's mountains green?
> And was the holy Lamb of God
> On England's pleasant pastures seen?
>
> And did the Countenance Divine
> Shine forth upon our clouded hills?
> And was Jerusalem builded here
> Among these dark satanic mills?
>
> Bring me my bow of burning gold;
> Bring me my arrows of desire;
> Bring me my spear; O clouds, unfold!
> Bring me my chariot of fire!
>
> I will not cease from mental fight,
> Nor shall my sword sleep in my hand,
> Till we have built Jerusalem
> In England's green and pleasant land.[26]

Blake understands this bilocation: the heavenly Jerusalem is real only to the extent that it is reflected among "these dark satanic mills" in England's green and pleasant land, or, more to the point, right here where you and I live today.

What Would the Spirit Say?

Pentecost Sunday

Acts 2.1–11
Psalm 104
Galatians 5.16–25
John 15.26–27; 16.12–15

Last week, I came across an unusual prayer in a little Anglican paper. The prayer seemed strangely appropriate for Pentecost Sunday, although it's not the kind of prayer that we usually think of praying or the kind of relationship that we usually think of having with God's Holy Spirit.

This is the anonymous lady's prayer:

Come, Holy Spirit, give me happiness and
contentment with my life.
And the Holy Spirit said no.
Your life is full of opportunities. Happiness is your choice.
Come, Holy Spirit, free me of pain and suffering.
And the Holy Spirit said no.
There are some things that only pain can teach you.
Come, Holy Spirit, make me grow.
The Holy Spirit said no.
I will prune you. I will cut you back
to make you more fruitful.
Come, Holy Spirit, give me patience.
And the Holy Spirit said no.
You learn patience in the midst of the trials and
troubles that come your way.
Patience is not free; it is earned.
Come, Holy Spirit, take away my pride.
The Holy Spirit said no.

Pride is a part of you. It may even prod you to excellence.
Just you control and direct it.
Come, Holy Spirit.

And the Holy Spirit said:

We wouldn't be having this conversation if I weren't already
here.

One of the most important early heresies in the church was
Pelagianism. It proposed that somehow we could earn salvation, that
we could work our way to heaven, that grace was not a free gift, that
God did not take the initiative in our salvation. On first reading, the
lady's prayer may sound Pelagian: "Patience is not free, it is earned."
"Pride is a part of you. Control and direct it." It's true, it could be read
in a Pelagian manner until we realize that it is the Spirit who is making
those challenges, those announcements, those commands. The Spirit is
clearly in charge here, however subtly. Our problem is that probably
too often we think of God being way out there, so that the Holy Spirit
needs to be coaxed into our lives. If we thought we could coax the
Spirit into our lives, that would really be Pelagian! The reality is that by
divine will and design the Holy Spirit is as close to us as our own
breath.

Perhaps it is this kind of sensitivity that "Come, Holy Spirit" prayers
reflect. We couldn't think of praying "Come, Holy Spirit" if we didn't
believe that the Holy Spirit was already present, close enough to hear
our prayers. Paradoxically, it is out of faith in the Spirit's presence that
we pray for the Spirit's presence. It's not that the Spirit isn't already
present. Rather, in our prayer we acknowledge the Spirit's presence
and turn our thoughts and consciousness towards accepting the possibilities that the Spirit brings.

Before the gospel was proclaimed, we sang an ancient sequence
that prayed much in the same way as the lady prayed, although perhaps
more eloquently. It would be worthwhile to make that sequence a
personal prayer sometime this week, stopping after each verse to listen
to what the Spirit might be saying in answer to your petitions.

Light most blessed, shine with grace
In our heart's most secret place,
Fill your faithful through and through.

What would the Spirit say to that?

Bend the stubborn heart and will,
Melt the frozen, warm the chill,
Guide the wayward home once more.

How is the Spirit responding to our prayer?

Just a couple of weeks ago we celebrated confirmation, and are looking forward to "graduation season." Children and young people are clearly on our minds. One of the key themes in catechetical and retreat work with these young people is the truth of their giftedness. We speak in terms of the gifts of the Holy Spirit; we speak in terms of talents and energies as "gifts."

Much as the Holy Spirit did in the dialogue with the lady whose prayer I read, I can imagine the Holy Spirit insisting that our young people "step up to the plate," that they take full responsibility for the exercise of their gifts and talents, to make the most of them in a spirit of joy and thanksgiving. And there's no time to waste. Did you know that Victor Hugo of *Les Misérables* fame wrote his first major work at age 15? That Raphael painted all of his masterworks by the time he was 37? That Tennyson published poetry at the age of 18? That Isaac Newton was 24 when he introduced the Law of Gravity? That Joan of Arc completed her work and was burned at the stake at age 19?

The French priest Michel Quoist wrote a wonderful "mini-mediation" for young people; it's entitled "The Swing."[27] In it he suggested that a swing was placed before each of them by God, but could be handled or ridden in any number of ways. Lazy drifting would be one, pushed to and fro by passing breezes. To stand up, take control of the ropes, brace your vigorous body and create a wind would be quite something else. And then, of course, there are all kinds of degrees in between where most of us fit in.

The Pentecost story is clearly about divine initiative, the Spirit being poured forth in wind and fire. It is likewise about human responsibility to be open to that Spirit, to be in touch with that Spirit, to breathe in sync with that Spirit breathing and burning within.

Let's take another quick look at today's text from Galatians. Paul notes that all of those things that are not of the Spirit and all that are of the Spirit are, in fact, somehow in our charge. We make decisions about those things. We say yes or no both to the works of the flesh and the gifts of the Spirit.

> The works of the flesh are obvious: fornication, impurity, licentiousness, idolatry, sorcery, enmities, strife, jealousy, anger, quarrels, dissensions, factions, envy, drunkenness, carousing, and things like these. (Galatians 5.19-20)

What a list. Almost makes us dizzy. So many potential problems. We all make decisions about these things. Do we make the right ones? As the Spirit said to the lady in response to her prayer, "Just do it." As Father Michel said to the young people, "Stand up on your swing."

> By contrast, the fruit of the Spirit is love, joy, peace, patience, kindness, generosity, faithfulness, gentleness, and self-control. There is no law against such things. And those who belong to Christ Jesus have crucified the flesh with its passions and desires. If we live by the Spirit, let us also be guided by the Spirit. (Galatians 5.22-25)

Can you feel it in yourself to be so guided? Is that what you want for your life? Do you feel called to belong to Christ, having crucified unworthy passions and desires? Recognizing the Spirit's presence in your life, can you pray, "Come, Holy Spirit"?

The wonderful text of the hymn that was chosen to open today's celebration really summarizes beautifully what I've been trying to say:

> Come down, O Love divine;
> seek thou this soul of mine,
> and visit it with thine own ardor glowing.
> O Comforter, draw near;
> within my heart appear,
> and kindle it, thy holy flame bestowing.

O let it freely burn,
till earthly passions turn
to dust and ashes in its heat consuming;
and let thy glorious light
shine ever on my sight,
and clothe me round, the while my path illuming.

And so the yearning strong,
with which the soul will long,
shall far outpass the power of human telling;
for none can guess its grace,
till Love create a place
wherein the Holy Spirit makes a dwelling

Bianco d Siena (d. 1434);
tr. R.F. Littledale (1833–1890), alt.
Set to music by Ralph Vaughan Williams (1872–1958)

The Circle Dance of the Trinity

Trinity Sunday

Deuteronomy 4.32-34, 39-40
Psalm 33
Romans 8.14-17
Matthew 28.16-20

Glory to the Father, the Son, and the Holy Spirit:
To God who is, who was, and who is to come.
(Gospel Acclamation)

Glory to the Father, the Son, and the Holy Spirit—
The complexity, the wonder, the mystery of God!

To God who is, who was, and who is to come—
The complexity, the wonder, the mystery of God relating to human history, to our time and space, to our experience as human beings! The mystery of eternity, the mystery of time, the mystery of God, the mystery of humanity brought together in two lines, the lines of a classic liturgical acclamation, so familiar, yet so mysterious!

I remember directing a retreat where someone asked me: "Why does our faith have to be so complicated? Why do we have to bother with theology? God is love. Isn't that enough?"

How would you have answered?

I don't remember exactly how I answered the lady. Our conversation didn't go too badly, but as I reflect on it in preparation for this great feast of the Blessed Trinity, I think I know how I should have responded. Hindsight is always 20/20.

I should have responded with another question, actually a series of questions something like these: What is the most important life decision you have ever made? Was it simple? Clear-cut? Unambiguous? Was it a decision that you could take on your own?

How is it being married? Living in community with a husband and two teenagers? Is it simple? Clear-cut? Unambiguous?

We human persons are pretty complex, especially when we are trying to sort out our most important values and trying to find ways to live in love and harmony with others. With experience we gain the insight that we are at our best when we are in the "give and take" mode, when we are in relationships that are generous and gracious, that have a certain rhythm and harmony about them—even though sometimes those relationships can get complicated. Interdependence can be complex and challenging.

The Bible itself, as well as every catechism I've ever seen, teaches about our having been created in the "image and likeness of God." If this is so, and if we recognize that we are at our best in relationship with others, that we are most godly when we are in communion with others, would you not guess that the inner life of God shares something of this relational complexity?

Let's go on. God is love. Is it possible to conceive of "love" living eternally in solitary splendour? Does not even the truth that GOD, who existed before all the ages, IS LOVE imply that there is some relationality within God's own inner being? Love simply cannot exist in some utterly transcendent eternal "oneness."

One of the catechisms on my shelf is a rather unusual one. Written in 1976, it is Andrew Greeley's *The Great Mysteries: An Essential Catechism.* I find his theological note on the Trinity to be quite wonderful:

> The doctrine of the Holy Trinity was not revealed to us to test our faith or to provide an abstruse puzzle for metaphysically inclined theologians. It was revealed to us to tell us something about God, and hence something about the purpose and meaning of human life. Briefly, the doctrine of the Trinity means that while God is one, he is not solitary. God is rational, God is interactive, God is a community, God is interpersonal love. The God who creates, the God who speaks, and the God who calls have been involved in an eternal love affair with one another and are now inviting us to join their dance of loving joy and joyous love. If the invitation is frightening, the reason

is that we are being asked to join very fast company. But we are free to bring our friends.[28]

What a wonderful metaphor. When we read today's scriptures again, can't we read between the lines and imagine Moses inviting a bewildered assembly to join the dance with him and God? Can we not imagine Jesus challenging the eleven, even the doubters, to get to their feet, to join him and the Father and the Holy Spirit, enlarging their circle dance to include the whole world?

There is a medieval English traditional carol entitled "Tomorrow Shall Be My Dancing Day" that echoes his insight about a dancing trinity, a dancing God. Jesus invites all humanity into its inner life through the mystery of his incarnation and subsequent ascension where, in his risen and glorified body, he takes the whole of creation with him to the "right hand of the Father." How's that for a dance routine? Here's the carol:

Tomorrow shall be my dancing day,
I would my true love did so chance
To see the legend of my play,
To call my true love to my dance.

Sing, oh, my love, oh! My love, my love, my love,
This have I done for my true love

Then was I born of a virgin pure,
Of her I took fleshly substance;
Thus was I born of a virgin pure,
To call my true love to the dance.

Sing, oh, my love, oh! My love, my love, my love,
This have I done for my true love

Then on the cross hanged I was,
Where a spear to my heart did glance;
That issued forth water and blood
To call my true love to the dance.

Sing, oh, my love, oh! My love, my love, my love,
This have I done for my true love

Then down to hell I took my way
For my true love's deliverance,
And rose again on the third day
Up to my true love and the dance.

Sing, oh, my love, oh! My love, my love, my love,
This have I done for my true love

Then up to heaven I did ascend
Where now I dwell in sure substance,
On the right hand of God, that man
May come into the general dance.

Sing, oh, my love, oh! My love, my love, my love,
This have I done for my true love.[29]

Isn't that amazing! Up and down and around with Christ in God! The Solemnity of the Blessed Trinity serves liturgically as a kind of postscript to our celebration of the Easter Season. This wonderful carol reaches back to include Christmas in its dance. It's about God's love affair with the world in Jesus, and an absolutely spectacular invitation to communion and harmony with all that is—to the "general dance."

Drinking the Cup
of the Covenant

Feast of the Body and Blood of Christ

Exodus 24.3-8
Psalm 116
Hebrews 9.11-15
Mark 14.12-16, 22-26

June 6, 1944 – D-Day

"Soldiers, sailors, and airmen of the Allied Expeditionary Forces: You are about to embark upon the Great Crusade, towards which we have striven these many months. The eyes of the world are upon you. The hopes and prayers of liberty-loving people everywhere are with you ..."

General Dwight D. Eisenhower

On or around June 6, 1994, on the fiftieth anniversary of this historic day, I remember that we prayed for peace in the world at our Sunday liturgy as we always do. We also prayed for a couple from our own parish who were in Europe for the anniversary observance in Normandy. When they got back, I had a chance to speak with the D-Day veteran's wife after mass. She was telling me about their trip overseas and how proud they were to be a part of what must have been a moving and memorable celebration. She remembered being at home with a young child and expecting another when her husband was fighting in the war, and how she worried and prayed, and was so relieved and thankful when it was all over. On that particular Sunday morning, however, she was concerned about her husband for another reason. He hadn't been sleeping very well since their return. He was proud of his military service and honoured to have been invited to be a part of the

169

group representing Canada, but being back there, having to relive the experience, was deeply troubling for him. In a way probably quite typical of most men, he was having a hard time talking about it even with his wife. Listening to her at the back of church, I realized that D-Day wasn't just way back there and then, it was right here in our own church.

Coincidentally, the very next day I met a lady in the mall who was telling me about an old family friend in Renfrew who had also been invited to France for the occasion. "He's really not very swift," she noted, "maybe even a bit retarded." I know that kind of language is probably not politically correct, but that's how she described the gentleman in question. Anyway, he had been invited over for the twenty-fifth anniversary of D-Day in 1969 and was invited again for the fiftieth, but refused both times to go. "Why not?" his friends and neighbours asked him. "I was over there once already and didn't like it much," was his quiet but determined reply.

World War II comes right into our own church in the lives and memories of people who experienced it, and who in some ways are still living it. We can share their story with them, we can sense its power. Even from their few hesitant words, we who have experienced none of the horrors of war can feel something of them. I get the sense, however, even from—and perhaps especially from—their silence that although the war was justified, even necessary, it wasn't okay with them. Their experience of such hostility against enemies left lasting unease, lasting scars.

Today, as we do every year at this time, we celebrate the Feast of the Body and Blood of Christ, and try to come to terms with the high ideals of holy communion that it proposes for our meditation and celebration. This year it doesn't coincide with the fiftieth anniversary of the end of a war, as it did that summer almost ten years ago. Today it falls in the midst of a war on terror and a time of profound economic uncertainty that highlight both the divisions in our world among races and religions and in the widening gap between haves and have-nots.

There is, of course, potential in all of this for men and women of all races and religions, perhaps even of the rich and poor to come together in genuine, honest and realistic ways to advance the cause of "holy communion" in the world. The opposite possibility is there as well. Times of tension can bring out the best and the worst in people. When our own personal way of life is challenged, the big picture becomes too easily clouded. Even in our own peaceful communities there have been recent examples of wholly irrational and self-defeating vandalism against synagogues and mosques. In times of tension we're all tempted to stick with our own kind and be increasingly suspicious of, and even to lash out at, other human beings who might look like or be even vaguely associated with "the enemy." In times of tension it's too easy to let go of the fundamental ideals of human equality and dignity held up, for example, as self-evident in the founding documents of the United States. It's too easy in times of tension to let such ideals shrivel up. It is here that the great central message of this feast comes on the scene.

There is no question that the feast is about the big picture of universal human communion as the ultimate goal of our life, the essence of the heavenly kingdom, profoundly holy, the will of God. It is equally clear, however, that this kind of communion doesn't come easily or cheaply. There's a price to be paid. There's sacrifice involved.

In the establishment of the covenant described in the wonderful story from Exodus, the best of the lambs of the flock are *slaughtered in sacrifice* to God. In a very graphic and dramatic image, the blood is first splashed on the altar where God is symbolically residing and then sprinkled upon the people as a sign of family bonding, a sign of the blood relationship that they have with one another and with God. The ritual pointed beyond itself to a dream as yet unfulfilled. The ultimate dream of Israel was that this covenant, imperfectly experienced among its own people, would one day extend beyond their nation to the whole of humanity. Think of the social, economic and ethical consequences of such a dream. How much grace, generosity and self-sacrifice would be required on everyone's part to bring about this dream? The blood of lambs can't do it on its own. Such was a central and recurring theme of the Hebrew prophets.

Today's Christian text from Hebrews is even more dramatic and explicitly universal. Jesus himself becomes the lamb. His blood is offered on the altar of the cross. That same blood is not splashed on the people, but taken into their very being in the cup of the covenant which is the eucharistic chalice, sealing believers as communicants in a blood relationship with one another and God, through, with and in Jesus Christ. It is this sacrifice that is renewed here in the eucharistic sacrifice, and in our communion with the body and blood of the Lamb of God.

> "This is my blood, the blood of the new and everlasting covenant. It will be shed for you and for all so that sins may be forgiven."

Can you see how important it is that we receive communion under both forms? That we take the cup of the covenant into our hands and taste its healing and reconciling grace? That we drink in the possibilities it offers? That our sense of covenant possibilities widen, especially when tempted to alienation and suspicion?

It's extraordinarily challenging to say "Amen" to the cup of the covenant in the blood of Christ! To do so involves a readiness to be drawn into his own way of being graceful, generous and sacrificial, to share in his own ongoing mission of reconciliation and of forgiveness of sins, or, to put it more positively, of covenant-making and covenant-expanding.

I find a beautiful new hymn in our Canadian *Catholic Book of Worship III,* "Break Not the Circle of Enabling Love" (#524), particularly appropriate for the Solemnity of the Body and Blood of Christ this year. This hymn contains some rich images: "This Lord who came and comes to teach the world the craft of hopeful craving" and "people of whatever race or nation will... see eye to eye with laughter and elation" are two good examples. Its wonderful imagery of the circle and of enabling love couldn't be more appropriate to the challenges of our time.

> Break not the circle of enabling love,
> where people grow forgiven and forgiving.
> Break not that circle, make it wider still,
> till it includes, embraces all the living.

> *Fred Kaan (Carol Stream, Illinois:*
> *Hope Publishing Company, 1975)*

We can say "Amen" to that, can't we?
I hope so.

172

A Mustard Seed and
a Heart Full of Prayer

Eleventh Sunday in Ordinary Time

Ezekiel 17.22-24
Psalm 92
2 Corinthians 5.6-10
Mark 4.26-34

He explained everything in private to his disciples. (Mark 4.34b)

I can't help wondering what kind of explanation of these parables Jesus would have given to his disciples and if, in fact, it would have been that helpful. Parables by their very nature are beyond explanation. They are more than rational. They speak to the heart and the imagination.

"The kingdom of God is as if someone would scatter seed on the ground, and would sleep and rise night and day, and the seed would sprout and grow." (Mark 4.26-27)

Explain that, please. How and why would you want to explain that? You need to feel it, sense it, experience it. You know how seeds are planted. We've all had parents who planted seeds, or maybe a particularly inspiring teacher from whose lessons we are still reaping benefits. How is that like the kingdom of God? Think about it; work with the image; let the image work with you. The parables are inviting us to allow our imaginations to be stirred up and to recognize how mysteriously and wonderfully the kingdom of God grows and develops and matures, if only we are open to believe in that possibility. Prayer and meditation are probably more important than analysis.

There's a wonderful story about an old rabbi who was sitting on the front steps of his synagogue poring over his Bible. There were kids around and kids will be kids—full of questions. At a certain stage they begin to wonder about things—sometimes they wonder deeply and question everything. (That's how our human nature works. It's how we develop into our own persons. At some stages it may get just a little obnoxious, but it's an inevitable part of the process of maturing.)

Now while this particular group was playing ball on the street, one of the boys interrupted his play to stop and question the rabbi about what he was reading. More to the point, I guess, was why he was reading it at all. He knew it must have been the Bible or something similar.

"Isn't that boring?" the boy asked. "Week after week after week, don't you get tired of that same old book, the same old stuff, the same old stories?" The rabbi answered: "I read them, and I read them again because I want to believe them."

The word of God was being nourished in the old rabbi's heart as he read his Bible and his prayers over and over. As for the boy with the ball, who knows what he thought of the answer? It's fun to imagine how the conversation might have developed between the two of them.

In telling why *he* was reading, the rabbi was not telling anybody else why *they* should be reading. Maybe the boy's curiosity would have led him further, to question just what made that old fellow tick. The rabbi was in a position to share his own faith. He was ready to explain his own reasons for being devout and observant, which is a lot more credible than anything he could have said about what others should do. Nobody, not even a teenage boy, can argue with a personal story.

How does the kingdom of God grow? In what way could the reign of God expand and fill our lives? Why would that matter?

The parables invite us over and over again to ask such questions in an ever-deepening way. We will never read the parables the same way twice. In what do we experience the kingdom of God as a seed that dies, sprouts, grows, produces, is harvested? Don't explain it to me. Tell me a story; give me an example. How does it work for you?

"With what can we compare the kingdom of God, or what parable shall we use for it? It is like a mustard seed, which, when sown upon the ground, is the smallest of all the seeds on earth; yet when it is sown it grows up and becomes the greatest of all shrubs, and puts forth large branches, so that the birds of the air can make nests in its shade." (Mark 4.30-32)

The kingdom of God is like that. The seed became a shrub; the shrub become a housing development for birds. Don't explain it to me. How is that true in your experience? Tell me a story.

Back in the 1930s, times were tough, particularly in Mexico. Romana didn't know what had happened to her husband. He was a proud man who maybe just gave up and ran away. She had only a few pesos, and only a few words of English, but she had a "heart full of prayer." She also had a distant relative in Los Angeles, where she was heading with her two kids, hoping for the best.

In Los Angeles, she started out washing dishes, saved $500, bought a tortilla machine and got busy. Eventually she became the manager of the largest Mexican wholesale food business in the world. That's what you call growth—from a few pesos, a few English words and a "heart full of prayer." Her children and grandchildren are still benefiting, "living in the nests she provided for them."

Is Romana what the mustard seed parable is all about? Is she living proof of its truth? Yes. It's not my way of reading the story, but *she* sees herself in it. Her story is not mine or yours, but it's a true story of faith, growth and transformation—from a "heart full of prayer." Something was planted, something flourished. Is that what the reign of God is like? Not totally—that's not the whole story and not everybody will have a story like that to tell, but "the kingdom of God is like a few pesos, a few words of English and a heart full of prayer." True?

President Eisenhower eventually singled out Romana Banuelos to become United States Treasurer. On the occasion of her swearing-in, he said: "We succeed only as we identify in life, or in war, or in anything else, a single overriding objective, and make all other considerations bend to that one objective."

That was his *explanation* for her extraordinary life. I guess it reflects something of her truth, but I like the parables better. I like the metaphors: a mustard seed and a heart full of prayer. I think they work better.

The reign of God defies definition or explanation. The reign of God is not lived fully in any one person's experience of it. The kingdom of God is coming. The kingdom of God is near. The kingdom of God is within you. With what can we compare the kingdom of God?

I still wonder what Jesus' explanations were like.

God Triumphs over Confusion and Chaos

Twelfth Sunday in Ordinary Time

Job 38.1-4, 8-11
Psalm 107
2 Corinthians 5.14-17
Mark 4.35-41

"Tell me, if you have understanding.
Who shut in the sea with doors
when it burst out from the womb?" (Job 38.8)

The disciples were filled with great awe and said to one another,
"Who then is this, that even the wind and the sea obey him?"
(Mark 4.41)

In the winter of 1995, a fishing boat began to sink in the rough, cold waters off Vancouver Island. The two men on board moved to a life raft that was tied to the sinking boat by a nylon rope. Unfortunately, the rope was tied so tightly that they could not untie it. All the pressure from the bouncing around only tightened the knot. As the fishing boat began to list and take on more water, they knew they couldn't reboard. At the same time, neither had a knife with which to cut the raft free. If the boat went down, it would pull the raft under water with them on it. They began frantically taking turns chewing the rope—even breaking teeth in the process. Minutes before the boat sank they had chewed through the rope. They and the raft were floating free. They still had a couple of fighting hours before they were rescued, but even at this point they knew they had a second chance.

Had Jesus been there, it would have been a lot simpler, right? And no broken teeth!

If that's how we read the story, I'm afraid our reading would be superficial. The sea is indeed a mighty and complex force. There's a lot more to biblical sea images than the miracle of a sudden calming. I suspect that even the two British Columbia fishermen came to recognize that what happened in their "salvation" from the sea went way beyond physical survival. Yes, they had survived, but they would never be the same people after such an experience.

Nothing so struck the imagination of ancient peoples as did the sea, stretching out before them without end: immense, with no known limits. One would venture into the sea only in absolute necessity, for crossings as short as possible, and in favourable seasons, for "You just never know."

The sea could erupt with little or no warning. There were stories of sea monsters that people swore they had encountered. The sea was the dwelling of capricious and tumultuous forces that could come to life at a moment's notice. This kind of terror is no laughing matter. Even today the sea remains most impressive and awe-inspiring.

In the remarkable text of today's liturgy, the Book of Job describes the sea bursting from the womb of God. Job challenges his questioners to tell him who it was that shut it in with doors. What images!

Almost every summer, I have the chance to spend a week or two on the shores of Lake Superior. The experience is always wonderful—awesome. Last summer was outstanding: during a week of what people up there find to be intense heat, the lake and the sky above changed so often and so dramatically! There would be, for example, a mass of black rain clouds making their way across the sky. I could see that it was already raining at one end of the property, but not at the cottage where we were staying. At one point it was raining at one end of the porch, but not at the other. The line was that dramatic. That night, after the front had passed, the stars seemed particularly bright, the northern lights particularly playful. I'm sure that meteorologists on TV were describing what I had experienced in their own language, but the ancients had their own ways of describing the wonder and complexity of earth, sea and sky, and I could well understand their seeing something personal, even divine, in what was happening.

Especially in the psalms, the Bible affirms that it is the One God who rules the sea and all the forces that break loose there: the wind, rain, thunder, lightning and darkness that can be so utterly frightening. This mastery over the waters is what God exercises when God decides to start and end the flood at the time of Noah, and to part the waters of the Red Sea so that Moses and the people could cross it "dry-shod," ordering the waters to come back together to prevent the Egyptians from doing the same. The same God "breaks the heads of dragons in the waters," in the poetic image of Psalm 74.

That Jesus shares something of this mastery is clearly a wonder for the disciples. Such mastery clearly extends to his mastery over other, less tangible ways in which believers can be tossed about, on the verge of shipwreck, about to be swallowed up. Do you know the feeling? I'm sure that if we all had a few moments, we'd be able to come up with "spiritual sea stories" big and small, perhaps even stories of "broken teeth"—yes, and stories of rescue and liberation.

The details that Mark offers his readers of this particular trip across the Sea of Galilee, which had a well-documented reputation for having a "mind of its own," are particularly interesting. This night voyage was Jesus' idea. It was to have been a leisurely sunset cruise to get away from the crush of the crowds. When the weather changed, the disciples had every reason to blame him for this "stupid idea."

To make matters worse, Jesus was sleeping through it all. "Teacher, do you not care that we are perishing?" Their anguish was well-founded. The boat was already being swamped, but Jesus was sleeping. Awakened, Jesus rose to rebuke the wind and the sea. "Quiet! Be still." He rebuked the wind and the sea the same way he had rebuked the demon who had possessed the man Jesus met in the synagogue at Capernaum. "Quiet! Come out of him." Once again Jesus sent the infernal powers to the depths. "Quiet! Be still." At the word of Jesus there was a great calm. Listen again to how Mark describes the power of his word:

> Jesus woke up and rebuked the wind, and said to the sea, "Peace! Be still!" Then the wind ceased, and there was a dead calm. He said to them, "Why are you afraid? Have you still no faith?" And they were filled with great awe and said to one another, "Who then is this, that even the wind and the sea obey him?" (Mark 4.39-41)

Particularly striking for me in Mark's telling of the story of Jesus is the contrast between this scene and another scene ten chapters later. For me it has always been one of the most poignant and touching scenes in the whole gospel. It is in Gethsemane, and this time it is the disciples who are sleeping and Jesus who is agitated.

> They went to a place called Gethsemane; and Jesus said to his disciples, "Sit here while I pray." He took with him Peter and James and John, and began to be distressed and agitated. And he said to them, "I am deeply grieved, even to death; remain here, and keep awake." And going a little farther, he threw himself on the ground and prayed that, if it were possible, the hour might pass from him. He said, "Abba, Father, for you all things are possible; remove this cup from me; yet, not what I want, but what you want." Jesus came and found them sleeping; and he said to Peter, "Simon, are you asleep? Could you not keep awake one hour? Keep awake and pray that you may not come into the time of trial; the spirit indeed is willing, but the flesh is weak." And again he went away and prayed, saying the same words. And once more he came and found them sleeping, for their eyes were heavy; and they did not know what to say to him. He came a third time and said to them, "Are you still sleeping and taking your rest? Enough! The hour has come." (Mark 14.32-41)

Once again the disciples have missed the boat. In the first case, they were wide awake when they should have been sleeping, and in the second they were sleeping when they should have been wide awake. In both cases they should have been able to take their cue from Jesus … but how could they? Can we blame them for panicking in the boat or for sleeping in the garden?

As always, Mark's gospel is being told for the sake of people like us who know the whole story even before we read it. Unlike the first disciples who walked with Jesus, we already know that Jesus is the "Messiah, the Son of God." Mark told us that at the very beginning. But, like the disciples, we're not always sure of our own place in the story as it continues to be lived among us. For the apostles, the garden seemed like a place to sleep, and the stormy sea a place to be wide awake, but the opposite proved true—typical gospel paradox. I suspect that in our own histories, we've all experienced such mistakes and missteps.

Both in passing through the storm at sea and passing through the garden to Calvary, we learn from Mark that chaos and confusion are no match for the reign of God, and that the last word spoken is going to be God's word of peace bringing light out of the darkness and life out of death.

The entrance antiphon and the opening collect today remind us that in all of our lives, punctuated from time to time by real storms, pseudo storms, and quasi storms, the key is prayerful reliance on God's covenant fidelity, hopeful confidence in the depth of God's love and providence, and steadfast love.

God is the strength of his people. In him, we his chosen live in safety. Save us, Lord, who share in your life

"From this world's uncertainty, we look to your covenant. Keep us one in your peace, secure in your love."

Wake Up and Get Up!

Thirteenth Sunday in Ordinary Time

Wisdom 1.13-15; 2.23-24
Psalm 30
2 Corinthians 8.7, 9, 13-15
Mark 5.21-43

> Jesus took the child's father and mother and those who were
> with him, and went in where the child was. He took her by
> the hand and said to her, "Talitha cum," which means, "Little
> girl, get up!" And immediately the little girl got up and began
> to walk about for she was twelve years of age. (Mark 5.40-42)

I was working with a group of young teachers who were just
finding their way in teaching scripture and religion. One of them was
commenting on how much she has been learning, not only in preparing her classes, but from children's responses. Sometimes they see more
in the texts than she does. Their sense of wonder and freshness can
bring the miracle stories, for example, to life in a new way. It's the first
time they've heard them. She used this particular miracle story as an
example.

After telling the story of the raising of Jairus' daughter, she asked
the children to make a drawing of the story and then to talk about
their drawings. One little girl's picture was particularly interesting. She
must have been impressed by the fact that the people were not allowed
in the room, because she had a big window in her bedroom with all
the people straining to look inside to see what was going on. They
were all twisted-looking, hands in the air, round heads with slits for
eyes and big frowns. As for the little girl herself, she was sitting straight
up in bed like a half-opened jackknife. Jesus was standing there with
his finger pointing to her. When she told the story of her picture, she
said that Jesus came into the bedroom where she was lying down,

shook her and said, "You get right up and out of that bed now, and go back to school where you belong." I have a feeling someone must have said something like that to her once or twice when she was feeling lazy. Humorous as it is, it is precisely what's going on in the story. The little girl is up and walking. She's to get something to eat and be on her way. "Get up and off to school, and here's your lunch."

It's a wonderful picture: the finger of Jesus pointing to that little girl. "Get up out of that bed and go back to school where you belong and here's a sandwich to take with you." That's really the message of the miracle stories. In every case there's more to being healthy than just having energy to walk around the room. There's more to being alive than being able to breathe.

The story itself is beautifully told. Jesus reaches out and touches the child, saying in Aramaic, "Talitha cum," which our text translates as "Little girl, get up." It has been pointed out that a more literal translation would read: "Lamb, get up!"—surely a tender, even cute way to talk to a little girl, but more deeply suggestive of the story being an allegory of the resurrection. Could Jesus himself be the lamb awakened and aroused from sleep by the hand of God? That might be pushing it, but this "wake up and get up" language is found in the earliest hymns to accompany baptismal liturgies.

> Sleeper, awake!
> Rise from the dead,
> and Christ will shine on you. (Ephesians 5.14)

The prayer of a contemplative Eastern Orthodox nun offers us a moving meditation on this story and its resurrection connotations:

> Master, you come near me and say to me as you said to Jairus' little girl, "Arise." And taking her by the hand, you called her back to life. The child whom everyone believed dead, immediately arose and began to walk. Here I glimpse the mystery and the power of the resurrection through the daily act of waking up. You too have risen up, living and glorious. And the glory of your Resurrection rests upon every one of our mornings ... It was "very early when the sun had risen." Lord, grant that no new morning dawn on me without my

going, in spirit, towards the empty tomb in the garden with my little bit of spices!

For it is the Risen Christ who comes to me, every day, at dawn. Whatever perplexities, whatever dangers surround me, the beginnings of all my days will be radiant if I remember, with all my soul and all my mind—that my Saviour has conquered the powers of evil and death. My first act of faith every morning will be an act of faith in your final victory.[30]

What a gift to experience your daily risings from sleep as resurrection calls, to experience every wake-up call as a herald of the last trumpet, to live all of your days in Easter faith! Somehow I think that this anonymous sister and our little "lamb" in Grade 3 might be soulmates. They know how to get into the miracle stories.

It's that same ability I wish for all of us as we enter into paschal word and paschal sacrament this Sunday morning.

When the Prophetic Word Comes Home

Fourteenth Sunday in Ordinary Time

Ezekiel 2.2-5
Psalm 123
2 Corinthians 12.7-10
Mark 6.1-6

"Mortal, I am sending you to the people of Israel ... I am sending you to them ... Whether they hear or refuse to hear, they shall know that there has been a prophet among them." (Ezekiel 2.3-5)

Jesus came to his hometown, and his disciples followed him. On the sabbath he began to teach in the synagogue ... They took offence at him ... he could do no deed of power there... (Mark 6.1-2, 3, 5)

Going home as an adult is virtually impossible. You never go back. You leave home for college and come home again—but it's only for a visit. Your parents, hard as they might try, still think of you as a child—their child—and yes, you are that, but ... Everything needs to be renegotiated. That is not an easy task.

Ordinarily a physician would not treat his own parents, a psychiatrist counsel his brother, or a priest minister to his own family. It just doesn't work well that way. I know a high school teacher who had one of his daughters in class. Neither of them was happy with that arrangement.

That Jesus should not be particularly well received when he goes home is no real surprise. The level of mistrust and hostility, however, would be surprising had not Mark prepared us so well for it.

184

We're now in chapter 6 and know that some Pharisees were ready to team up with the Herodians in a conspiracy to destroy him. That lay leaders from Galilee and Jerusalem "temple people" would team up in this way points to how serious a threat they considered Jesus to be.

Jesus' family had already come out to "restrain him," thinking he was "beside himself." Some scribes from Jerusalem thought one explanation for his "seemingly" divine power was that he might be in cahoots with the prince of demons.

And here he is, in his hometown on the Sabbath, and teaching in the synagogue. Is he looking for trouble or what? "They took offence at him." Literally they "stumbled over him."

> "Prophets are not without honour, except in their hometown, and among their own kin, and in their own house." (Mark 6.4)

Both Ezekiel and Jesus have to confront people close to home, and it's not easy for either of them. In both cases, the good news sounds to their hearers like bad news; God's call for transformation and renewal demands some radical surgery that may well be painful. Both Ezekiel and Jesus have to confront their own people with their sinfulness. The response in both cases is "Who do you think you are?" If you don't like the message, discredit the messenger.

The call experienced by both Ezekiel and Jesus, however exalted, brings discomfort, unease—psychological, personal, spiritual pain. None of us thinks of ourselves as a prophet or messiah, but a lot of us know something of the tensions Ezekiel and Jesus are feeling. Parents have had to call their own children to task, have had to tackle topics that might be very sensitive. They may even have been written off as "old fashioned," or worse. If you don't like the message, put down the messenger. For all the discomfort, however, good parents know that they have to deal with some of these things even if their interventions may not seem very successful.

Teachers, as well as employers, can find themselves in that kind of position. You find that sometimes you just have to tell it like it is, and lay down the law despite the labels you may be stuck with as a consequence.

In one parish where I was pastor (not this one, of course!), I once had to shake down one of the parish committees that was overstepping its mandate and causing all kinds of mayhem in the dynamics of overall parish life. I was called a "tyrant."

Prophets and messiahs we're not, but all of us share in certain aspects of what those titles entail. Being a parent, a teacher, an employer or a pastor is a happy privilege that brings moments of discomfort when the word isn't always positive or good. At those times we need special sensitivity to the power and grace of God. We need wisdom, discernment and courage.

Looking at it from the other side is important, too. I've been suggesting that there are ways of identifying with Ezekiel and Jesus in their prophetic mission, but I'm afraid there are ways we can identify with those who took offence, who stumbled over Jesus. Our own ways of thinking and seeing things may from time to time need a prophetic nudge. And it's not impossible to imagine that even *we* might write off prophets.

The July/August 2002 issue of *Sojourners Magazine*, for example, reported a case of "If you don't like the message, discredit the messenger." The management of a group of Florida nursing homes filed objections with the National Labor Relations Board that organizers had used voodoo practices to intimidate a largely Haitian workforce into voting to unionize at one of their homes. Marie Jean-Phillipe, a Haitian-American and one of the staff of 86 who was encouraging others to vote for the union, was portrayed as a "priestess" who used "voodoo beads." In fact, this quiet little lady was a daily communicant who carried a rosary and sometimes prayed it walking the corridors when things got quiet. The real issues were low wages, unaffordable health insurance and mistreatment from management, not voodoo beads, but it's not always easy for people to deal with the truth, especially when there's money involved. These people were "taking offence at Marie," tripping over her on a major issue. They didn't like her message, so she must be "beside herself" or even in cahoots with the devil. Who does she think she is?

It's not easy to be either on the giving end or the receiving end of a prophetic word. Both speaking and listening can be tough. All of us need to discern when, where and how to do both.

The Third Call

Fifteenth Sunday in Ordinary Time

Amos 7.12-15
Psalm 85
Ephesians 1.3-14
Mark 6.7-13

Jesus called the twelve and began to send them out two by two, and gave them authority over the unclean spirits. He ordered them to take nothing for their journey except a staff; no bread, no bag, no money in their belts; but to wear sandals and not to put on two tunics. (Mark 6.7-9)

This is the third time that Jesus called the apostles.

The first call came in chapter 1: he called Simon and Andrew from their fishing boats, and James and John from their fishing boat, their father and his hired men. He called them to a new profession and a new family, but without a lot of clarity about just what that might mean.

Chapter 3 recounts a more solemn call. Jesus calls the disciples to the mountain where he designates the twelve whom he calls apostles (those to be sent), that they might be with him, and that he might send them to preach and have authority.

Chapter 6 presents the third call. "Jesus called the twelve and began to send them out two by two." The sending now becomes real. The apostles actually become that which they are called. They are *sent*, as their name implies.

As I have worked with seminarians over the last few years, I have found this third calling especially rich. It applies not only to their own sense of vocation and direction, but to all of us, too. The sense of call is more striking in the Rite of Christian Initiation of Adults, but even in the Rite of Infant Baptism the infant is named, called and anointed for his or her own unique share in the mission of Christ, in the "apostolate."

The commentaries I've checked all agree on four points that are key to the apostles' commissioning and to our own understanding of the Christian life and vocation.

First, the apostles are doing not their own work, but God's. They are not only authorized by Jesus, but are engaged in a venture that belongs to him. They not only follow his directions, but are empowered with his spirit. He is acting in and through them.

Last year I rediscovered a little meditation written in the 1950s by Michel Quoist, a French priest. In his "Prayer of a Priest on a Sunday Night," he pictures Jesus speaking to a tired young priest who is discouraged and lonely.

> Son; you are not alone.
> I am with you.
> I am you.
> For I needed another human instrument to continue
> my Incarnation and my Redemption,
> Out of all eternity, I chose you. I need you.[31]

Have you ever felt that you needed Jesus to speak to you like that?

One day I stepped out into the street from Union Station in downtown Washington, D.C, looked up the street and saw this wonderful text carved into the façade of a building:

> Messenger of sympathy and love,
> Servant of parted friends,
> Consoler of the lonely,
> Bond of the scattered family,
> Enlarger of the common life,
> Bearer of news and knowledge,
> Promoter of mutual acquaintance,
> of peace and goodwill
> among peoples and nations.

Was the building a church or synagogue? No, it was the United States Post Office. Exalted language like that usually refers to the Spirit of God, but to the postal service? Why not? God's work is being carried out whenever any of this is happening. I wonder if the man who comes up and down our street every day to deliver the mail recognizes the loftiness of his vocation. Jesus' explicit sending of the apostles invites that kind of connectedness with his spirit animating and ennobling our human lives and activities.

Second, Jesus recommends that the disciples travel light. They are to dispense with extra food, clothing and money. It's not a question of asceticism or sacrifice here as much as it is a question of simplicity and trust. They are to be working, not primarily with the contents of their purses, but with their inner resources. Jesus is saying something like this: "You have what it takes; it will be given. Just go and get on with it."

Just a week or so ago I was talking with a lady who didn't have a lot of confidence in herself or her own judgment. She had been reading every self-help book and parenting manual that she could get her hands on. Only gradually did she come to realize that she could have written them herself. She had to learn how to go down into the well of her own wisdom, to trust the resources offered by the Spirit to her own inner being.

Third, take seriously the possibility of failure. Sometimes you just have to leave things alone and move on. You may even have to shake the dust off your feet and leave the situation in God's hands. You gave it your best shot. This is Amos' experience in the first reading. He is being mocked and sent on his way. Nobody needs his kind of prophesying in the king's sanctuary at Bethel. He should just cool it and go home. His response is to say, in effect, "I'm just doing what I can here—but mark my words."

> "I am no prophet, nor a prophet's son; but I am a herdsman, and a dresser of sycamore trees, and the Lord took me from following the flock, and the Lord said to me, 'Go, prophesy to my people Israel.'" (Amos 7.14-15)

The word is God's; the work is God's. I'm giving this thing my best shot; take it or leave it. It's hard when you've invested a lot of yourself to think like that and shake the dust from your feet, but sometimes that's exactly what needs to be done. Truth is truth; it needs to be said; it needs to be done. The final outcome is in God's hands.

Finally, Jesus called the twelve and began to send them out *two by two*. He seemed to sense in all of this that the greatest asset of a disciple along the way will be a fellow disciple. Isn't that true for all of us as well? Is not your greatest source of strength and faith the person walking beside you? What a blessing friendship is!—having a partner, a soulmate, a companion on the journey. Jesus is telling us something very important as he sends out his disciples, not as lone rangers, but in pairs.

Four points: It's God's work, not yours. Travel light and trust that you will be gifted with all that you need. Be ready for struggle, even failure. Your greatest asset in all of this will be fellow believers, companions on the journey. There's a lot of wisdom here! Think about it. Pray about it as we did in the opening prayer of today's liturgy:

Father, let the light of your truth guide us to your kingdom through a world filled with lights contrary to your own. Christian is the name and the gospel we glory in. May your love make us what you have called us to be.

Amen!

Experiencing Christ's Compassion

Sixteenth Sunday in Ordinary Time

Jeremiah 23.1–6
Psalm 23
Ephesians 2.13–18
Mark 6.30–34

The apostles returned from their mission. They gathered around Jesus, and told him all they had done and taught. He said to them, "Come away to a deserted place all by yourselves and rest a while." (Mark 6.30–31)

The apostles, who had gone out in their pairs with nothing but one tunic, a staff and sandals, were back. They had lots to say. It was time for a debriefing. They gathered with Jesus, sharing with him what they had done and taught—actually a little summary of what Mark considers the three marks of discipleship:

• being with Jesus
• doing works that reflect his goodness and power
• proclaiming his word.

They were checking back in with the basics. That they were in a deserted or desolate place recalls the origins of Jesus own ministry: the place of John's initial call to repentance, which led to his baptism, and the place of Jesus' temptation.

Before the apostles could go forward any further, they had to step back. It's interesting that our word for retreat, originally a religious event or experience, is now used in government and in the corporate world. It means stepping back for a fresh look at the basics. With Jesus, the apostles will be able not only to report on their first "assignment," but to reconnect their own core values with God's plan in the person of Jesus.

In his book *Mere Christianity*, C.S. Lewis suggests that a healthy Christian life needs this kind of reflection daily:

> The real problem of the Christian life comes where people do not usually look for it. It comes the very moment you wake up each morning. All your wishes and hopes for the day rush at you like wild animals. And the first job each morning consists simply in shoving them all back; in listening to that other voice, taking the other point of view, letting that other larger, stronger, quieter life come flowing in… coming in out of the wind.[32]

Mark makes it quite clear that the apostles had precious little time for their retreat, for listening to that other voice. It doesn't sound as though they had any time at all for the debriefing they had looked forward to. I hope they had a nice boat ride, because by the time they got to the other shore, the crowd had already made its way there on foot.

> As Jesus went ashore, he saw a great crowd. He had compassion for them, because they were like sheep without a shepherd; and he began to teach them many things. (Mark 6.34)

Perhaps this was all the retreat the apostles really needed: being with Jesus and experiencing his compassion, hearing his teaching, and witnessing his feeding of the crowds. Being in touch with his way of being, of teaching and of shepherding could revitalize all three aspects of their discipleship. Being with him and observing him were their best chances of getting in touch with the other voice, and coming in out of the wind. Debriefing would have to come later.

Jesus had compassion for them…

The word for compassion is especially powerful. The Greek word translated as "compassion" points not just to an emotional feeling, but to an experience that is literally physical. It is a gut-wrenching experience; it means having your stomach tied in knots; it is a feeling that arises out of the "womb"; it is a bridge between seeing and acting. Jesus' compassion already had him halfway towards teaching, shepherding and feeding the crowd. The apostles couldn't have helped experiencing something of that energy.

When he stepped ashore, Jesus' compassion made him ready to meet the crowd. They could sense and feel it, assuring them that they could count on him. They could believe in him. By stepping ashore with Jesus, the disciples could deepen their connectedness with his way of being, thinking and acting. It was not the kind of retreat they had planned, but it would have to do.

That the people believed in Jesus, that they were genuinely eager to be in contact with him, that they knew they could count on him, was very important both for them and for Jesus. Having experienced so much hostility from some of the Pharisees, scribes and folks back home, Jesus was happy to be able to count on the people for their openness and readiness to be drawn to faith.

A lovely, sensitive lady, the grandmother of one of the children who received first communion during the Easter Season, was telling me how impressed she was with her little granddaughter. "You know," she said, "she doesn't know all the things about holy communion that I think I knew when I was her age, but she really loves Jesus and you should hear her pray at home." I was so pleased at what she had to say; I wish now that I had asked her to write to the pope, the bishop, the school board and anybody else who has anything to do with our catechetical programs. It really is important for children—and all of us—to learn how to believe in Jesus and love Jesus. What we learn *about* Jesus and how he is present to us are important too, but secondary.

To experience the compassion of Jesus, to sense his shepherding deep in our own person is such a wonderful gift. I'm sure that's why Psalm 23, second only to the Lord's Prayer, is far and away the most popular biblical prayer. It speaks to the heart. Even though people might not experience it, they would like to:

Nothing shall I want.
He leads me.
He goes before me with rod and staff.
He feeds me.
He anoints my head.

Only goodness and kindness shall follow me.
In the Lord's house shall I dwell forever.

I'm never going to be poor; I'm never going to be lost; I'm never going to be hurt; I'm never going to be hungry; I'm never going to be laughed at; I'm on my way to heaven. The Lord is my shepherd.

Jesus has compassion for the crowd; he teaches them; he feeds them.

That "my cup is overflowing" is a pledge that there will always be more than enough energy and grace, no matter what. Even when poor, hungry and lost, we have received riches, food and direction deep within that no one will be able to take away. To be able to experience the compassion of Christ is a wonderful gift indeed.

After their mini-retreat on the boat, the apostles got to experience that compassion in action, although they could not possibly have understood it at the time. In the language of C.S. Lewis, they were hoping to be with Jesus "out of the wind." Instead they found themselves "in the wind," the wind of Jesus' shepherding spirit that only gradually would become their own—and ours.

How Many Loaves Have You?

Seventeenth Sunday in Ordinary Time

2 Kings 4.42–44
Psalm 145
Ephesians 4.1–6
John 6.1–15

John's gospel stands apart from the synoptics, Matthew, Mark and Luke, in a number of very important ways. One is how he deals with Jesus' miracles. John does not call them miracles at all, but "signs." In fact, the first part of his gospel has been called the "Book of Signs."

There are seven of these signs. The first is the transformation of water to wine at Cana; the last is the raising of Lazarus from the dead, all of which lead into the "Book of Glory" that presents the great eighth sign.

Numbers are significant for John. In this case, seven denotes fullness and completeness. There are seven days in a week, for example, and the seventh day is the Sabbath, for contemplation and appreciation of all that has gone before. The eighth sign is something altogether new; it is eschatological; it is of a new world; it is the death and resurrection of Jesus himself.

Miracles tend to draw attention to themselves, but these signs point beyond themselves to something more. Over the next five Sundays we'll be reading from chapter 6 of John's gospel, which presents one of these signs in all its fullness.

The chapter begins with the multiplication of loaves and fishes, but moves quickly to questions, discussions, even confrontations around the "bread of life." It's clear that the multiplication of the loaves and fishes is designed to set us up for something more: hearing a whole lot over the next few weeks about the "bread of life."

Of particular interest to me are the three persons who share the stage with Jesus as the story opens: Philip, the practical analyst; Andrew, the cynic; and a nameless little boy who has an open and generous heart.

> When he looked up and saw a large crowd coming toward him, Jesus said to Philip, "Where are we to buy bread for these people to eat?" He said this to test him, for he himself knew what he was going to do. (John 6.5-6)

Philip starts up with his calculations. "Six months' wages wouldn't even buy enough bread for everybody to have even a little bit." He estimates how many people are out there, he estimates costs, he estimates what would be required for each person to have a decent meal, he knows what six months' wages are and knows he doesn't have that kind of money in his pocket. He knows that the whole thing is preposterous and reports back. That's Philip.

Andrew comes up and says, "There's a kid over there. He has five barley loaves and two fish." He makes a joke of it. "What's this among so many?" Ha ha! Nothing can be done.

And finally there's a little boy who is nameless. He offers his lunch and, in the hands of Jesus, that's enough—more than enough. I think I've mentioned before that when a person is nameless, it usually means he's bigger than himself. We're somehow supposed to see ourselves or at least our own possibilities in these nameless characters.

Father Joseph Donders, a wonderful preacher and teacher, published a homily he gave to school kids in Kenya. He was trying to get the sign value of the story across to them. This is how he reads between John's lines to fill out and interpret the full meaning and direction of the sign that begins to take shape in this little boy's gift:

> There is a big hush and a great silence. People look at one another. There must have been quite a few in that crowd with some food, but they kept their mouths shut. Nobody admitted to having a crumb of bread or a bit of fish. They were afraid they were going to lose it.

> And then there is that small boy. He had been looking at Jesus with an open mouth and a wet nose. He patted his pockets, he felt under his shirt, and he shouted, "Yes, sir, over here." Out he

came with five barley loaves and two fishes, small ones, very small ones, the ones little boys catch.

The whole crowd laughed. Jesus did not. He took those five rolls, and he took those two fish, and he told the people to sit down.

There was a great deal of noise and everyone sat down. Only the small boy was still standing there with Jesus, looking with eyes full of wonder at his fish and his bread.

Jesus gave his fish and his bread to those big apostles of his and said, "Divide it among them." They said: "Divide what?" He said again: "Just start, will you?" They started to break and break and break and break until everybody had enough, even more than enough—so much so that they still had pieces in their hands when their stomachs were full.

Jesus said, "Can you please collect the leftovers?" They collected twelve basketfuls, and Jesus must have given them to the small boy, after all it was his bread, his fish. The people praised Jesus. They even wanted to make him king. I think Jesus praised the small boy who had given all he had. For Jesus that was the attitude of a proper king. Those who give will receive, and receive in abundance.[33]

Then Jesus "withdrew again to the mountain by himself." It is in the people's hunger and the little boy's gift that the sign begins. Jesus took the loaves, and when he had given thanks, he distributed them to those who were seated; so also the fish, as much as they wanted. Sounds a little like the Mass, doesn't it? It's supposed to. See what I mean by *sign*? Eventually the church starts using a more technical word—*sacrament*.

The sign begins with the little boy's gift, moves ahead with Jesus' acceptance of the gift and his prayer of thanksgiving to God and, in a way to the little boy himself. The boy served as an instrument of God's own generosity for which Jesus was truly thankful. This little boy had "the spirit." Jesus was able to work with him and with what he had—

stretching it into food for a multitude, a "sacrament" of God's own abundance.

In conclusion, let's look again at how the three contrasting personalities in the story responded to the challenge at hand: Philip satisfied himself with the reasonable analysis that said the project was just too big to handle and that he and his friends simply didn't have the resources to handle it. Andrew became cynical, even bitter, that this challenge was presented in the first place. We should have known better than to allow ourselves to get into this predicament. The little boy simply offered what he had. He put his resources into the hands of Jesus.

It's pretty clear that his is the preferred response. It is he who has the spirit of faith and hope … and love. Jesus can work with him.

Let's see what Jesus can make of our five loaves and two fish today. Let's pull them out of our little lunch boxes and offer them as bread for this eucharist. Let's see what can become of the food that we offer, how it can be transformed and come back to us with such abundant grace.

Check Your Depth Perception

Eighteenth Sunday in Ordinary Time

Exodus 16.2-4, 12-15, 31a
Psalm 78
Ephesians 4.17, 20-24
John 6.24-35

"I am the bread of life. Whoever comes to me will never be hungry, and whoever believes in me will never be thirsty." (John 6.35)

Again today we have to dig into the text to see just what the evangelist really has in mind. Jesus performs a sign. He takes the bread and the fish and they are multiplied and there's plenty left over: twelve baskets. A miracle? Sure, it's a miracle, and Jesus did it! But—it's a sign.

The crowds were stunned, and rightly so, but they didn't seem to get it. They saw the miracle but did not perceive the sign. "Keep it up, Jesus," they seemed to be thinking. "We'll never be hungry again. How about we make you our king? If you can break bread and fish like there's no tomorrow, you can probably do just about anything!" Jesus fled to the mountain.

The people sought him out, and when they found him Jesus reprimanded them.

"Very truly, I tell you, you are looking for me, not because you saw signs, but because you ate your fill of the loaves. Do not work for food that perishes, but for the food that endures for eternal life, which the Son of Man will give you." (John 6.26-27)

Like Nicodemus before them, these people needed to learn that there was more to being born than being born. Like the woman at the well, they had to learn that there was more to being thirsty than being thirsty. Physical birth, physical water and, in this case, physical bread are

199

more than they appear to be on the surface. They are signs. Meditation on the physical gives rise to spiritual insight. John's readers need to look under the surface of the text and, perhaps more importantly, under the surface of their own lives and experience to recognize what real life, real thirst and real hunger are all about and what Jesus might have to do with these deeper layers of their personal needs. Born again in water and the spirit, they recognize a source of water that can become a fountain within, leaping up to eternal life. In this case they recognize Jesus himself as the bread of life.

Just after Christmas a couple of years ago, I was speaking with a young man who had a four-year-old daughter. He made an appointment to see me because he wanted to have his daughter baptized and enrol her in the neighbourhood Catholic school. He hasn't been involved in the church since his parents took him when he was a child. They don't go anymore either. It seems that he went to church because his parents made him go, and *they* went because they thought it would be good for him. Neither he nor his parents went to church because they really wanted to go—on their own, for their own spiritual purposes. They were getting something out of it, I suppose. They were exercising a certain amount of discipline, they were fulfilling expectations arising out of their traditional Irish roots, but rebirth and renewal in water and the spirit? Discovering an internal fountain of youth or the bread of eternal life? Clearly not.

I'm not passing judgment on them. They were and are good people, solid upright people with sound values and morals, but they had never been in touch with the transformative signs of the sacraments. "Church" is about real stuff, deep spiritual stuff. "Being born again of water and the spirit" is what church baptism is all about. Baptism and eucharist are springs and fountains for eternal life. Eucharist is "bread of life." Church stuff is real—cleansing, renewing, thirst quenching, hunger satisfying.

The young father and I went over these Johannine stories and signs together over several sessions. He was vaguely familiar with them, but it was as if he had never really heard them. It dawned on him as we went along that this religious stuff was real, and he found himself getting hungry and thirsty in new and deeper ways. He was starting to get it! In the meantime, I suggested he sit in with us on a few RCIA sessions where there was a man of about the same age whose eyes were also being opened. They would have a lot in common. He celebrated the sacrament of reconciliation just before Easter and was quite ready for his daughter's baptism when the time came a few Sundays later.

In the light of our reading of John 6 over five Sundays, maybe we ourselves need to take a fresh look at some of these same issues and check our own depth perception. Do we see the signs? Do we see through the signs and beyond the signs?

Maybe we need to ask ourselves—no—maybe I need to ask myself—no, better—maybe I need to let Jesus ask *me* a few questions, let him challenge me as he did the crowd:

"Are you looking for food, or are you looking for God?"

"Are you happy with a full stomach or are you longing for the bread of life?"

"Sure, you're coming to Mass, but do you get it?"

I Am Bread—and You?

1 Kings 19.4–8
Psalm 34
Ephesians 4.30–5.2
John 6.41–51

"No one can come to me unless drawn by the Father who sent me; and I will raise that person up on the last day. It is written in the prophets, 'And they shall all be taught by God.' Everyone who has heard and learned from the Father comes to me. Not that anyone has seen the Father except the one who is from God: he has seen the Father. Very truly, I tell you, whoever believes has eternal life." (John 6.44–47)

Last week I spoke about a young father and his unbaptized daughter. Nominally Catholic but non-practising, he had come to see me because he wanted his daughter baptized. Only after his contact with John's gospel and some faithful members of our parish community was he drawn to deeper faith. He was ready to discover Jesus as a source of life-giving water, as the light of the world, as the bread of life, as the way, the truth and the life for him.

The word *drawn* is a wonderful one. It makes me think of a magnet. However, during these five summer weeks when we are reading from John's gospel, we'll discover that not everyone is as ready to be drawn as this man was. There will be those who, for whatever reason, are pulling away from Jesus, resisting the magnet, refusing to be drawn.

On the way back to Ottawa from my Uncle Norbert's funeral in Detroit a few years ago, I took the train from Windsor, Ontario. En route to Toronto, I was sitting next to a Catholic school trustee from one of the larger boards in the province who had a lot to say about his life and accomplishments. When he found out that I was a priest, he told me that he had been the godfather at the baptism of his infant nephew just a couple of months ago, and that he had had to go to a "class." At that class, the priest had asked him to do something that blew his mind: write a letter to his nephew, a letter that he would not read until his eighteenth birthday. In this letter, the godfather was asked to express what he hoped for his nephew in terms of his life, values and, especially, his relationship with Jesus. He had to put in writing who Jesus was for him, why this relationship matters to him, and why he hopes it will matter to his godson as he becomes an adult.

Here was another man dealing with raising a child in the faith, but coming at it from a very different position. This man was a practising Catholic, but when he had to take pen in hand he wasn't quite sure why and what that meant. Suddenly, and a bit awkwardly, he found himself in a position where he had to share his personal faith, even put it down in writing. It was a real struggle for him.

I remember a high school teacher of mine who called on one of the students in our class with a question. He responded that he knew the answer, but just couldn't explain it well. The teacher retorted: "If you can't explain it well, you don't know the answer."

When you really stop to think about it, what difference would it make anyway for this child to have Jesus in his life? Why shouldn't the godfather just hope that his nephew will turn out to be a decent human being? Why even bother being a godfather? Why not be just a nice, friendly uncle?

John's gospel—and all four gospels, for that matter—make absolute claims for Jesus. "Everyone who has heard and learned from the Father comes to me." (John 6.45b) In other words, if you're not coming to me, you're not listening to God. Even more striking in John are the "I AM" sayings, connecting Jesus explicitly to the revelation of God to Moses in the burning bush. "I AM" is the divine name.

> "*I am* the way, and the truth, and the life. No one comes to the Father except through me." (John 14.6)

These absolute claims are indeed off-putting. They sound arrogant. They are clearly divisive and have even been interpreted by fundamentalists to exclude from salvation all who are not explicitly Christian. Jesus' claims are surely extraordinary, but, in my mind at least, the approach is to enter into the metaphors that he himself chooses.

I am bread—unless you eat of this bread ...

I am light—unless you follow this light ...

I am the way, the truth, and the life. No one can come to the Father except through me.

I'd like to suggest that the key to understanding these absolute claims is the metaphor. Let's look at two examples.

I am the bread of life. I am about being food for others. I am nourishment. I am a nurturing presence who is consumed in the process of giving life. Could my friend on the train explain to his nephew that this is the only way to go? What are the alternatives? Would you rather eat your way through life, or go through life being food for others? "I am bread. That's what I am," Jesus says. How about you?

I am the light of the world. I am about brightness and clarity, openness, integrity and wisdom. I'm about curiosity and knowledge of the truth. Could my friend on the train explain to his nephew that this is the only way to go? There needs to be light even in your most secret places. Character is what you are even when nobody else can see you except yourself and God. Personality is what you are when there are a lot of people around; character is what you are when everybody goes home. "I am light. That's what I am," Jesus says. What about you?

It is true, of course, that many good people discover and live out these truths in their own way, even apart from God's revelation in Jesus, but that's not the point. In Jesus we see and recognize divine revelation, and respond in faith and love. We learn to recognize the truth of the absolute claims that he makes in the process of living them in communion with him.

Jesus is drawing people to himself in a vast open field where bread and fish have been broken and shared with the multitudes. Let's move to another table, a more intimate venue where his absolute claims are made again, where once again he is drawing disciples to himself, this time on the night before he died:

"I am the way, and the truth, and the life. No one comes to the Father except through me. If you know me, you will know my Father also ... The words that I say to you I do not speak on my own; but the Father who dwells in me does his works. Believe me that I am in the Father and the Father is in me; but if you do not, then believe me because of the works themselves. Very truly, I tell you, the one who believes in me will also do the works that I do and, in fact, will do greater works than these, because I am going to the Father." (John 14.6-7, 10.12)

Let us move now to our own table, this eucharistic table where we, too, are being drawn to Jesus once again, drawn into communion with his way of being bread and light—the way the truth and the life, being drawn into the works that our faith and communion with him imply.

The Consequences
of Eucharistic Faith

Twentieth Sunday in Ordinary Time

Proverbs 9.1-6
Psalm 34
Ephesians 5.15-20
John 6.51-58

"I am the living bread that came down from heaven. Whoever eats of this bread will live forever; and the bread that I will give is my flesh for the life of the world." (John 6.51)

It's just so physical, isn't it?

I am *bread* … Whoever *eats* of this bread … The bread that I will give is *my flesh* … Unless you *eat the flesh* of the Son of Man and *drink his blood,* you have no life … Whoever *eats me* will live because of me…

It's all so physical: when you stop and think about it and emphasize those key words, it's even rather hard to take … even for us Catholics who are so accustomed to the images of bread and wine, and who stand in such a long faith tradition that discerns in them the real presence of Jesus Christ: "body, blood, soul, and divinity."

Sometimes I think, however, that this language and our familiarity with it can obscure something of its radical content and stand in the way of our really understanding. For many of us who come to the eucharist weekly, even daily, it may have become too easy to take.

Last October, it was my turn to preside at the seminary eucharist on the feast of Saint Ignatius of Antioch, bishop and martyr. As Peter's successor as bishop of Antioch, Ignatius was condemned to death and thrown to wild animals under the authority of the Emperor Trajan in 107. In the course of his journey to Rome to face his death, he wrote seven letters, one of which is featured in the Liturgy of the Hours for his feast day. It's truly a remarkable document. It seems as though some of his friends in Rome were trying to appeal his case, or at least win for him a stay of execution. He would have none of it.

> I am writing to the churches to let it be known that I will gladly die for God if only you do not stand in my way. I plead with you: show me no untimely kindness. *Let me be food* for the wild beasts, for they are my way to God. *I am God's wheat and shall be ground by their teeth so that I may become Christ's pure bread.* Pray to Christ for me that the animals may be the ultimate means of making me a sacrificial victim for God … Give me the privilege of imitating the passion of my God. If you have him in your heart, you will understand what I wish. You will sympathize with me because you will know what urges me on … I am no longer willing to live a merely human life, and you can bring about my wish if you will. Please, then, do me this favour, so that you in turn may meet with equal kindness. Put briefly, this is my request: believe what I am saying to you. Jesus Christ himself will make it clear to you that I am saying the truth … If I am condemned to suffer, I will take it that you wish me well. If my case is postponed, I can only think that you wish me harm.[34]

His eucharistic theology and spirituality couldn't be clearer, nor could his eagerness for its ultimate fulfillment in his own life. Ignatius of Antioch sees the meaning of his own life and death as an echo of Jesus' own gift of his flesh and blood as food and drink for the life of the world. The flesh of Ignatius too, consumed by wild beasts, becomes bread of life for the world. As wheat is ground to become bread, so he will be ground by the teeth of beasts to become the pure bread of Christ.

At that same liturgical celebration, we prayed over the gifts:

> Lord, *receive our offering* as you accepted Saint Ignatius when he offered himself to you as the wheat of Christ formed into pure bread by his death for Christ.

As Jesus goes, so goes Ignatius. As Ignatius goes, so go we. As his offering was accepted, so may ours be received. Wow! Our participation in the Holy *Sacrifice* of the Mass really comes to life when we think about it this way. What a spirit Ignatius must have had—full of zest and eagerness.

As Jesus is wheat, so Ignatius is wheat. As Jesus is bread, so Ignatius is bread. Just stop and think how sacrificial these images are and how demanding they are as metaphors for the Christian life.

Unless the grain of wheat is planted in the ground and dies ...
Unless the wheat is threshed and ground ...
Unless the flour loses itself in the dough ...
Unless the dough is kneaded and punched down ...
Unless the loaf is baked in the fire ...
Unless the loaf is cut by the knife ...
Unless the bread is chewed by the teeth ...

It is in dying and rising that a grain of wheat becomes itself, reaches its destiny. It is in dying and rising that bread becomes itself reaching its destiny.

Unless, unless, unless ...

Isn't that what our tradition is saying when we speak of "Body, blood, soul, and divinity of Jesus Christ really present in the grain of wheat, in the bread and wine"? That's clearly what Ignatius believed, and he was fully ready to see and embrace the consequences of his eucharistic faith for his whole life.

Last fall, the Baltimore Museum of Art held a special exhibit featuring ancient Antioch. Located in what is now Turkey, near the Syrian border, the ancient metropolis of Antioch ranked as one of the great cities of the Roman Empire and early Christian world. Decimated centuries ago by earthquakes, plagues and military invasions, the city, for all practical purposes, was lost until a team of archeologists began excavating the site in the 1930s. Among others, the Baltimore Museum of Art and the Louvre participated in the project, unearthing Antioch's past, which had been buried beneath fields and olive groves for almost 1500 years. The excavation yielded a collection of high-quality Roman domestic floor mosaics dating from the time of Ignatius himself.

Of particular interest were the dining room floors, which were the most elaborate. The dining room at the time of Ignatius was clearly the most important room of the house. At meals in the dining room, neighbours gathered, poetry was read, and politics and philosophy were discussed and debated. It's as if they had their own tradition of "liturgy around the word" and "liturgy around food." Both elements were clearly combined culturally, as they are today. What's a meal without conversation? One can only imagine Ignatius discussing the eucharist in such a room, at such a table, perhaps even in the context of a eucharistic celebration. John's gospel was almost surely not finalized at the time, but the images of John 6 that we heard proclaimed today were clearly front and centre in his teaching and faith during these first formative years of eucharistic practice and theology.

Among the other treasures on display in the Antioch exhibit were an ancient eucharistic plate, or paten, and a chalice. They were huge! The diameter of the plate was almost three quarters of a metre, and the chalice was correspondingly large to make a matching set. Pretty impressive! It made me wonder what the bread was like, what the experience of breaking the bread and pouring the wine must have felt like at the time of Ignatius.

We'll never know for sure, but it's interesting to wonder. Certainly his experience of the eucharist was impressive enough to form his whole way of understanding his life and death in communion with Christ.

From his early witness we can learn to receive the eucharist with reverence and devotion, with faith and hope and courage.

"My flesh is true food and my blood is true drink. Those who eat my flesh and drink my blood abide in me, and I in them." (John 6.55–56)

Amen.

Eucharist as Decision

Twenty-first Sunday in Ordinary Time

Joshua 24.1-2a, 15-17, 18b
Psalm 34
Ephesians 4.32–5.2, 21-32
John 6.53, 60-69

"Far be it from us that we should forsake the Lord to serve other gods; for it is the Lord our God who brought us and our ancestors up from the land of Egypt, out of the house of slavery, and who did those great signs in our sight. He protected us along all the way that we went, and among all the peoples through whom we passed. Therefore we also will serve the Lord, for he is our God." (Joshua 24.16-17, 18b)

"Unless you eat the flesh of the Son of Man and drink his blood, you have no life in you." When many of his disciples heard this, they said: "This teaching is difficult; who can accept it?" ... Jesus asked the twelve, "Do you also wish to go away?" Simon Peter answered him, "Lord, to whom can we go? You have the words of eternal life. We have come to believe and know that you are the Holy One of God." (John 6.53, 60, 67-69)

This Sunday, as our reading from John 6 comes to a close, I'd like to continue focusing on the challenge of eucharistic participation. Ignatius of Antioch clearly had his take on sacrifice. He knew that his whole life had to be in tune with what he was celebrating in the eucharist or his life in Christ would have no real integrity. In the context of that real-life approach, let's look at the eucharist this Sunday from a slightly different but complementary angle. Let's look at it as a decision, a transforming decision.

Amen. As for us, we will serve the Lord, for he is our God. Amen. To whom shall we go? We have come to believe that you are the Holy One of God. Amen.

Traditionally the church has understood the eucharist as the third sacrament of initiation. Baptism was once and for all; confirmation was once and for all; but eucharist goes on until its completion at the table in the kingdom of heaven when all will be one, when communion will be complete. Our Amen to the eucharist involves an ongoing and deepening affirmation of the fundamental commitments we make to Christ and to each other in baptism and confirmation. Our eucharistic Amens echo through our whole lives as affirmations of a foundational life decision to be in communion with the Body of Christ, dying and rising with him, faithful to and in continuity with the life of a believing people with whom we stand in communion.

At the beginning of this homily I cited key sections of two of the readings for today that describe such choices. The first sounds like a covenant renewal ritual. It is a religious assembly of people gathered before God, probably before the ark of the covenant. After Joshua, their leader, testifies to his own faith and commitment, he invites and witnesses the proclamation of faith and commitment arising from the whole community. Joshua and the people stand in solidarity with each other in their "Amen" to the Lord, who brought them up from slavery.

The second describes Peter stating his own personal decision to stick with Jesus. Later on he, too, will become a leader of faith whose own witness and commitment will invite and confirm the faith and commitment of others.

I have two beautiful editions of the Haggadah, the description and ritual for the celebration of the Passover, in which the Jewish people yearly reaffirm their faith in the God who brought them up from slavery. One of them contains a particularly touching entry from a journal that was discovered in the liberation of the Bergen-Belsen concentration camp in the aftermath of World War II. It's in the form of a prayer and must have been written by a man who would die there and was writing on the occasion of Passover. It came out of his desire to celebrate in tune with his tradition and in solidarity with his people, but it was just impossible. He didn't even have the basic elements of unleavened bread and wine. It is in this context that he prayed:

Our Father in heaven, behold it is evident and known to thee that it is our desire to do thy will and to celebrate the festival of Passover by eating matzah and by observing the prohibition of leavened food. But our heart is pained that the enslavement prevents us and we are in danger of our lives. Behold, we are prepared and ready to fulfill thy commandment: "And ye shall live by them and not die by them."

We pray to thee that thou mayest keep us alive and preserve us and redeem us speedily so that we may observe thy statutes and do thy will and serve thee with a perfect heart. Amen.

His prayer may not have been answered as he had hoped, but it was answered. This man lives. What a remarkable testimony to the power of faith and tradition!

Our family has pictures of my uncle, who is also my godfather, taken during the same war, serving Mass. If I remember correctly, it is on the tailgate of an army Jeep.

Both cases display a seriously felt need to be in touch with ancestral rituals and the commitments they represent and contain. There is in each case a determination to confirm a sense of self, a sense of community, and a sense of divine vocation. These rituals both *express* faith and *build* faith by their unique grace and transforming power.

I referred earlier to Terry Anderson's book *Den of Lions,* from which I quoted from one of his poems. You may remember that Terry was an Associated Press journalist with roots in Ohio and Michigan, who was held captive for seven years in Lebanon. Five years after his release, he went back to Lebanon and was subsequently interviewed on CNN about just how that felt, and just what being back there was like.

During his captivity, he was often blindfolded so he could not see his jailer's faces. On his trip back he sat face to face with a leading figure in Hezbollah, the "Party of God," the organization blamed for his kidnapping. Today these people are being named as a terrorist organization. When Anderson asked the man what he thought of hostage-taking now, his question was met with polite indifference—silence—and then: "I'm not prepared to say whether these methods are good or bad, right or wrong. These actions were short-term, with short-term objectives. I can't make an absolute judgment."

In spite of everything he went through, Anderson continues to be a man of faith. He chooses to respond to the gift of faith planted deep within him. As a devout Christian he continues to believe in the call of God to universal communion in Christ and to see that reality fore-shadowed in the eucharist.

> "As for me, I will serve the Lord,
> who brought us up for slavery."
> "Lord, to whom can we go?
> You have the words of eternal life."

Listen to his description of eucharist in a Lebanese dungeon:

Five men huddled close
against the night and our oppressors
around a bit of stale bread
hoarded from a scanty meal
and a candle, lit not only as
a symbol but to read the text by.
The priest's as poorly clad
as drawn with strain as any,
but his voice is calm, his face serene.
This is the core of his existence,
the reason he was born.
Behind him I can see
his predecessors in their generations
back to the catacombs,
heads nodding with approval,
hands with his tracing
out the stately ritual,
adding the power of their suffering
and faith to his, and ours,
the ancient words shake off
their dust and come alive.
The voices of their authors
echo clearly from the damp, bare walls.

The familiar prayers come
straight out of our hearts.
Once again Christ's promise
is fulfilled; his presence fills us.
The miracle is real.[35]

Like the prayer of the Jewish man in Bergen–Belsen, this represents a truly remarkable profession of faith.

Today's responsorial psalm fits perfectly with the readings:

Taste and see the goodness of the Lord.

I will bless the Lord at all times;
His praise shall continually be in my mouth.
My soul makes its boast in the Lord;
Let the humble hear and be glad.

Many are the afflictions of the righteous,
but the Lord rescues them from them all.
He keeps all their bones;
not one of them will be broken.

Taste and see the goodness of the Lord. (Psalm 34)

As for me—Amen. To whom shall we go? What is your decision?

Higher Standards

Twenty-second Sunday in Ordinary Time

Deuteronomy 4.1-2, 6-8
Psalm 15
James 1.17-18, 21-22, 27
Mark 7.1-8, 14-15, 21-23

Moses spoke to the people: "So now, Israel, give heed to the statutes and ordinances that I am teaching you to observe, so that you may live to enter and occupy the land that the Lord, the God of your ancestors, is giving you ... You must observe them diligently, for this will show your wisdom and discernment to the peoples... (Deuteronomy 4.1, 6)

"This people honours me with their lips, but their hearts are far from me." (Mark 7.6)

There's something wonderful about people who are serious about the practice of their faith, and who genuinely strive to shape their lives around core beliefs and values.

At the time of Jesus, pious Jews who were serious about fidelity to the law were asking the experts for guidance. The scribes were among these experts. They were called upon to help ordinary believers interpret the implications of the law for situations not foreseen at the time of its writing. The ancient biblical texts could not possibly provide answers for any and every eventuality. Over the years the reasoning of the scribes had not been written down but had instead been passed on by word of mouth, to avoid any possibility that their reflections and applications would be confused with or given the same dignity as the written word. The oral tradition was not to be confused with or held in the same respect as the scriptures themselves. Known as the "tradition" or the "tradition of the elders," this material was finally codified and written down sometime after AD 200 in the two Talmuds.

All of this is surely to the good. The kind of discussion carried on among the scribes continues in the work of theologians to our own time. In the *Catechism of the Catholic Church*, for example, the Ten Commandments, which can be printed in less than half a page, are treated over the course of 115 pages. They are expanded, interpreted and applied in light of the church's tradition and the realities of our own time. The commandments have a dignity that their further explanation does not have, but the interpretation is necessary for us to understand them in reasonable and meaningful ways appropriate to our own time.

The roots of the controversy between Jesus and certain of the scribes and Pharisees of his day was not the need to keep the legal system up to date, and interpret it well in light of new developments, but exaggerations and excesses. The pile-up of commentary around the law can sometimes obscure the initial purpose of the law. Both the text and its spirit can be buried in commentary.

Other issues were hypocrisy and corruption. In the text just prior to today's text, Jesus had very harsh words to say about very knowledgeable people who find certain religious loopholes that they could use to avoid important responsibilities, even that of looking after aged parents. Clever people have always been able to find ways to twist and abuse the law for their own benefit; finding tax loopholes is a prime example. Their careful attention to detail is not directed to understanding and obeying the law, but controlling it for their own benefit, while continuing to appear as upstanding citizens.

People in leadership positions in Jesus' day as well as in our own need not only to know their stuff, but to live accordingly—to live honestly and responsibly in spirit and truth. There's no room for hair-splitting the law for one's own advantage, nor is there room for hypocrisy and double standards. Every once in a while very public cases involving both the personal affairs of individuals, as well as those of large corporations, give plenty of evidence that these kind of temptations haven't gone away.

At a recent seminar on preaching, one of the permanent deacons gave a little example from his own life that can pull some of this together. It was his turn to preach at his parish and he decided to focus on the theme of justice. He began with the commandment "Thou shalt not steal." First he discussed the personal meaning of the commandment in terms of respect for the property of others, and then stretched it to include larger issues of social justice. Sometimes, for example, we think we're getting a terrific deal on a purchase and don't realize the subsistence wages that workers in a Third World country might have been paid in the course of the item's production. Somebody else paid the price; we are stealing. The morning after he gave his homily he got on the bus and realized that he had forgotten his pass and would have to pay cash. He hurriedly gave the driver two dollars, got his change and went to find a seat. Looking at the change he realized he had too much. "The bus company will never miss a quarter," he thought to himself, but then thought better of it and gave the quarter to the driver as he got off the bus. The bus driver thanked him for the quarter as he commended him on his good homily the morning before. Aha! "Practising what you preach" suddenly came home to roost—and was he ever glad to have made the right choice.

The story is told of two men who met on the street. One man said to the other, "Have you heard about Harry? He embezzled half a million dollars from the company." The other man said, "That's terrible. I never did trust that so-and-so."

The first man continued, "Not only that, he left town and took Tom's wife with him." The other man said, "That's awful. What a sleaze."

The first man said, "Not only that, he stole a car to make his getaway." The other man said, "Unbelievable."

Finally, the first man said, "Not only that, he was drunk when he pulled out of town." The other man, hardly able to believe his ears, just shook his head.

After a few moments he said, "But who do you suppose is going to take over his Sunday School class?"

I hesitated to use this second example because it's so preposterous that it might even distract from our need to search our own hearts for any hypocrisy or double standard that may be operative in us. The scriptures today describe true righteousness and holiness not as simply being faithful to the practice of religious faith, but as living the whole of life in a way that's consistent with faith—being truly faithful in all things.

Let's take a closer look at being faithful, at faithfulness. It strikes me that a distinction between obedience and faithfulness may be helpful. Both are important, but faithfulness is always prior to obedience and essential to its proper understanding and practice.

We obey laws and regulations. We are faithful to an ideal or set of values.

We obey certain traditions. We are faithful to tradition.

We obey religious rituals and requirements. We are faithful to the person of God.

The other day, as I was walking from the rectory to the church under the covered walkway, I stopped to pull some weeds and trim out the rose bed near the bell tower. Two boys on their bikes came roaring into the parking lot and slammed on their brakes, skidding to a circular stop. I'm sure you can picture it. They had their baseball caps on—backwards as is the style. The doors of the church were open and they were half peeking in. I thought maybe they were looking for a bathroom or a drink, so I went over and said hello to them. They were just curious. They had been around here often before but had never been inside. So I gave them a little tour, asking them to take their caps off, because it was a church. Both were going into Grade 9 the following year and both were Jewish. One of them observed that in synagogue they had to wear something on their head, and here they weren't supposed to. Why was that? I told him it was tradition—a sign of respect. That was fine as far as he was concerned, but, to tell you truth, I was glad he didn't pursue that line of questioning. The boys were very nice and polite. Maybe they'll stop in again. But their visit raises a question: What's more important—hats in church or hospitality?

That was an easy case. Let's look at another, more complex one.

A couple of weeks ago I was speaking with a young couple about being married here in our parish. Neither of them goes to Mass here or anywhere else, but both seem like very nice people and are clearly crazy about each other. They have been living together for almost a year. What do we do about that? Can just anybody expect to be married in church?

Getting registered in the parish, getting back to Mass, and yes, taking a set of church envelopes—*and*—separating until they're married: Are those the issues?

Why had they come to see me? Who is God for them? Jesus? They're both baptized and confirmed. What is their family background? What has their Catholic faith felt like for them growing up? What are their hopes for children and for the faith-nurturing they would hope to offer them?

This is a much bigger question than "When was the last time you were at Mass?" and an even bigger issue than figuring out what more suitable living arrangements might be until the knot is officially tied. Such questions reflect fidelity to God as a higher value than obedience to specific prescriptions; personal integrity as a higher value than conformity to traditional standards, however noble and desirable. No serious couple would want to begin their married life with a ritual that has no authenticity for them, in a religious context that has no meaning for them, in a building that is not their home.

By and large, people respond very well to such real questions of faith and integrity. Sometimes a couple like that will nod their heads, thank me, and leave—respectfully—as friends. At other times, they stay and come back so that we can move forward together.

The second reading, from the letter of James, gives us some wonderful spiritual images with which we can pray as we ponder our own desire to be faithful to God and God's ways made known to us by Jesus and lived in the tradition of our church.

God is the Father of Lights.
God gave us birth by the word of truth.

So:

Welcome with meekness the implanted word that has power to save your souls. Be doers of the word. Religion that is pure and undefiled before God, the Father, is this: to care for widows and orphans and to keep oneself unstained by the world. (James 1.21b-22, 27)

You couldn't ask for higher standards than those.

Astounded Beyond Measure

Twenty-third Sunday in Ordinary Time

Isaiah 35.4-7
Psalm 146
James 2.1-5
Mark 7.31-37

They brought him a man who was deaf and who had an impediment in his speech. (Mark 7.32)

I remember a sister telling us as schoolchildren that there was a good reason God gave us two ears and only one mouth. We're supposed to do twice as much listening as talking.

There's a wonderful expression of this truth in one of Isaiah's servant songs, the one proclaimed on Passion Sunday:

The servant of the Lord said:
The Lord God has given me the tongue of a teacher,
that I may know how to sustain the weary with a word.
Morning by morning he wakens—
wakens my ear to listen as those who are taught.
The *Lord God has opened my ear,*
and I was not rebellious, I did not turn backward.
(Isaiah 50.4-5)

It's pretty clear in Sister's comments on God's design of our heads, as well as in the passage from Isaiah, that there's a lot more to hearing, really hearing, than not being deaf. In the Bible, hearing often serves as a metaphor for openness—openness to the truth, openness to communication with God who speaks.

Hearing—hearing with the mind and heart, hearing a word with transforming potential—is stressed over and over in the scriptures, perhaps most notably in Israel's pre-eminent prayer that was to be said daily and serves as the core of faith:

> Hear, O Israel: The Lord is our God, the Lord alone. You shall love the Lord your God with all your heart, and with all your soul, and with all your might. Keep these words that I am commanding you today in your heart. Recite them to your children and talk about them when you are at home and when you are away, when you lie down and when you rise. Bind them as a sign on your hand, fix them as an emblem on your forehead, and write them on the doorposts of your house and on your gates. (Deuteronomy 6.4-9)

Hear, O Israel. Hearing the word of God is clearly prior to speaking it or writing it. In the scriptures hearing the word, being open to the word, and allowing the word to penetrate the depths of our being is foundational for right thinking and right living. When Jesus says, *"Ephphatha!"*—"Be opened!"—he is standing within and working out of that broad sense of what hearing really involves, the hearing that leads to faith and hope. That the man, as well as those who brought him to Jesus and those in the crowd, is anonymous is another signal that Jesus' opening of ears transcends the particulars of the story. It is a metaphor for the kind of healing and opening that any person will need to absorb the content of the good news, to speak it, celebrate it, and live its consequences.

In a fourth-century homily, Saint Ephraem speaks eloquently of Jesus' touch that opens the ears of the heart:

> The deaf mute healed by Christ felt his fingers of flesh touch his ears and tongue; but when his ears were unstopped, he reached the inaccessible divinity through the intermediary of this finger that his senses perceived. The very artisan of his body, the maker of his limbs had come to him; he had found him deaf, and with a soft voice, without the slightest pain had opened his hard ears. Immediately his blocked throat, up to now unable to let any sound through, burst out in praise of him who, with one word, had cured him of his helplessness.[36]

In the Rite of Christian Initiation of Adults, we still celebrate a "Rite of Opening" that is based on this story from Mark. Even today the priest touches the ears of persons preparing for baptism with the command "Be opened." In discussing the theology behind such an ancient sacramental practice in class last spring, I came across the text of a sermon given by Saint Ambrose, the fourth-century bishop of Milan, asking his congregation to remember and reflect on the significance of this very rite that had taken place the previous Saturday.

> What did we do last Saturday? The opening. These mysteries of the opening were celebrated when the bishop touched your ears and nostrils. What does this mean? When a deaf mute was brought to him, Our Lord Jesus Christ in the gospel touched his ears and mouth: the ears because he was deaf, the mouth because he was mute. And he said "Ephphatha." This is a Hebrew word that means "Be opened." Therefore, the bishop touched your ears so that they might be open to his words and speech —his sharing of the gospel with you … But you ask, "Why the nostrils?"—in order that you might receive the good odors of divine goodness, so that you might say, "For we are the aroma of Christ for God," as the holy apostle says (2 Corinthians 2.15), and so that there might be in you all the perfumes of faith and devotion.[37]

The work of Christ goes on. Openings are still happening. Ears are unstopped and tongues are loosened for witness and praise. Once again we see how inclusive Mark's telling of the gospel is. The good news goes on; it moves forward; it enters our own time and place. We are all invited into the story. Sometimes we may find ourselves bringing others to Jesus; sometimes we're the one being brought to him for new and deeper openness to his truth and wisdom; sometimes we're ministering in his name as instruments of opening for others; sometimes we're just marvelling as we see this happening around us.

I suspect that even the description of his circuitous travelling that is linked to this story has something to do with its universal application. People in the crowd from here, there and everywhere are caught up in the story. They refuse to be silent about the marvellous good news which they, too, are hearing as they see Jesus at work. "Astounded beyond measure," they say: "He has done everything well; he even makes the deaf to hear and the mute to speak." (Mark 7.37) Astounded beyond measure, they may be discovering new possibilities for their own ears, new possibilities for personal and spiritual openness for them-selves.

Another ancient source, this time a hymn, summarizes this well:

Deafened ears, of sound unconscious,
every passage blocked and closed,
at the word of Christ responding,
all the portals opened wide,
hear with joy friendly voices
and the softly whispered speech.
Every sickness now surrenders,
every listlessness departs.
Tongues long bound by chains of silence
are unloosed and speak aright.[38]

Ephphatha—Be Opened!

Take up the Cross

Twenty-fourth Sunday in Ordinary Time

Isaiah 50.5–9
Psalm 116
James 2.14–18
Mark 8.27–35

Among the items in the Mark Twain Memorial in Hartford, Connecticut, are these neatly framed words:

Always do right. It will gratify some people and astonish the rest.

Truly yours,
Mark Twain
New York, February 16, 1901

True enough. Challenging enough. But listen to this:

Jesus called the crowd with his disciples, and said to them, "If any want to become my followers, let them deny themselves and take up their cross and follow me. For those who want to save their life will lose it, and those who lose their life for my sake, and for the sake of the gospel, will save it." (Mark 8.34–35)

To take up the cross involves more than just doing right. It reflects a conscious choice to bend over backwards, go out on a limb, take an extraordinary risk, be selfless for the sake of Jesus and the gospel, whether or not others are gratified or astonished.

Today's text is the centrepiece of Mark's gospel, both literally and figuratively. Standing as it does at the centre of the gospel, it serves as a real turning point. From here, Jesus will pass through Galilee for the last time on his way to Jerusalem, where his ministry will come to an end.

At first sight it seems to begin harmlessly enough. Sounds like an informal test of public opinion. How am I doing? How many am I gratifying? How many am I astonishing?—but that's not the issue. The question is "Who do people say that I am?" There's a difference. Even public opinion recognizes perhaps Elijah, or John the Baptist, or one of the other prophets, all of whom suffered mightily for their faith and convictions.

It was Peter's turn: "You are the Messiah"—not like those others. You're God's chosen one. When Jesus began speaking of the suffering and rejection that would link him to the other prophets, Peter rebuked him for not seeming to know what a real messiah's life would be like. Jesus in turn rebuked Peter. "Get behind me, Satan! For you are setting your mind, not on divine things, but on human things."

The liturgy links Mark's proclamation of the nature of Jesus' sense of what being messiah will entail for him to the mysterious "suffering servant" of Isaiah.

> "The Lord God has opened my ear,
> and I was not rebellious,
> I did not turn backward.
> I gave my back to those who struck me,
> and my cheeks to those who pulled out the beard;
> I did not hide my face from insult and spitting.
> The Lord God helps me;
> therefore I have not been disgraced;
> I have set my face like flint,
> and I know that I shall not be put to shame;
> he who vindicates me is near." (Isaiah 50.5-7)

Peter doesn't like that picture. Can you blame him? He would prefer something more modest like "doing what is right, gratifying some, and astonishing others." And yet, despite all his protesting, there is something beautiful about the picture. The unwavering attachment to God's will in the midst of suffering that we see in the servant's face, the certitude with which he fully expects to see his righteousness rewarded, his incredible dignity and hugeness of spirit have a kind of grandeur to them, as will the messiah's own self-offering on the cross.

Joseph Ton is a remarkable example of someone who took the imitation of Jesus and the carrying of the cross quite literally. He ran away from his native Romania to study theology at Oxford. As he prepared to return home as an independent missionary, his fellow graduates were sure he was foolish, that he'd probably be arrested at the border even before opening his mouth. He got back into the country the same way he had gotten out, a kind of reverse escape, and took up his preaching until he was arrested. As he was being harassed and interrogated, he replied very simply: "Your supreme weapon is killing; mine is dying."

> "Who will contend with me?
> Let us stand up together.
> Who are my adversaries?
> Let them confront me.
> It is the Lord God who helps me;
> who will declare me guilty?" (Isaiah 50.8–9a)

> "If any want to become my followers, let them deny themselves and take up their cross and follow me. For those who want to save their life will lose it, and those who lose their life for my sake, and for the sake of the gospel, will find it." (Mark 8.34–35)

To take up the cross involves a conscious moral, ethical, personal choice. To take up the cross is a decision. It is not accepting the inevitable tragedies of life, big and small, that come into people's lives. You've all heard people say—and may have said yourself at some unexpected turn of events, "This must be my cross to bear"; or "God must have sent me this cross for a purpose." Notice that Jesus does not say: "Accept your cross." He says: "Set your mind on divine things." "Take up the cross." "Follow me." The cross involves a very active and conscious decision.

Of course, we're invited to accept our crosses and offer up our sufferings, but this is not what Jesus is suggesting here. It's more radical than that. His cross is actually something that we're called to look for, not simply accept. Taking up the cross and following Christ is a conscious and ongoing decision that invites us to discover in ourselves a potential for the highest imaginable nobility of spirit reflected in his own.

You may have heard the children's story about a woman who once found an eagle's egg and put it into the nest of a barnyard chicken. The eaglet hatched with the brood of chicks and grew up with them. All his life, the eagle did what the chickens did. It scratched the dirt for seeds and insects to eat. It clucked and cackled. And it flew no more than a few feet off the ground, in a chicken-like thrashing of wings and flurry of feathers.

One day the eagle saw a magnificent bird far above him in the cloudless sky. He watched as the bird soared gracefully on powerful currents of wind, gliding through the air with scarcely a beat of its powerful wings.

"What a beautiful bird," the young eagle said. "What is it called?" The chicken next to him said, "Why, that's an eagle—the king of all birds, but don't pay any attention to him." So the young eagle returned to pecking dirt, and died thinking it was a barnyard chicken.

Looking up to Jesus, following him to Jerusalem, watching him setting his mind on divine things, not human things, is awesome—both scary and wonderful at the same time.

To set our own minds on heavenly things, to take up the cross and follow, is to fly high—very high.

"Who do people say that I am?"

"Who do *you* say that I am?"

Who *you say Jesus is* says a lot about *who you think you are* and can become in him.

Becoming Like Children

Twenty-fifth Sunday in Ordinary Time

Wisdom 2.12, 17–20
Psalm 54
James 3.16–4.3
Mark 9.30-37

Then they came to Capernaum; and when he was in the house Jesus asked them, "What were you arguing about on the way?" But they were silent, for on the way they had argued with one another about who was the greatest. Jesus sat down, called the twelve, and said to them, "Whoever wants to be first must be last of all and servant of all." Then he took a little child and put it among them; and taking it into his arms, he said to them, "Whoever welcomes one such child in my name welcomes me, and whoever welcomes me welcomes not me but the one who sent me." (Mark 9.33-37)

It's particularly significant that this text follows immediately upon Jesus' second prediction of his passion:

"The Son of Man is to be betrayed into human hands, and they will kill him, and three days after being killed, he will rise again." But they did not understand what he was saying and *were afraid* to ask him. (Mark 9.31-32)

One of the intriguing features of the whole gospel is the relationship of Jesus with his disciples, how they're called, taken aside, privileged to share intimate moments with Jesus—and still miss the point. In Mark, they're presented as mirrors in which we are invited to see ourselves. Even those of us who are closest to the church and to the practice of faith can get things mixed up pretty easily.

A couple of weeks ago, I came across a loose clipping containing a touching but sad prayer written by a white minister from South Africa who had served his church for 35 years, but was not involved at all in the process of transformation and reconciliation that finally came to pass and is still a work in progress. He was looking back over his career as a minister of the gospel, at what he stood for and what he didn't stand for, at what he said, and what he didn't say. His own analysis of his career was that it was mixed up. This is his prayer that he offered publicly in the midst of his congregation:

> Loving God, you asked for my hands, that you might use them for your purpose. I gave them a little bit, but withdrew them when the work was hard. You asked for my mouth to speak out against injustice. I gave a little whisper, that I might not be heard. You asked for my eyes to see the pain of poverty. I closed them because I was afraid to see. You asked for my life that you might work through me. I gave a little bit, but I didn't want to get too involved. Lord, forgive my calculated efforts to serve you only when it was convenient and safe for me, only in those places where it was safe to do so and only with those persons who made me welcome. Lord, forgive me. Renew me. Send me out now as a useable instrument that I might take seriously the meaning of your cross.

That he would share this prayer with his congregation is truly remarkable and courageous. His prayer may not relate directly to our own experience of faith, but I still think we can see ourselves in his mirror. At least I know that I can.

Dealing with our own positions, our own safety, our own status within the community, our own reputation can sometimes keep us from what is of God—what is truly noble. It's true as well that the pace of life, its demands and routines, including regular hearing of the scriptures and participation in the eucharist, can insulate us from more fundamental questions that need to be raised. It's those fundamentals that Mark just won't let us avoid.

The experience of this minister and that of the disciples in mixing up their priorities can invite us to reflect on who we are and where we stand: whether we're in it with both feet, both hands, both eyes, both ears and our heart, mind and mouth. Whether we're involved in our personal affairs, in our families, in our job, in our world, in our political situation with all of the truth that we have. Whether we have embraced the cross of Christ, whether we live in his spirit, whether we dedicate ourselves in his style to what is real, what is true and what is honest, or whether we're in fact hedging our bets a little bit—or a whole lot.

We all need to make sure that ten years or twenty years from now we're not going to be looking back and saying: "Gee, you know, I didn't really do much with my life. I wasn't really my best. I let so much of life slip through my fingers."

That's what happened to the minister. He had to write a lament and a prayer for transformation into a more fitting instrument of God's justice, love and mercy. What's wonderful about the prayer is both its honesty and the hopefulness he expresses in the ongoing power of God's fidelity to him and to the world.

In the gospel passage, Jesus uses a child as a living parable to dislodge the disciples from their preoccupation with their own status. Roman Palestine was not post-Enlightenment Europe, with its romantic cult of the innocence and importance of children. Children were at the low end of the social ladder; only slaves were below them. Children thus served as a symbol of both lowliness and powerlessness as well as of the trust and simplicity that deeply understand God's kingdom.

The text "Whoever welcomes one such child in my name welcomes me and whoever welcomes me welcomes not me but the one who sent me" moves Jesus' point even further in focusing on the up-side-down nature of the kingdom and of how Jesus understood his own mission. Instead of wrangling about their own status, the disciples must be concerned for the weakest members of the community with whom Jesus identifies himself. That identification will be most complete as he enters into the passion and embraces the cross.

New York's Penn Station was demolished in 1963 to be buried underneath what is now the Madison Square Garden Complex. In a coffee-table book for railroad aficionados, I found reference to a plaque that used to hang there. It was dedicated to one of its early station masters.

Friend to mankind
William H. Egan
Station master

Beloved by all who journeyed through this station,
by all who served its millions of patrons,
devoted guardian of the lonely wayfarer,
of presidents, princes and prima donnas.
The lowly and the celebrated in all walks of life
were proud to know him.
He Loved People.

The Pennsylvania Railroad

Whether he was a Christian or not, this man saw his life in terms not of being station *master*, but of recognizing the common humanity of all travellers and serving them generously. To be hospitable and welcoming is a really good start: who knows where the rich and poor are to be found? There can be real poverty in a prima donna just as there can be real richness in the ordinary wayfarer.

The gospel is moving us to something even deeper than the shared humanity that the station master observed so clearly in the travellers he served. In receiving others as human beings, we recognize and receive them as children of God. Even further, we recognize, especially in the most vulnerable, the "Beloved Son." In the great judgment scene in Matthew, this "Whatever you do to the least" will come through in great detail, but already in Mark the seed is planted.

Let's join with the minister in asking that we all get it right—that we all get at least a little better at getting it right.

Lord, forgive me. Renew me. Send me out now as a useable instrument that I might take seriously the meaning of your cross.

Unlicensed Prophets

Twenty-sixth Sunday in Ordinary Time

Numbers 11.16-17, 25-29
Psalm 19
James 5.1-6
Mark 9.38-43, 45, 47-48

The Lord said to Moses, "Gather for me seventy of the elders of the people" … When the spirit rested upon them, they prophesied. But they did not do so again. Two men remained in the camp, … and the spirit rested upon them … and so they prophesied in the camp … Joshua son of Nun, the assistant of Moses, one of his chosen men, said, "My lord Moses, stop them!" But Moses said to him, "Would that all the Lord's people were prophets, and that the Lord would put his spirit on them." (Numbers 11.16, 25-26, 28-29)

After Jesus had finished teaching the disciples, John said to him, "Teacher, we saw someone casting out demons in your name, and we tried to stop him, because he was not following us." Jesus said: "… Whoever is not against us is for us." (Mark 9.38, 40a)

Who's who and what's what?—and who has a right to say or to do what, when and where? Who's in and who's out? That's certainly a key question in today's scriptures. As petty as it sounds, questions like that continue to be asked.

In the text from Numbers, Moses took seventy elders outside of the camp for what sounds like an ordination. For whatever reason, two elders remained in the camp. The spirit came upon the seventy and they prophesied—once but never again. The two who had stayed in the camp and were not "ordained" prophesied anyway. It seems that the gift of prophecy also remained with them. Somehow, it wasn't right! Among the seventy-two theirs are the only names that have come down to us: Eldad and Medad.

Joshua was Moses' right-hand man and successor who finally led the people into the promised land. At this point, however, he wants these two silenced. Not properly ordained or licensed, they could become alternative teachers, a threat to the position of Joshua and Moses. But Moses said:

> "Are you jealous for my sake? Would that all the Lord's people were prophets, and that the Lord would put his spirit on them!"

In the gospel there are also some unlikely prophets, evangelists and exorcists. They seem out of control. They are speaking and operating without permission. Jesus' response to the situation is to go beyond the issue of control. He may even be referring to his own lack of "credentials," and to the inevitability of the cross which, as far as any political or religious system goes, would remove any credentials that anyone may have thought he had. The "scandal" to which he points is that anyone would even consider denying the working of this spirit in his ministry for the benefit of "little ones" who believe.

> John said to him, "Teacher, we saw someone casting out demons in your name, and we tried to stop him, because he was not following us."

Imagine. There are people casting out demons. Clearly something good is happening here: demons could have been just about anything from genuine possession to some kind of personal or psychological disorder. It doesn't matter. People were being liberated. What's the problem?

The problem: it's out of control. The spirit is out of control. For Jesus, like Moses before him, it's not a problem. Control is not the issue. If it's really God's spirit, it will be beyond our human control anyway. The question isn't the licensing or control of the spirit, but watching for it and letting it speak wherever it is found.

When I was pastor in Kanata I used to visit Mrs. Dickie every month for five years, so I got to know her pretty well. Some of you may, in fact, know her. She drove a taxi in Ottawa for 35 or 40 years.

Her stand was on Albert Street right across from the Colonial Bus Terminal, which no longer exists. I'm not sure that we can imagine a woman driving taxi in the 1930s and 40s, but she was trying to support herself, her children and her invalid husband, who owned the business. She had wonderful stories to tell about everyone from Prime Minister MacKenzie King to anyone else she may have met in her travels. Sometimes crudely told, and peppered with swear words in both official languages, they were always lively and interesting.

Mrs. Dickie was a person of deep faith and prayer. When I visited her, she had a prayerbook: a little black book that she read from beginning to end every day. The pages were brown and starting to break. Crippled up as she was, totally dependent on her family for even her most basic needs, she had a wonderful perspective on life. When I think of unlikely people prophesying, I think of her. It's true that I was the ordained one, the licensed one, but I'm sure that over the years she gave more to me than I gave to her. She witnessed faith more effectively to me than I did to her.

A couple of weeks ago I was visiting one of our parishioners at the Queensway-Carleton Hospital. I stopped by the pastoral care office to take a look at the list of patients, just in case there was someone else I knew there. Mrs. Dickie's name was on the list. She had been admitted to the long-term care unit. She had declined a lot. She didn't know me, and when I started talking about her family, she didn't seem to know who I was talking about, but before long she launched into one of her stories. I asked her where her prayer book was, but she didn't remember she had one. I offered a few prayers with her, and at the end she said, "Amen. Amen. Amen. That's how I pray, Mister. Amen. Amen. Amen. Is that okay with you?"

Of course it was okay. She, the unlikely, unordained, unlicensed prophet was back to the basics in her faith and prayer. The word "Amen" means "It's okay." It means "So be it." I'm fine with what is. I'm at rest. It's what a baby would say nestled contentedly at her mother's breast. It's the most basic prayer we have, a prayer of trust, even abandonment, to God's love and care. The word had special meaning coming from Mrs. Dickie. She died shortly after my visit. I have a feeling "Amen" was her last word.

Joshua and John's questions about who's who and what's what are not the important questions about prophecy, faith and prayer. The real signs are not in your pedigree or your ordination certificate, but in the prophetic, prayerful and faithful ways in which people live their lives— giving cups of cold water to others, caring for "little ones," and watching their life carefully, really minding their own business—the hands and the eyes that may cause you to stumble. That's where the "spirit" will be found—inside and outside the camp.

That's Not Funny!

Twenty-seventh Sunday in Ordinary Time

Genesis 2.7-8, 18-24
Psalm 128
Hebrews 2.9-11
Mark 10.2-16

Wives, be subject to your husbands as you are to the Lord. For the husband is head of the wife just as Christ is the head of the church, the body of which he is the Saviour. Just as the church is subject to Christ, so also wives ought to be, in everything, to their husbands. Husbands, love your wives, just as Christ loved the church and gave himself up for her, in order to make her holy by cleansing her with the washing of water by the word, so as to present the church to himself in splendour, without a spot or wrinkle or anything of the kind—yes, so that she may be holy and without blemish. In the same way, husbands should love their wives as they do their own bodies. He who loves his wife loves himself. For no one ever hates his own body, but he nourishes and tenderly cares for it, just as Christ does for the church, because we are members of his body. "For this reason a man will leave his father and mother and be joined to his wife, and the two will become one flesh." This is a great mystery, and I am applying it to Christ and the church. Each of you, however, should love his wife as himself, and a wife should respect her husband. (Ephesians 5.22-33)

You're probably wondering where I got that reading. It's not a part of today's liturgy, but we did hear this from Mark, who is quoting Genesis:

"From the beginning of creation, 'God made them male and female.' For this reason a man shall leave his father and mother and be joined to his wife, and the two shall become one flesh.'" (Mark 10.6-8)

Jesus quotes this text in his teaching about divorce, and the Letter to the Ephesians quotes it as well in the section I just read.

The text from Ephesians did come up on a weekday not long ago, and a lady stopped me after Mass and asked why readings like that were read in church if they were not going to be explained. What she was really saying is that I should have explained it that morning instead of giving a homily on the gospel. The last time it had been read the priest had commented that "he wouldn't touch that one with a ten-foot pole"—and laughed. She didn't think it was funny. She was right—so here goes.

Texts such as this one and today's text about the rib of Adam and Jesus' absolute prohibition against divorce are not laughing matters. They need to be dealt with and studied. These ancient texts, which emerge from a culture so far removed from ours, need to be examined and reflected on for what they are. Then they must be interpreted for our own time. Let me be bold enough this morning to take a crack at it, however briefly.

The text about husbands and wives in the Letter to the Ephesians addresses the first of three sets of relationships that the author is treating: wives and husbands, children and parents, slaves and masters. In none of the cases does the author tackle the rightness or wrongness of underlying structures—wives, children and slaves as property, for example. He presumes the structure. Why? Probably because from the author's vantage point, the world as he knew it was short-lived. The end of the world was expected during his generation. In addition, he probably didn't have the power or influence to change anything, whatever he might say, write or do. That's hard for us to understand today, believing as we do that religious and spiritual leaders need to take a more prophetic stance. When you look at the text more carefully, however, you see that it calls for a prophetic transformation even though it leaves social structures unchanged.

In each set of relationships, the author works with an A–B structure. There's an A and a B in a wife's relationship with her husband, an

A and a B in a child's relationship with his parents, and an A and a B in a slave's relationship with his master.

In each case, A reflects the culture and calls for obedience. In each case, B moves beyond the culture and completely absorbs obedience into a higher value, a higher experience. "Wives, be submissive to your husbands": that's the A part. "Husbands, love your wives as Christ loves the church" ironically makes the whole notion of submission irrelevant. "Husbands, love your wives as you do your own bodies"—even with maternal categories like nourishing and tenderness—puts submission in a perspective that virtually makes it disappear. It's still in the cultural rule book, but is transcended in the Christian life. Even the language is changed to "respect."

Let's look at the next example: Children, be obedient to your parents. That's the A part, but B: Parents, look your children in the eyes; they're persons. You don't really own them, and if you act as if you do, you'll lose them. *Persons.* In the cultural rule book, children are owned by their parents, but in the Christian life the rules are transcended.

Slaves, be obedient to your masters. That's A, but B: Masters, you better look at this whole thing again, because there is only one master—the Lord in heaven.

The author does not tackle the cultural rule book, but goes over and beyond it. He is in no position to alter the social structures, but he does call believers beyond them. The cultural question of ownership of other human beings is not tackled, but for believers who wait in joyful hope for the final coming of Christ, the categories no longer function; they have become meaningless, transcended in faith.

That it took centuries to abolish slavery and that the rights of women and children are still a work in progress in a culture where Christians have been in power is a whole other issue. Misunderstanding Paul may even have contributed to our delays.

Now let's tackle two of the other thorny issues presented in the scriptures today—the rib business, and divorce.

A medieval Jewish rabbinic tradition looks at the story in a very interesting way. How could Adam have been male? Maleness only makes sense relative to femaleness. "Man" is neuter. In the original, the word "rib" is the whole rib cage, the whole midsection of the person that is divided in half. The "man" is divided in half, and now has a companion.

Now there are two of us, he says. Now we can live. The male is not prior to the female. The two are created together—bone of bone, flesh of flesh.

Jesus' absolute prohibition against divorce arises from a very particular concern. "Moses said" that a man could write a certificate of divorce and dismiss his wife. Moses says nothing about what a woman could do. For a woman to dismiss her husband evolved into a long, complicated and public process, while a man could simply write up a certificate. In Jesus' view, that's not what God had in mind. In affirming the sacredness of the bond, men and women are placed side by side in his teaching—no longer two, but one flesh—and the consequences of divorce are the same for each of them. His teaching affirms the equality of man and woman.

My friend who stopped me after Mass that morning is right. None of this stuff is funny. These ancient texts continue to invite profound reflection on values that go beyond the specifics of their particular cultural framework. It's quite true that they have been used to beat up people—divorced people and gay people, to keep women in their place, and even to condone slavery. They have been misused and abused.

These important texts and others like them are proclaimed to invite serious, even profound, reflection on the mystery of human life, the mystery of human sexuality and the possibility of permanent covenant relationships between men and women that are creative and life-giving, and that somehow reflect the presence of God in the world.

Firmly rooted in the Catholic tradition of biblical study and interpretation, we read these ancient texts with discerning minds and hearts, praying for wisdom.

All Things Are Possible

Twenty-eighth Sunday in Ordinary Time

Wisdom 7.7–11
Psalm 90
Hebrews 4.12–13
Mark 10.17–30

I prayed, and understanding was given me;
I called on God, and the spirit of wisdom came to me.
I preferred her to sceptres and thrones ...
I loved her more than health and beauty,
and I chose to have her rather than light,
because her radiance never ceases.
All good things came to me along with her,
and in her hands uncounted wealth. (Wisdom 7.7–8, 10–11)

Jesus, looking at him, loved him and said, "You lack one thing;
go, sell what you own, and give the money to the poor, and
you will have treasure in heaven; then come, follow me." (Mark
10.21)

The word of God is living and active, sharper than any two-
edged sword, piercing until it divides soul from spirit, joints
from marrow; it is able to judge the thoughts and intentions of
the heart. (Hebrews 4.12)

The strength of the imagery in Hebrews gives us a wonderful
point of departure to look at both the quality of wisdom herself and
Jesus' challenge to the rich man.

The personification of God as living and active, sharp like a sword,
suggests critical thinking, careful discernment. It has to do with right
judgment. It is piercing and discriminating.

At other places in the Bible, the personification of the word of God runs swiftly (Psalm 147). At other times, wisdom arrives quietly and simply as an answer to prayer, and rests, radiant in her beauty (Wisdom 7). But listen to this. It's more like what Hebrews is describing:

> While gentle silence enveloped all things,
> and night in its swift course was now half gone,
> your all-powerful word leaped from heaven,
> from the royal throne,
> into the midst of the land that was doomed,
> a stern warrior
> carrying the sharp sword of your authentic command,
> and stood and filled all things with death,
> and touched heaven while standing on the earth.
> (Wisdom 18.14–16)

That's the image at work here. There's no rushing about, or abiding in radiant beauty, but instead, leaping and cutting.

In Mark's typical fashion, the story of Jesus and the rich man stands as a kind of mirror. We can see ourselves and our own lives reflected there. The man's religious heritage, his prosperity, his sincerity, his demeanor, his politeness are all admirable qualities. He could be virtually any of the gentlemen here in our own church today.

Watch what he does. He runs to Jesus and kneels at his feet. He poses his question, clearly eager for the answer.

> "Good Teacher, what must I do to inherit eternal life?"

When Jesus responds by referring to the commandments, the rich man replies that he's been keeping them since his youth. Don't you think that most of us could reply in the same way? There's nothing arrogant about that. Of course, we're not perfect, but all in all we're a pretty decent lot. This guy, too, is a pretty decent sort. In no way does Jesus question his sincerity or integrity. Instead,

> Jesus, looking at him, loved him and said, "You lack one thing; go, sell what you own, and give the money to the poor, and you will have treasure in heaven; then come, follow me." When

the man heard this, he was shocked and went away grieving,
for he had many possessions. (Mark 10.21–22)

The Bible and its ethical demands are usually rather reasonable.
They are responsible and balanced. Honour your parents; don't lie,
cheat or steal. Fine. Do unto others as you would have them do unto
you. That sounds fine, too.

In a couple of weeks we'll meet another man, a scribe. He'll be
asking about the "greatest commandment." As is the case this Sunday,
Jesus will receive him and his question with respect. The twofold commandment of love that will be Jesus' answer is challenging, to be sure,
but the scribe will be able to accept and affirm its wisdom, even its
balance and inner logic. Jesus' answer will be quite acceptable to him.

There's something else going on today. This grouping of texts moves
us beyond "acceptable" ethical challenges to complete surrender. Ordinary human ways of doing things, ordinary securities and props, will
need to be put aside. The response to God envisioned here moves
drastically beyond any notion of balance or conventional morality.

After the man in question has gone away shocked and grieving,
even Jesus admits that the project of salvation is "impossible" apart
from God's own action. It's interesting that he won't even allow himself to be called "good." "No one is good but God alone." It's troubling.

Over the centuries, others have proposed that the "one thing lack-
ing" is freedom from "stuff." Henry David Thoreau was one of them.
This nineteenth-century writer and philosopher was a great propo-
nent of simplification. He simplified his own life by building a cabin in
the woods near Walden Pond in Concord, Massachusetts, where he
lived for two years observing, studying, thinking and writing. He refused even the gift of a mat for his door when he realized that he'd
have to shake it out from time to time. Why not use the grass outside?
It's free and there need be no extra expenditure of money, time or
energy.

Here are a few of his more famous quotes:

Beware of all enterprises that require new clothes.

Many go fishing all their lives without knowing that it is not fish they are after.

Most of the luxuries and many of the so-called comforts of life are not only not indispensable, but positive hindrances to the elevation of mankind.

From his cabin in Walden, Thoreau wrote of the pleasures of withdrawing for a time from mainstream society. While at the cabin he sought to be free of the hurry and anxiety of those who were, in his words, "employed as it says in an old book, laying up treasures which moth and rust will corrupt and thieves break in and steal."

Why should we be in such desperate haste to succeed, and in such desperate enterprises? If a man does not keep pace with his companions, perhaps it is because he hears a different drummer.

The story of Jesus' encounter with the rich man invites us to consider a different drumbeat for ourselves, or at least to recognize that we can't be too sure of our own rhythms and priorities. We can't write off Jesus, or Thoreau for that matter, as marginal sorts—gadflies, people who have nothing better to do than poke around at the edges of things with all their idealistic thinking. They don't have wives and families, jobs and responsibilities. It's easy for them.

John Paul II chose to begin his encyclical on Christian morality with an extended meditation on this encounter of Jesus with the rich man. We're not to take it as an isolated event safely lodged back there in Jesus' ministry that involves just one person. That Mark has Jesus look around and say to his disciples, "How hard it will be for those who have wealth to enter the kingdom of God!" is a typical device that he uses to universalize what went before.

I like to picture Jesus "looking around" even today, looking around in the midst of our own assembly, at each one of us with our own unique history and complex psychological and spiritual makeup, looking deeply into our hearts. We can well imagine him saying as he looks around: "How hard it is to enter the kingdom of God." We can also imagine ourselves saying to one another as the first disciples did, "Then who can be saved?" But Jesus overhears our whispering and declares: "For mortals it is impossible, but not for God; for God all things are possible."

> The word of God is living and active, sharper than any two-edged sword, piercing until it divides soul from spirit, joints from marrow; it is able to judge the thoughts and intentions of the heart.

The living and active word of God is the person of Jesus himself. As we encounter him again in this liturgy, let us know that his presence is not just imaginary. Let us allow his presence, both challenging and reassuring, to sink deeply into our being and judge the thoughts and intentions of our hearts.

Redemptive Suffering

Twenty-ninth Sunday in Ordinary Time

Isaiah 53.4, 10-11
Psalm 33
Hebrews 4.14-16
Mark 10.35-45

The servant of the Lord has borne our infirmities
and carried our diseases …
It was the will of the Lord to crush him with pain …
through him the will of the Lord shall prosper …
The righteous one, my servant,
shall make many righteous,
and he shall bear their iniquities. (Isaiah 53.4, 10, 11)

"The Son of Man came not to be served but to serve, and to give his life as a ransom for many." (Mark 10.45)

Statements such as these arise often and are very difficult for us to understand. What kind of God would demand such pain, the suffering of the innocent to pay for the sins of the guilty? It's not easy for us to get our heads around the mystery of our redemption in Christ, our being bought back by his blood. In fact, we don't like a God who would make such demands until we start thinking about our own experience as human beings and how we are saved, how we are redeemed, how we are graced.

I watched parts of the funeral of the Haitian justice minister who had killed in cold blood. The memorial Mass was broadcast from the cathedral in Port au Prince. There was high energy in that place. It was clear that this man's death was an energizing and purifying power for renewal in the community.

Think, too, of the dignity of Nelson Mandela, jailed for so many years. One wonders whether the history of South Africa would have unfolded as it did without his suffering. An imprisoned Mandela haunted the world in ways that free men and women could not.

Have you ever gotten up with a kind of "funk" in your heart—depressed, discouraged, frustrated for no reason? You're just going around with this—and then you see a crippled man laughing and you feel stupid, cheap. I can't tell you how often patients whom I've visited in the hospital talk about the liberating power of other people's suffering. Just last week I was talking to a lady who was recovering from surgery and thought that it was taking "forever." She was walking a little bit in the hall and saw somebody in far worse shape who was in a better mood than she was. In a sense she was liberated by suffering well-borne in another.

Perhaps these examples help us understand how the innocent suffering of Christ, the Servant of God, can call us beyond ourselves, can be personally and spiritually redemptive for us by calling us beyond our crazy little funks—and even our sin, selfishness and pride—to fullness of life.

Father John Catoir, author of the Christopher News Notes, once told the story of a time when he was preaching a homily at St. Patrick's Cathedral in New York. It was the feast of a martyr and the theme of his homily was how Christians are invited to share in the sufferings of Christ and how the sacrifice of Christ can be renewed in real life. His homily was disrupted by the entrance of a feeble old man and two people who were helping him get seated near the front of the cathedral. As the liturgy progressed, Father Catoir noticed the strength and dignity in the old man's face, and at the sign of peace made it a point to go down into the assembly and offer him the peace of Christ.

When he went back into the main aisle again to offer him communion, the man didn't respond with the usual "Amen," but thanked Fr. Catoir three times.

At the end of mass, the priest greeted the old man as he left the church. Noticing that he was wearing a clerical shirt but no white collar, he asked him if he was a priest. "No," said the man, "I am a Lutheran pastor." It turned out that the man had been in a concentration camp in Eastern Europe for fourteen years. His name was Richard

Wermbrandt, and he was the author of the book *Tortured for Christ,* which has sold more than three million copies. A week later, Catoir received a signed copy of Wermbrandt's book. It bore this inscription: "Christians, each one has the same mission as Jesus the Lord, to suffer in their own bodies so that others might live."

Upon further reflection, Catoir believed that it was the Lord himself who sent Wermbrandt to him in St. Patrick's Cathedral on that martyr's feast day—yes, to worship, and even unexpectedly to receive holy communion at his hands, but even more to draw the priest himself into communion with the sacrifice of Christ still being lived out and renewed in the life of his unexpected visitor. Wermbrandt was a living homily.

It's a wonderful story of how the real-life sufferings of another person unexpectedly drew this good priest into deeper communion with the crucified Christ. Father Catoir believed himself "graced."

> This is the cup of my blood, the blood of the new and eternal covenant. It will be shed for you and for all so that sins may be forgiven.

If we have eyes to see, we'll be able to discover reflections of Jesus' sacrificial redemptive death all around us. We'll even have our own turn to reflect it to others—to be ongoing instruments of redemption through him, with him and in him, in the unity of the Holy Spirit, for the glory of God.

Son of Honour

Thirtieth Sunday in Ordinary Time

Jeremiah 31.7-9
Psalm 126
Hebrews 5.1-6
Mark 10.46-52

"See, I am going to bring them from the land of the north, and gather them from the farthest parts of the earth, among them those who are blind and those who are lame, those with child and those in labour, together; a great company, they shall return here." (Jeremiah 31.8)

Jesus said to him, "What do you want me to do for you?" The blind man said to him, "My teacher, let me see again." Jesus said to him, "Go; your faith has made you well." Immediately the man regained his sight and followed Jesus on the way. (Mark 10.51-52)

Look, see what I am doing. Don't you get it? Can't you see? Don't you understand? Open your eyes!

They're nearing Jerusalem at this point in the gospel drama. Although he has predicted his passion three times, Jesus seems to be the only one who has his bearings, who knows where he is going. The twelve affirm that he is the Christ, but don't understand what that means, They move forward only hesitatingly. The Pharisees and the scribes are critical, disturbed and threatened. The crowds, well, they're just curious—a part of the parade. The walk, the parade, the procession is interrupted.

"Jesus, Son of David, have mercy on me!"

The cry comes from a blind beggar sitting along the roadside. Some in the crowd try to silence him. Remember how they tried to stop the Syrophoenician woman? She, too, refused to be silenced. Jesus responds to his cries; he stops and calls him. This is more than a healing. It's a vocation story.

So throwing off his cloak, he sprang up … and *followed* Jesus.

As a beggar, he probably spread out his cloak, onto which generous people tossed their offerings. Like Peter, Andrew, James and John nine chapters earlier, this blind beggar left his profession behind. As they left their boats, so he left his cloak, springing up into something new.

The social and economic dimensions of the story are heightened by its placement after the story of the rich man. Ironically, the one who has nothing finds it easier to leave behind even the nothing he had than the rich man his many possessions. Though sincere, respectable and religious, the latter could not break with his many possessions. He resisted Jesus' call and wound up a regretful, grieving non-disciple. In contrast the beggar abandoned his one possession and gladly responded to his new vocation in life. The adage that "the first will be last and the last first" is already coming true.

Another fascinating detail in the story is the man's name: Bartimaeus, meaning *Son of Honour*. The leper, the paralyzed man coming through the roof, the Syrophoenician woman, the daughter of Jairus: all are nameless. The "son of honour" acclaims the "son of David" as he approaches the holy city to fulfill his royal destiny. Even in the darkness of his poverty, the blind beggar sees more and has more than anyone else on the scene. Gifted with sight, he follows Jesus on "the way," which is the oldest Christian word to describe the following of Christ, who, in John's gospel calls himself the "way, the truth, and the life."

I was biking around Washington, D.C., once during cherry blossom time. The blossoms were past their peak and an early morning breeze was blowing, sending the pink petals swirling through the air and covering the bike path like snow. People were slowing down along the parkway to watch—everybody, that is, except the park attendant. Armed with broom and dustpan he was frantically trying to sweep up the petals as they floated down. The expression on his face was such that I was sure he saw nothing of the delicate beauty of those petals, only litter. He missed the moment.

A blind man was invited to attend a friend's wedding. The couple was being married in a village church that was well-known for its picturesque qualities and beautiful grounds. So many commented about all of it at the reception and again when the photos came back. "But didn't they hear the bell?" the man thought to himself. For him, the bell that pealed to welcome the bride and celebrate the marriage had been magnificent. The air was filled with its vibrating jubilation. Even the ground seemed to tremble at its song. Not used to the sound of a bell, he was amazed at the atmosphere of joy and solemnity that it created for this occasion. Everyone else seemed to have missed that part of the ceremony.

I give these two examples just to indicate once more that what is really important in Mark's telling of miracle stories is their spiritual foundation and universal applicability. They call us to consider levels of sight, hearing and movement beyond the physical.

In this case, where do we need greater depth perception or spiritual insight? Do we really want that kind of knowledge and insight, or are we happy with the way things are for us? After all, what you don't know can't disturb you. Sometimes insight can be disturbing. Would recognizing ourselves as blind beggars and admitting that reality in our lives make us "children of honour"? Would that give us courage to spring to our feet in a leap of faith, leaving the old wrappings behind? Even in his darkness, Bartimaeus knew where he needed to be going. He knew what he was looking for. He got right what others missed. He heard the call, sprang to his feet, and was on the road with Jesus.

Our prayer for the week might well be that which opened our celebration today:

Almighty God, Father of our Lord Jesus Christ, faith in your word is the way to wisdom, and to ponder your divine plan is to grow in the truth.

Open our eyes to your deeds, our ears to the sound of your call, so that our every act may increase our sharing in the life you have offered us.

Hear, O Israel

Thirty-first Sunday in Ordinary Time

Deuteronomy 6.2-6
Psalm 18
Hebrews 17.23-28
Mark 12.28-34

"You are not far from the kingdom of God." (Mark 12.34)

From the very beginning, this scribe was open and interested. Jesus seemed to notice and respect that. He wasn't like some of the others. He hadn't been sent by anyone to trip up Jesus, nor was there anything fishy about his question.

At this point he and his companions were involved in a spirited conversation with Jesus; he was going to ask the question that might just cut right through to the heart of the matter: "Which commandment is first of all?"

Six hundred and thirteen prescriptions were tied with and related to the traditional Ten Commandments. Some were demanding; others were less so. Sorting through and applying them wasn't always easy. Among other things they dealt with such matters as worship, diet, personal and communal hygiene, family life, divorce, property rights, and dealings with foreigners or immigrants.

In our culture and legal system we'd think 613 regulations were nothing at all. Imagine how many laws and sub-laws and by-laws regulate so much of what we do. If this conversation were going on today, such "scribes" might well be discussing welfare reform, health care, education or immigration policy. They could be discussing the legalization of marijuana for medical purposes, or a new juvenile crime bill. Whatever the topic, the discussion was hot and heavy, and Jesus seems to have been in the thick of it.

"Which commandment is the first of all?" the scribe asked him. Jesus answered, "The first is, 'Hear, O Israel: The Lord our God, the Lord is one; you shall love the Lord your God with all your heart, and with all your soul, and with all your mind, and with all your strength.' The second is this, 'You shall love your neighbour as yourself.'" (Mark 12.28b–31a)

The scribe's preoccupation was a good one. It wasn't that he was looking simply for the most important among many prescriptions of law or commandments; he was looking for a unifying principle. As a religious man, he was looking for foundational material that could both support and help to sift all of this complexity. Jesus' answer was just what he was looking for.

Jesus' answer lies not in specific details, but in underlying foundations—an underlying attitude, conviction, passion or commitment. Jesus' answer reaches to the level of the spirit, the level of the soul—the deepest part of a person's being. Only there can a unifying principle for morality and law be found.

The commandment "Hear, O Israel" is itself a key element of this soul foundation. Deuteronomy's command to *hear* is not just about hearing with your ears; it's about hearing with your whole being, being fully and completely attentive, on the edge of your seat with anticipation for what will be said.

I'm sure you remember the potentially disastrous coal-mine accident in Pennsylvania last summer. All nine miners who were trapped in that wet darkness got out alive. One of them had a sister in Chicago who was nervously awaiting news of her trapped brother. She couldn't sleep. Her stomach was upset. She was shivering. She had diarrhea. The miners were down there for 72 hours. Finally the phone rang. He was out! They were all out; all nine of them were out. He was okay—they all were okay. She shuddered and broke down crying.

That's what listening is all about, a kind of passionate attentiveness to and alertness for a word that will affect the whole heart, soul, mind and strength. Throughout those 72 hours, she was listening, really listening. The first part of the commandment involves getting into that kind of posture, having that kind of readiness to hear the word of God.

Such listening and the subsequent commitment to love God and neighbour come out of the depths of the whole person: the heart, which is the seat of will and intellect; the soul, which is the life principle itself; and strength, which is the seat of action, energy and commitment. It is the whole person, on the edge of the seat, alert and attentive, ready to move. That kind of posture is foundational for good ethical judgments. People can sometimes surprise us with their "gut sense" of morality that really does arise from their personal foundations.

The moment was a tense one. Rosalie Elliott had made it to the fourth round of a national spelling contest in Washington. The 11-year-old from South Carolina had been asked to spell the word *avowal*. In her soft southern accent she spelled the word, but the judges were not able to determine if she had used an *a* or an *e* as the next-to-last letter. They discussed the issue among themselves for several minutes as they listened to playbacks of the tape recording. The crucial letter was too accent-blurred to be deciphered. Finally the chief judge put the question to the only person who knew the answer. "Was the letter an *a* or an *e*?" he asked Rosalie. By this time, surrounded by whispering young spellers, she knew the correct spelling of the word, but without hesitation, she replied that she had misspelled the word and walked from the stage. The entire audience stood and applauded, as did some 50 reporters. The moment was a proud one for her and her parents. "I knew in my heart what I had said, and so did God," was what she said to her mother later. She was responding in the realm of foundations such as those represented by the "greatest of the commandments."

I remember reading somewhere about Jewish prisoners in the Nazi period reciting or chanting this prayer even as they were being led to death: Hear—Know—Love—with your whole heart, soul and strength. Let God be the passion in your bones.

> I love you, O Lord, my strength.
> The Lord is my rock, my fortress, and my deliverer.
> My God, my rock in whom I take refuge,
> my shield, and the source of my salvation, my stronghold.
> (Psalm 18)

In Mark's gospel, Jesus adds a phrase to the traditional prayer "Hear, O Israel": "and with all your mind."

"'Hear, O Israel: The Lord our God, the Lord is one; you shall love the Lord your God with all your heart, and with all your soul, *and with all your mind,* and with all your strength.'"

"With all your mind" is not in the original from Deuteronomy, but is added in Mark. Although implied in the "heart," Jesus adds specific reference to curiosity and questioning in his answer.

I find it troubling, even a bit sad, that among some people who believe themselves to be faithful Catholics, there's a mistrust and suspicion of biblical scholars and theologians, as if their questioning and critical work makes them suspect, perhaps even disloyal to the tradition that they take seriously enough to probe and question.

The second commandment stands side by side with the first.

"Love your neighbour as yourself."

It, too, deserves to be probed and questioned. Notice that it's not "Treat your neighbour fairly." It's not even "Do unto others as you would have them do unto you." It's not primarily about activity, but about what is prior to activity—conviction, decision and commitment. The commandment invites believers to deal with their neighbour's well-being in the depths of their souls in the same way that they are dealing with their own well-being; to long for their neighbour's good from within their hearts just as they long for their own.

As always in Mark's gospel, this story is a mirror in which we are invited to see ourselves, ask our own questions—good questions, deep questions—and find our answers in Jesus.

"You are right, Teacher; you have truly said that 'he is one, and beside him there is no other'; and 'to love him with all the heart, and with all the understanding, and with all the strength,' and 'to love one's neighbour as oneself,'—this is much more important than all whole burnt offerings and sacrifices."

When Jesus saw that the scribe answered wisely, he said to him, "You are not far from the kingdom of God." (Mark 12.32-34)

Not far! What's left in going the whole distance is the ongoing fulfillment of what he has heard—a lifelong process for him and for all of us. Hear, O Israel. Live on the edge of your seat.

The Widow's Mite

Thirty-second Sunday in Ordinary Time

1 Kings 17.10–16
Psalm 146
Hebrews 9.24–28
Mark 12.38–44

Elijah asked: "Bring me a little water … [and] a morsel of bread."

The woman replied:"As the Lord your God lives, I have nothing baked, only a handful of meal in a jar, and a little oil …"

Elijah said to her:"Do not be afraid." (1 Kings 17.10–13)

"Beware of the scribes," Jesus said. "They devour widows' houses …"

Jesus sat down opposite the treasury … Many rich people put in large sums. A poor widow came and put in two small copper coins … all she had to live on. (Mark 12.38–44)

Many of us live in a context in which we are constantly being asked to give: church, United Way, Red Cross, disaster relief funds, Christmas Exchange. Those of us who live in cities are also very likely to encounter people on the streets looking for handouts. Many of us even budget for these gifts; we count them among our planned and foreseen "expenses." In all of this, most of us feel that we give what can, and try to be discriminating and reasonable in doing so.

The widow in the gospel story presents a very different picture. She doesn't find ways to fit her charitable giving into her budget. She gives it all. The money deposited in the temple treasury was not for the poor, but for the upkeep of the temple and its worship. It was preached about and solicited as an offering made directly to God. She responded wholeheartedly to what she was taught. She gave all she had to live on. In all giving, it is the gift of self that matters, and if this is the point of the widow's mite story in Mark, it is made very well!

If this is the content and intention of Jesus' teaching, it could even be supported by close parallels in the teaching of other rabbis, such as the following:

> Once a woman brought a handful of fine flour [for a meal offering—Leviticus 11.2], and the priest despised her, saying: "See what she offers! What is there in this to eat? What is there in this to offer up?" It was shown him in a dream: "Do not despise her! It is regarded by God as if she sacrificed her own life." (Leviticus Rabbab, iii, 5)[39]

Another wonderful tradition supports this line of reasoning and interpretation quite well. Since the Romans destroyed the temple in 70 CE, all that remains is the Western Wall, sometimes called the Wailing Wall, which supported the huge platform on which the temple was built. The tradition says that when the temple was being built, Herod financed one supporting wall. The priestly caste financed another wall; the legal or teaching class financed the third wall. The last wall was financed with the gifts of the poor. It was the Western Wall. When the Romans came in to devour the temple, all that remained was the Western Wall. The spirit of God left the holy of holies to reside in the wall of the poor.

There's also a story told about a church in England that owns a very unusual chalice—unusual because mounted in its base are four pennies and a halfpenny. At four years of age, a little boy lay dying, but before he said his last goodbyes, he asked for his small bank and gave it to his father for God. When his father opened the bank, he found the five coins; it was his father who had the chalice made.

All these examples point to the nobility of sacrificial offering, especially from the poor, but is this actually the point of the widow's mite story? If this kind of noble sacrificial generosity is the point of the story, then I guess we should all feel a little guilty. We just don't give that way. The story does contrast people who give out of their abundance with the woman who gives out of her poverty—she gives all she has to live on. Contrasting "out of abundance" and "out of poverty," she would appear to have the moral high ground. Her gift could even be spiritualized as an act of trust, abandonment to providence, deep surrender to God—even a foreshadowing of Jesus' own gift of self on the cross.

All of these interpretations, while possible, are not probable in the story's context. The positioning of the story between Jesus' rebuke of the scribes who *devour the houses of widows*, and the prediction of the *temple's ultimate doom* suggests that Mark's intention is not to have his readers admire the woman and feel guilty about their own paltry generosity. His intention instead is to stir up anger and disgust at the system that manipulated, even brainwashed, her into thinking that such a gift was appropriate and praiseworthy.

The word *devour* is a good translation from the Greek original. It's used of the wild animals who attack and devour their prey. Is the fact that the woman feels she can and should make such an offering an example or a case of the scribes devouring people by teaching them that such a gift would be expected? Should she not have been stopped from making such an offering? Could some of the temple's resources have been rechannelled to serve her and those like her?

Jesus was sitting in one of the two outer courts of the temple, the Court of Women, where thirteen trumpet-shaped collection boxes were placed to receive the offerings of worshippers. The woman in question deposited two *lepta*, the smallest coin in circulation. It was one-third of an *as*, which was one-tenth of a *denarius*, which would have been a fair day's wage. These two *lepta* were all she had to live on. Should she be commended for her generosity, or is there something wrong with a system which would even suggest that she should sink her livelihood into one of those trumpets?

We don't know what Jesus' body language or tone of voice might have been as he watched and commented. If we take the poor widow's story apart from what comes before and after, we might think he was speaking in glowing terms about her generosity. When we see it in the context of his condemnation of the official teachers and leaders of the temple who devour widows' houses, another interpretation suggests itself—especially when we read what follows:

> As he came out of the temple, one of the disciples said to him, "Look, Teacher, what large stones and what large buildings!"

Then Jesus asked him, "Do you see these great buildings? Not one stone will be left here upon another; all will be thrown down." (Mark 13.1-2)

In this context, is not the widow's mite story really a condemnation of the scribes' lack of humanity, which would allow her to be duped by a system that would have her support a temple that is doomed in any case—and with her whole livelihood?[40]

The pairing of the widow's mite story with the story of Elijah and the widow is particularly interesting.

She went and did as Elijah said, so that she as well as he and her household ate for many days. The jar of meal was not emptied, neither did the jug of oil fail, according to the word of the Lord that he spoke by Elijah. (1 Kings 17.15-16)

In the Book of Kings, far from devouring the widow's resources, Elijah the prophet leaves her with more than she had when he arrived. His word to her reflects what will evolve into a rich prophetic tradition, always on the side of the poor. Today's psalm reflects that rich tradition beautifully.

It is the Lord who keeps faith forever,
who executes justice for the oppressed;
who give food to the hungry.
The Lord sets the prisoners free.

The Lord opens the eyes of the blind
and lifts up those who are bowed down:
The Lord loves the righteous
and watches over the strangers.

The Lord upholds the orphan and the widow,
but the way of the wicked he brings to ruin,
The Lord will reign forever,
your God, O Zion, for all generations.

It is this same prophetic tradition in which Jesus stands, and which colours his words and deeds throughout the gospel.

Get out of the Groove

Thirty-third Sunday in Ordinary Time

Daniel 12.1–3
Psalm 16
Hebrews 10.11–14, 18
Mark 13.24–32

"Heaven and earth will pass away, but my words will not pass away." (Mark 13.31)

Imagine it—Jesus looking from the Mount of Olives across the valley to what must have been a magnificent sight: the temple standing in all its splendour, the meeting place of the culture, history and faith of his people. For all of its magnificence, it was vulnerable. As is possible with all civilizations and cultures, fatal flaws can develop by which they can rot from within. It's true as well that strong, hostile forces can attack from without. Looking out over the temple, Jesus seems to be sensing that, in its case, both factors are at work. Jesus clearly does not have a very high opinion of the temple leadership—and is very aware of the power of Rome. For all of its magnificence, the temple stands on shaky ground, as do the religious and cultural structures that it represents. The world of the temple was coming to an end.

Jesus invites his hearers to take the long view with him—to look beyond the temple, the city, even the heavens and the earth, as they knew them. He points to the sun and the moon and the stars being shaken. He speaks of a final judgment, not so much as a threat, but as a vindication of all righteous people. "After the suffering" they will see "'the Son of Man coming in clouds' with great power and glory. Then he will send out the angels, and gather his elect from the four winds, from the ends of the earth to the ends of heaven." (Mark 13.26–27) Jesus invites his hearers into a vision that goes beyond structures and civilizations, beyond the worlds that they know and seem able to control, beyond even the magnificence of what they see and can imagine.

The significance of this passage for Mark's gospel cannot be overstated. Located just prior to the passion narrative, it heralds what is to come. From this same vantage point of the Mount of Olives, he himself would suffer his agony of discernment, where he would have to definitively embrace the end of his own "world." The same view would be out there before him "on the night before he died," "on the night he was betrayed."

Jesus' admonition to watch and be alert is particularly poignant as he enters into this last stage of his ministry. Now his constant, alert watching will lead him to the cross, which, for all its pain, will be his ultimate triumph.

> They went to a place called Gethsemane [on the Mount of Olives] … He took with him Peter and James and John, and began to be distressed and agitated. And he said to them, "I am deeply grieved, even to death; remain here, and keep awake." And going a little farther, he threw himself on the ground and prayed that, if it were possible, the hour might pass from him. He said, "Abba, Father, for you all things are possible; remove this cup from me; yet, not what I want, but what you want." He came and found them sleeping; and he said to Peter, "Simon, are you asleep? Could you not keep awake one hour? Keep awake and pray that you may not come into the time of trial; the spirit indeed is willing, but the flesh is weak." (Mark 14.32-38)

On both occasions, Jesus is inviting his disciples to join him in genuine discernment, however painful, of what matters and what does not, of what will last and what will not, of the inevitable end of many worlds.

In the texts themselves we can see various layers of world-endings: his own death, the destruction of the temple, the final consummation of the world as we know it. In our own lives, too, we need to be discerning and watchful for the endings of our own worlds. We can be mindful of the reality of death, of the bankruptcy of Enron or WorldCom, of the horror of September 11—the "worlds" in which people live can pass away in so many ways. It's important for all of us to heed Jesus' invitation to look out over the valley with clear eyes, to "watch and pray."

It's too easy for us to get stuck in a groove. I hit on a televised science program one evening in which a biologist was describing his experiment with what he called "processional caterpillars." He had lined them up on the rim of a pot holding a tasty plant so that the lead caterpillar was head-to-tail with the last caterpillar, leaving no break in the parade. The tiny creatures walked around the rim of the pot for a full week before all of them died from exhaustion and starvation. Not once did any of the caterpillars break out of the line and venture over to eat the plant. Food was only inches away, but the follow-the-leader instinct was even stronger than the drive to eat and survive.

It's too easy for us humans to become processional caterpillars, almost mindlessly going around in our own daily circles, presuming that this is the way it is and the way it should be. Being in the groove may not be the place to be. Being in the groove might mean being in a rut. Clarity of vision—wisdom—discernment—prayer. The importance of these values is clear, isn't it? Especially when we take Jesus' advice and look around with one eye and look within with the other.

An article covering the resignation of Bill Galston as a domestic policy advisor to President Clinton ran in the *Baltimore Sun* a few years ago. He announced plans to return to his teaching career at the University of Maryland—"to strike a new balance" in his life. He had been living a very productive life, but had to make changes to his own "big picture." He had had a hand in the formation of the National Campaign Against Teen Pregnancy, and was working on education reform and promoting new legislation to strengthen Head Start programs. He tried hard to make time for his own son, Ezra, and even brought him to his White House office in the evening. Still, he was hounded by the fact that, more often than not, he came home too tired to really enjoy being there. There was a contradiction between his "Putting Children First" theme and policy initiatives, and his own relationship with his son. What finally brought his world to an end was a note from his son: "Baseball's not fun when there's no one there to applaud you."

Typical of Mark's whole approach, this theme of watchfulness in chapter 13, and in the passion account as well, is directed to and includes us all. We live in God's time, under God's reign, and are invited to see and understand our lives accordingly—in communion with Jesus who has gone before us and goes before us for all time.

"Truly I tell you, this generation will not pass away until all these things have taken place." (Mark 13.30)

In some sense, every person in every generation experiences the end of the world and the last things. The issues that Jesus raises are truly perennial. His questions need to become our questions; his way of discernment needs to become our own. What will last and what won't? What's worthwhile and what's not? These are timeless, ageless questions that call for real vigilance and prayer, struggle and sacrifice.

"Heaven and earth will pass away, but my words will not pass away."

Kingdom of God or Utopia?

Christ the King

Daniel 7.13-14
Psalm 93
Revelation 1.5-8
John 18.33b-37

"My kingdom is not from this world. If my kingdom were from this world, my followers would be fighting ... You say that I am a king. For this I was born, and for this I came into the world, to testify to the truth. Everyone who belongs to the truth listens to my voice." (John 18.36-37)

He will come again in glory to judge the living and the dead, and his kingdom will have no end. (Nicene Creed)

The language of kingdom-building is often heard among Christians. Fashioning the kingdom of God right here and now, making "heaven on earth," is an exciting and wonderful project, but is that really what the scriptures are asking of us? Jesus himself announces the kingdom, and points it out. His miracles and signs are breakthrough moments for the kingdom to manifest itself. Jesus teaches his disciples to pray for the kingdom, but does he build it or invite others to take on kingdom building?

Dreaming about and working to build a utopia is the stuff of idealists; it has never succeeded. What is the real Christian hope? What is the real Christian mission? Clearly it's not enough to sit on our hands and wait for the kingdom to descend from on high—but can we build it?

In all four gospels, Jesus uses language and images that have political and social overtones. There's a city built on a hill, a house built on strong foundations, competing armies. Believers and non-believers alike marvel at his works of power.

The word "power" conjures up an almost endless array of images: military armaments, economic influence, personal charisma, hydroelectric plants, freakish events of nature. For those outside the circles of power, moving inside seems the key to success and happiness, even the key to making the world a better place. Politicians and social reformers, even highly idealistic religious leaders like St. Francis of Assisi, exercised political and social power, and in doing so experienced its limits.

The scene from Jesus' trial before Pilate turns any ordinary understanding of power or use of power on its head. There is perhaps more dramatic irony at work in this story than anywhere else in the New Testament. Pilate, who thinks he has power, in fact has none. The power that he seems to have (to put Jesus to death) is politically the only expedient thing to do. Pilate is powerless and knows it. Jesus, who appears utterly powerless, is strangely powerful in his nobility; he seems to understand where real power comes from and what it means. His power transcends political status and social influence; his kingdom is "not of this world."

The story itself is structured around the physical movements of Pilate in and out of his headquarters. The Passover was so near that the religious authorities couldn't come inside without ritual defilement; their piety is contrasted with their scheming to bring the Word-made-flesh, the Messiah, the King of Israel, to his ultimate end as Lamb of God. The power they think they have to bring this whole "Jesus thing" to an end actually brings it to fulfillment. Ironically, their impiety towards Jesus accomplishes God's work.

Jesus' saying that "my kingdom is not of this world" does not imply that Jesus and his followers have no role to play in human affairs or in the ongoing human quest and struggle for justice and peace. Instead, the claim distinguishes Jesus' rule from the various forms of power that mark human institutions—even human love stories. Domination, force, economic manipulation—even personal manipulation—are common and, some would hold, inevitable weapons for achieving progress and for holding and maintaining power. Jesus' power obviously derives from a different source.

That Jesus wants to talk about truth is utterly disconcerting for Pilate. Pilate operates in a carefully maintained world of illusion. The presence of one who came into the world to testify to the truth and who affirms that everyone who belongs to the truth hears his voice is clearly a threat to him. Disillusionment is precisely what Pilate needs most if he is to be set on the road to truth, but it is also what he fears most.

The last time I was in New York, I saw *Urinetown*, a musical comedy that is really quite unusual. It's a parody, a satire. It pokes fun at environmental protection, the power of love, power to the people—you name it. It begins by inviting the audience into a futuristic society where water has to be controlled to such an extent that "public amenities" are strategically placed throughout the town. There are no private baths or private toilets, and there are fees for the use of all such "amenities."

You won't be surprised to learn that the whole system is regulated by the You're in Good Hands Corporation owned and managed by Caldwell B. Cladwell, a corrupt and wealthy autocrat.

As the action begins, the company announces a price increase for public toilets. A rebellion breaks out, led by Bobby Strong, who falls in love with Cladwell's daughter, Hope. If you're not yet too mixed up, I'm sure you can see the potential for lighthearted allegory and moralizing—maybe even a happy ending. Even the names of the characters indicate heroes and villains: Cladwell, Hope, Bobby Strong, Miss Pennywise, and police officers Lockstock and Barrel.

During the course of the uprising, Bobby Strong, who is clearly a "Christ figure," is killed, but Cladwell, too, is toppled. Hope takes over the You're in Good Hands Corporation, all fees for the use of amenities are dropped, Amenity Number Nine is named after Bobby Strong, and Hope leads the whole town in what reads and sounds like a gospel spiritual. Each stanza invites the audience into a new relationship with the river:

> I see a river flowing for freedom …
> Come to the river flowing for justice …
> Sisters and brothers, fight for the river …
> Step in the river. Wade in the river
> Soak in the river, through and through …

You are the river. I am the river.
He is the river, She is too. ...

We see a river flowing for freedom ...

And—they live happily ever after? Indeed not! Without the heavy-handed supervision of Cladwell and Pennywise, the water goes brackish and the whole place becomes "Urinetown." It won't be long before there's no more river of freedom, river of justice, or water of life—only "Urinetown."

Believe it or not, it's a comedy. I wish I had time to tell you about some of the other characters and scenes of the show. But what does all of this have to do with Christ the King?

The musical parodies human ideals, human structures, human loyalties and human ideals. The musical is very funny, but its basic contention, as you've already heard, is not a laughing matter. In its own quirky way, it may be able to communicate something of the truth communicated by this sober gospel picture of Jesus and Pontius Pilate standing together.

We humans are very prone to systems, even to ideals that become idols—that become the answer to all the problems of the world. If only this, then this. "If onlys" are just too simple. All our "if only" wishes and dreams, even if fulfilled, would only be provisional. We know that, but have a hard time accepting it.

There is only one God—and capitalism isn't it. There is only one God—and democracy isn't it. There is only one God—and romantic idealism isn't it. There's only one God—and the church isn't it. The distinction between the visible church and the kingdom of God is a constant feature of Catholic theology.

This doesn't mean that we don't jump right into life with both feet, and engage the political and economic processes of our own time with as much enthusiasm and creativity as we can gather up. Rather, we do so with the kind of realism and humility that recognizes that we just don't have all the answers. Parents and teachers are at their best when they're ruling the roost with a bit less than absolute confidence that they have all the answers for their children. Heads of schools, churches and corporations are at their best when they recognize their

limitations and don't function as if they were absolute, infallible mon-
archs—all knowing, all wise and all powerful.

All of us are invited to be engaged in the work of the kingdom as
builders, yes, but perhaps better as believers and seekers. A perfect world
is not ours to build; there always needs to be room in our thinking for
what transcends even our best plans and programs. What is important
is that in faith and hope we move towards the kingdom promised. God
reigns. Jesus is king—and one day we and the whole world will see and
recognize him. It's what we call "eschatological hope"—big words to
describe the ultimate goal of biblical faith. As for now, the kingdom of
God on this earth is, and will always be, a work in progress until that
great day when the dream and visions of Daniel will be fulfilled:

> I, Daniel, had a dream and visions as I lay in bed. As I watched
> the night visions, I saw one like a human being coming with
> the clouds of heaven. And he came to the Ancient One and
> was presented before him. To him was given dominion and
> glory and kingship, that all peoples, nations and languages should
> serve him. His dominion is an everlasting dominion that shall
> not pass away, and his kingship is one that shall never be
> destroyed. (Daniel 7.13-14)

In the meantime, in the midst of our hard work and best efforts,
we stand with open hands and open hearts to pray as Jesus taught us:

> Our Father, who art in heaven, hallowed be thy name; thy
> kingdom come; thy will be done on earth as it is in heaven.
> Give us this day our daily bread; and forgive us our trespasses
> as we forgive those who trespass against us; and lead us not
> into temptation, but deliver us from evil.

The prayer has a wonderful ring about it on this Feast of Christ
the King, on this last Sunday of the church's year of grace. We move on
in hope—and in humility.

Notes

1   John R. Donahue, S.J., and Daniel J. Harrington, S.J., *The Gospel of Mark* (Collegeville: The Liturgical Press, 2002), 41–46. Consistent with the whole *Sacra Pagina* series, this commentary is an excellent resource for preachers, providing sound critical analysis without any loss of sensitivity to the spiritual and religious meaning of the texts.

2   Paul J. Achtemeier, *Mark: Proclamation Commentaries* (Philadelphia: Fortress Press, 1986). This short book designed for preachers gives a fine overview and has separate chapters dealing with important themes such as "The Christology of Mark," "Jesus as Teacher," "Jesus as Miracle Worker," and "The Parousia in Mark" that are very useful when these themes come up in the lectionary texts.

3   Eugene LaVerdiere, S.S.S., *The Beginning of the Gospel* (Collegeville: The Liturgical Press, 1999), 9. The whole of this author's 18-page commentary on Mark 1.1 (A title for the Gospel, a preface to the Readers) is well worth study and sets up preachers and teachers for an invitational and inclusive approach to the good news.

4   Terry Anderson, *Den of Lions: Memoirs of Seven Years* (New York: Crown Publishers, 1993), 5.

5   Terry Anderson, *Den of Lions*, 1.

6   Terry Anderson, *Den of Lions*, 268.

7   Karl Rahner, S.J., *The Great Church Year* (New York: Crossroad, 1993), 101–106.

8   See Huub Oosterhuis, *Times of Life* (New York: Paulist Press, 1979), 15–17.

9   Bonnie Bowman Thurston, *Preaching Mark* (Minneapolis: Fortress Press, 2002), 21.

10   Bonnie Bowman Thurston, *Preaching Mark*, 22.

11   Tom Harpur, *God Help Us* (Toronto: McClelland & Stewart, 1992), 95.

12   Cf. Walter Brueggemann, "The Prophet as a Destabilizing Presence," in *A Social Reading of the Old Testament,* Patrick D. Miller, ed. (Minneapolis: Fortress Press, 1994), 221–225.

13   Bonnie Bowman Thurston, *Preaching Mark*, 34.

14   Tom Harpur, *God Help Us*, 65.

15   Quoted in Robert Atwan, George Dardess and Peggy Rosenthal, eds., *Divine Inspiration* (New York: Oxford University Press, 1998), 102–103.

16   Tom Harpur, *God Help Us*, 124.

17   See Huub Oosterhuis, *Your Word Is Near* (New York: Newman, 1968), 144.

18   From the hymn *Vexilla Regis prodeunt,* Venantius Fortunatus c. 530–609.

19   The image "tread in relays" is taken from "Prayers on the Way of the Cross" in Michel Quoist, *Prayers,* (New York: Sheed & Ward, 1963), 179.

[20]   Robert Bridges and W.H. Gardner, eds., *Poems of Gerard Manley Hopkins* (New York: Oxford, 1948), 95.

[21]   For further commentary on this amazing ending, cf. John Donahue, S.J., and Daniel J. Harrington, S.J., *The Gospel of Mark*, 457–461.

[22]   The Canticle of Zechariah, chanted every morning in the Liturgy of Hours, has special energy on Easter morning. The Easter Vigil, presuming that it was ending at dawn, once concluded with a form of morning prayer that featured this canticle.

[23]   Annie Dillard, *Teaching a Stone to Talk* (New York: HarperCollins, 1982), 41-42.

[24]   Quoted in Atwan, Dardess and Rosenthal, eds., *Divine Inspiration*, 389.

[25]   Joseph Donders, *Praying and Preaching the Sunday Gospel* (Maryknoll, NY: Orbis, 1990), 114.

[26]   William Blake, "And Did Those Feet," quoted in the *Norton Anthology of World Masterpieces* (New York: Norton, 1999), 549.

[27]   Michel Quoist, *Prayers*, 27.

[28]   Andrew Greeley, *The Great Mysteries: An Essential Catechism* (New York: Crossroad/Seabury, 1976), 36.

[29]   Elizabeth Poston, ed., *The Penguin Book of Christmas Carols* (Harmondsworth, England: Penguin, 1965), 118.

[30]   Quoted in Robert Gantoy and Romain Swaeles, eds., *Days of the Lord, V* (Collegeville: The Liturgical Press, 1993), 124-125.

[31]   Michel Quoist, *Prayers*, 66.

[32]   C.S. Lewis, *Mere Christianity* (San Francisco: HarperCollins, 2001), 198.

[33]   Joseph Donders, *Praying and Preaching the Sunday Gospel*, 132.

[34]   Ignatius of Antioch, Letter to the Romans, Chapter 4.1-2, 6, 3, Quoted in *Liturgy of Hours*, vol. IV (New York: Catholic Book Publishing, 1975), 1490-1492.

[35]   Terry Anderson, *Den of Lions*, 145.

[36]   Ephraem (306–373), *Sermon sur Notre Seigneur*, quoted in Robert Gantoy and Romain Swaeles, ed., *Days of the Lord, V*, 215.

[37]   Ambrose, *De Sacramentis l: 1-3*, quoted in Robert Gantoy and Romain Swaeles, eds., *Days of the Lord, V*, 214.

[38]   Prudentius, quoted in Bonnie Bowman Thurston, *Preaching Mark*, 90.

[39]   Quoted by Richard Viladesau, *The Word in and out of Season* (New York: Paulist, 1990), 120.

[40]   For a fine summary of these points of view, cf. Bonnie Bowman Thurston, *Preaching Mark*, 139-145.

Also available
from Father Corbin Eddy

Who Knows the Reach of God?
Homilies and Reflections for Year A

Father Corbin Eddy explores Year A, the year of the Gospel of Matthew, through engaging, thought-provoking and down-to-earth reflections on scripture.

- 270 pages
- paperback

Who Knows the Colour of God?
Homilies and Reflections for Year C

Father Corbin Eddy explores Year C, the year of the Gospel of Luke, through engaging, thought-provoking and down-to-earth re-flections on scripture.

- 200 pages
- paperback

NOVALIS

To order these and other fine books, contact NOVALIS
at 1-800-387-7164 or cservice@novalis.ca